HOOKED ON ART!

265 Ready-to-Use Activities in Seven Exciting Media

JENEAN ROMBERG

Prentice Hall

Library of Congress Cataloging-in-Publication Data

Romberg, Jenean.
    Hooked on art! : 265 ready-to-use activities in seven exciting media /Jeanean Romberg.
        p. cm.
    ISBN: 0-13-042603-2
        1. Art—Study and teaching (Elementary)—Activity programs.   I. Title.
N350.R557 2001
372.5—dc21   2001133057

Acquisitions Editor: Susan Kolwicz
Production Editor: Sharon L. Gonzalez
Interior Design: Nicola Evans
Composition/Layout: Celestial Engineering

Printed in the United States of America

10 9 8 7 6

ISBN 0-13-042603-2

ATTENTION: CORPORATIONS AND SCHOOLS

Prentice Hall books are available at quantity discounts with bulk purchase for
educational, business, or sales promotional use. For information, please write to:
Prentice Hall, Special Sales, 240 Frisch Court, Paramus, NJ 07652. Please supply:
title of book, ISBN, quantity, how the book will be used, date needed.

PRENTICE HALL
Paramus, NJ 07652

On the World Wide Web at http://www.phdirect.com

In Memory of

my mother, Sebieanne V. Romberg,
and
my aunt, Marie V. Howes,
who always loved and encouraged me

Acknowledgments

Special thanks to my sister, Sandra R. Kincaid,
for help and support from the beginning.
To Special Friends
who care, share, and listen daily—Jo Anne Wilshire and Glenda Renshaw;
Donna Husbands, a friend for all seasons
and reasons, who moved and I miss daily.

About the Author

Jenean Romberg has taught all six elementary grades in California and Scotland, was the Elementary Art Specialist for the Newport-Mesa Unified School District and taught art for teachers at Pepperdine University. She has directed arts and crafts for summer city recreation programs, as well as summer camps in the mountains. She left teaching to pursue more personal creative outlets. At present she is teaching Folk Art, designing and publishing instructional packets for both painting and sewing, and has published in *Better Homes and Gardens* crafts publications. She also designs and produces gift items for retail stores in her studio high in the California mountains, and returns each year to Wilshire's of Oak Glen to help, enjoying the friends and people who share apple season in autumn.

About This Resource

We have entered the new "millennium" with all kinds of new materials and ways to creatively express oneself. Still, crayons . . . paper . . . paste . . . scissors . . . paint . . . the first art materials for children, never changes. Each generation needs and wants to experience creative activities. The joy of creating something is exhilarating. Making art fulfills children's real need for self-expression. They are eager to experience and participate actively and imaginatively in it. The value of the activity isn't measured by the finished product, rather in the pure enjoyment and learning along the way. It is important to take the time to explore the uses and limitations of different media, materials, and techniques, become skillful in their uses, and learn what we, personally, can or cannot do.

Hooked on Art provides a broad exploration of basic materials, utilizing a wide variety of tools and techniques as well as manipulative and organizational skills. Each of the seven sections includes dozens of activities selected to meet special moods and occasions; are sequentially organized to allow a progression from very simple techniques in one media to more complex techniques involving several media. The techniques are designed to enable anyone to achieve fascinating and intriguing effects so that those "initial" experiences with a particular medium are positive and rewarding. After gaining confidence and knowledge, we then feel secure enough to be inventive, to express individual ideas, and take pride and gain satisfaction in creativity. By choosing and creating colors, textures, and shapes, we share something of ourselves.

Use the activities in this book to explore various media and techniques, as well as a starting point for your own ideas and variations. Experiment, change, and push the limits of each activity or media you try.

When beginning an art activity with children, the following things are very important and need to be considered and shared:

- Each activity begins with a list of materials needed for *each individual.*
- Try the activity yourself before presenting it; you will be more aware of the techniques and the knowledge needed as well as the pitfalls to be avoided.
- Do demonstrate. Your free use of materials and your approach will encourage others; care, use of materials, and basic skills can be demonstrated at the same time.
- Don't be afraid if a demonstration turns out a failure; if it does, discuss why.

- All supplies listed are generally available in schools, easy to find, or inexpensive. Directions are simple and to the point, with illustrations to demonstrate each step.

- The captions are simply for suggestion. Show samples, demonstrate, and give examples, but then let the students go from there and they will—beautifully!

- Always have everything you will need for the activity READY!

- Allow plenty of time in which to complete each project; divide into two or more working periods if necessary so no one will feel pressured.

- Encourage the students to share their work with each other either while they are working or when the activity is completed. It's exciting and often motivating to see what others are doing.

Now, let's explore, experiment, create! Most of all, make art a happy, exciting experience.

Jenean Romberg

Contents

1. About Crayons   1

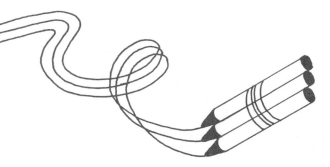

2. About Paper 53

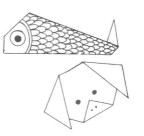

3. About Tissue   113

Techniques with Tissue   114

Materials   115

Activities

4. About Tempera   163

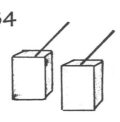

Fold Prints

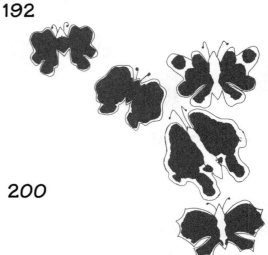

About Fingerpainting   198

Painting with Sponges   204

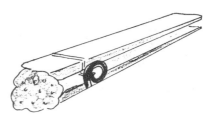

Resists with Crayon   207

Impasto

With Other Media

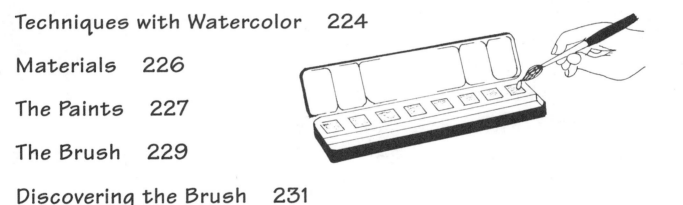

5. About Watercolor   223

6. About Printing 271

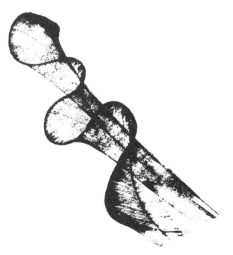

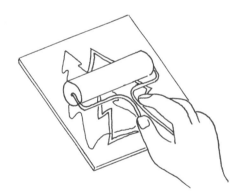

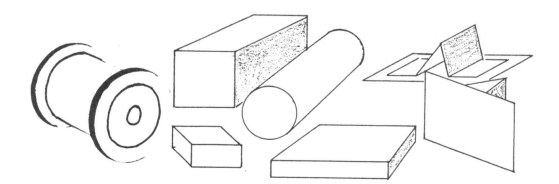

7. About Mobiles   331

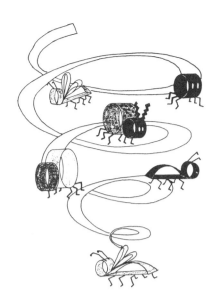

About Crayons

There's something magical about the crayon, made of color pigment and wax. It's generally the first drawing tool one uses and yet too rarely are children and adults aware of the full potential and versatility of the crayon. There are certain things a crayon can do better than any other art material. Just taking the wrapper off the crayon offers endless possibilities! Often, as children and adults, we are encouraged to keep crayons "nice" when, in fact, broken, peeled crayons are best for creating lines, curves, textured effects, and filling spaces. Crayons lend themselves to many different techniques and combine well with other media. Crayons, something like the ones we use today, have been used by artists for hundreds of years. Many famous artists have used crayons for drawing and sketching.

In this section, we will attempt to explore the many exciting possibilities in the world of crayons, from very simple line drawings to pictures to designs with techniques involving crayon and other media. Sometimes there will be several variations of the same technique, each involving a little more skill and coordination, while others will have only one example with suggestions for variations. There has been no attempt to dictate how or what to draw. It is both unnecessary and unwise to show a child how to draw. The titles and examples are merely hints for motivation. The techniques are designed to enable anyone to achieving fascinating and intriguing effects which do not demand any particular skill or ability.

Techniques with Crayons

The following techniques will be used in the crayon activities in this book. Here is a brief summary of each:

line scribbling   designs, patterns, free forms

line drawings   on paper and/or cloth

rubbings   Place objects with textured surfaces under paper and rub over the top surface with the flat side of an unwrapped crayon to bring the design through.

stenciling   A stencil is a thin sheet of cardboard, paper, or metal cut out so that when it is laid on paper or cloth and color is applied by making short brisk strokes from the edge of the stencil on to the paper or cloth, the design or pattern that has been cut out will be reproduced on the surface.

scratchboard   Put bright patches of thick crayon all over the paper; pat surface with chalk dust from the chalk eraser. Then color over the bright colors and chalk dust with a thick coat of black crayon. With pointed tools scratch out a planned picture. Don't just outline; fill in shapes with lines to give textured effect.

etching   Same as scratchboard except that instead of black crayon a coat of black tempera paint mixed with a few drops of liquid soap is painted over the bright-colored crayon and left to dry thoroughly. Then scratch in picture or design.

resists   Draw in picture, design, or pattern with crayon, leaving some areas and background uncolored. Then apply a thin coat of tempera or watercolor paint over the total picture. If the crayon has been applied heavily enough, the areas colored with crayon will repel the tempera.

with watercolor   Color picture with crayon. Use strong lines and combination of lines, leaving some areas of white paper. Fill in uncolored areas with watercolor.

with fingerpaint   Color the entire surface of paper brightly with crayons; apply in strips or area blocks. Then cover entire surface with fingerpaint using any one color, and fingerpaint over surface to make a picture or design.

overlay   Paint a design or drawing first; when dry, color over the paint with crayons. Remove some of the areas of the drawing with a sharp pointed object for interesting variations.

chalk transfer	Cover a piece of paper with chalk; with white crayon color all over the chalk. Take another color of crayon and cover up the white crayon. Then place this paper face down on a piece of smooth paper and, using a hard pencil or ball-point pen, draw a picture or design on the back of the paper with the chalk and crayon on it. This will transfer the colors and picture or design to the smooth paper.
transparencies	Crayon shavings, made with a vegetable or cheese grater, are placed between layers of wax paper or plastic wrap and pressed gently with a warm, not hot, iron. A piece of paper on top of the wax paper will ensure that the transparency is not scorched.
paper batik	A design is colored with bright-colored crayons; a thick coat of wax is then applied, covering the entire paper. Then place the paper in water, gently crumple into a ball, open flat and paint completely with a dark color tempera paint. Rinse paint off with water. Tempera paint will penetrate into the cracks created when you crumple the paper and this results in a batik effect.
fabric batik	A design or drawing is painted on cloth using melted crayons mixed with paraffin, and a paintbrush. The wax must go through the cloth. When the painting is completed and the wax is dry, crumple the cloth gently and then dip in a pail of dark-colored dye or paint entire surface of cloth with India ink. The dye or ink will cover all parts of the cloth not covered with wax. To remove the wax, put the cloth on a pad of newspaper and then lay newspaper on top. Iron with a warm iron. The heat will draw the wax out. Do this several times, changing the paper each time, until all the wax is absorbed by the paper.
on wood	Color a design or picture heavily on a piece of wood such as soft pine; place a piece of construction paper on top and iron with warm iron. The wax will melt into the wood and also make a print on the paper.
on sandpaper	Draw a design or picture on fine-grained sandpaper, coloring heavily. Cover design or picture with a piece of white drawing paper and then newspaper. Iron over the top surface with a low temperature and the design will transfer to the white paper, giving a "pointillism" effect.
lettering	The flat crayon is excellent for lettering posters and signs. The crayon does not have to be turned to vary thickness or lines. Try notching the crayon in several places so that several parallel lines can be drawn at once.

Materials

The following materials are needed to do the activities in this section:

crayons

watercolors

tempera paint

India ink

white drawing paper

construction paper

manila paper

newsprint

electric skillet

iron (Get one at a thrift shop.)

old newspapers

plastic wrap

wax paper

fabric: old handkerchiefs,
     pieces of old sheet,
     muslin

paraffin wax

etching tools

thick cardboard (Cut up used boxes.)

scrap wood

Additional Materials

- New crayons with the paper on look nice but are not very useful; take off the paper and store in plastic containers, margarine tubs, or a small box.

- Save those crayon scraps! Cut-down milk cartons can be placed in a shoe box, a soda bottle cardboard 6-pack, or on a tray for easy storage and portability.

- Crayon marks can be easily removed with any liquid spray cleaner.

- Vegetable or cheese graters work well for making crayon shavings.

- A sheet of newspaper will always protect the working surface. This eliminates worry about coloring over the edges and makes clean-up easier and faster.

- Make a collection of things that have textured surfaces for crayon rubbings such as:

leaves	string	fine grasses	cutouts
burlap	sandpaper	window screen	fabric
textured fabric	cheese grater	corrugated paper	

Encourage observation of surroundings and objects that have textured surfaces that could be added to the collection.

- Make a collection of objects to be used as etching tools:

toothpicks	sharp sticks	paper clips
bobby pins	different combs	pen points

Technique: Linear patterns and designs

Materials:

- (1) 18″ x 24″ colored newsprint
- unwrapped crayons

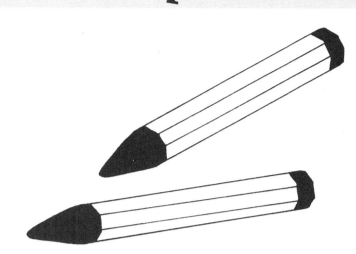

Steps:

1. Fold the 18″ x 24″ newsprint in half and in half again, widthwise and lengthwise, so there are 16 rectangles.

2. To better understand and appreciate the full potential of the crayon, experiment with the following techniques, trying a different one in each of the 16 rectangles on the paper.
   - Using the pointed or blunt end of the crayon, make lines that are straight, curved, wavy, zigzag or looped; thin, delicate, strong, and heavy.

   with the point . . .

   with the blunt end . . .

- Create textures and linear patterns by repetition of certain strokes, dots, circles, squares, etc.; connect, overlap, or space these in a variety of ways.

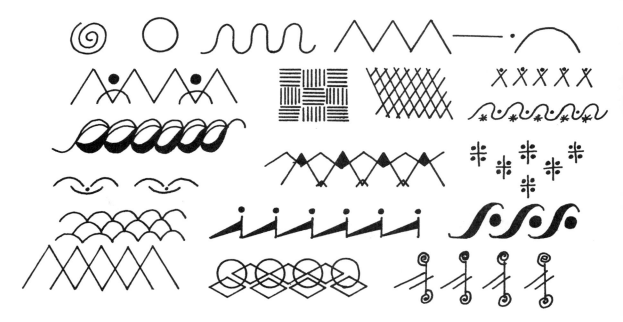

- Use the end or side of the crayon; applying more pressure at one end than at the other end of the crayon will give a shaded (dark to light) effect as well as lines varying in thickness.

- Lay the crayon on its side and twist around to make circles and bows.

- Use a notched crayon for interesting effects. Try this for lettering.

- Tape two or three crayons together to make parallel lines.

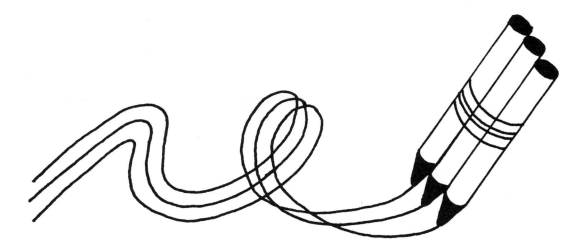

3. Encourage varying degrees of pressure, including the heaviest possible for bright, deep colors. A good build-up of wax is often the secret to success with many projects.

4. Coloring in one direction is not always the best way to apply color. Follow the contour of the object, or show crayon strokes purposely to create mood or movement.

5. Apply the color with the side of the crayon as well as with the end.

6. Blend colors by using one over another or many together. A good way to teach blending of colors is to make an entire design of one color, using the side of the crayon only. Then apply different colors over parts of the design, sometimes using other shades of the same color, entirely different colors, or only black and white.

A Point or Line

Materials:

- (3) 6" x 6" pieces of white drawing paper
- black crayon

Steps:

1. Have the children make a collection of natural forms which have surface patterns such as rocks, shells, seed pods, the feathers of birds, or leaves. Observe and discuss the variety of different textures and linear patterns.

2. Give each child three 6" x 6" squares of white drawing paper. Using a black crayon, create a different texture or linear pattern on each square. Remember, a line begins with a point or a dot; line is the track made by a moving point.

3. Here are some examples of patterns which could be made. (You might wish to draw similar ones on 9" x 12" white drawing paper to use as examples.)

unbroken line

points or circles at random; parallel lines flow gently around these

bent zigzag lines in repeated patterns

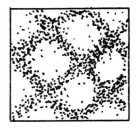

points of equal size

hatched lines

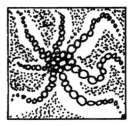

two sizes of dots or tiny circles

Variations:

— Use 9" x 9" paper folded into 3" squares; draw a different pattern on each.

— Recreate a pattern as seen in a natural object such as a shell, spider web, seed pod.

Technique:
Linear designs

Accent on Pattern

Materials:

- crayons
- (1) 9" x 12" white drawing paper
- 4 crayons, different colors

Steps:

1. Select one geometric shape:

2. Select four colors of crayons; suggest the use of shades of a color, complementary colors, warm or cool colors.

3. Draw one shape in the center of the paper with any color crayon. Repeat the shape inside the original, each time with a different color, until the center is reached.

  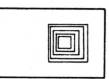

4. Draw the same shape again, either larger or smaller, next to the first and color it in the same manner. Repeat these shapes until the entire paper is covered. Sometimes it will be necessary to draw half a shape to fill in areas.

Bulletin Board:

Mount each design on a piece of 9" x 12" construction paper of a complementary color. Pin up in checkerboard fashion, one right next to the other with the caption "Accent on Pattern."

Spinning Wheels

Technique: Line drawing

Materials:

- (1) 9" x 12" black construction paper
- crayons

Steps:

1. Begin the design by making points or dots at various intervals all over the black paper.

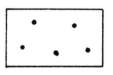

2. Then around each point or dot, with any color, make a circle consisting of short straight lines. Do this around each point or dot on the paper.

3. Continue by putting another ring around each circle with another color. Keep adding more rings of short straight lines around each circle, changing the colors.

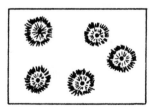

4. When the circles begin to touch each other, decide which ones will complete their circles, stopping the rings of the other circles where they meet. Completely fill the paper.

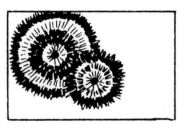

Variations:

— When the coloring is completed, a watercolor wash of a bright color such as yellow can be painted over the entire paper to create an unusual effect.

— Try using a pastel-colored paper instead of black paper and only two or three bright-colored crayons.

Line Pictures

Technique: Line drawing

Materials:

- (1) 9" x 12" white drawing paper
- crayons

Steps:

1. Illustrate the various types of pictures that can be made by simple line drawings on the chalkboard. The variety of pictures shown and the time used for demonstration will depend on the grade level of the class. The following can be used for illustration:

2. I recommend that the picture be something familiar such as a house, a tree, or an underwater scene. Use short straight lines to create the picture. Contrast in the picture can be achieved by varying the length of lines, changing the width of lines, and by putting some close together and some far apart.

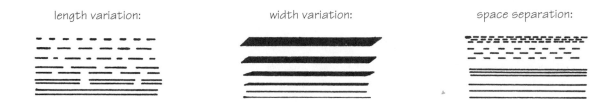

length variation: width variation: space separation:

Variation:

Try recreating the picture using only dots of various sizes, i.e., pointillism.

Technique: Linear patterns

Materials:

- (1) 9" x 12" x ¼" graph paper
- crayons

Steps:

1. Using a black crayon, divide the graph paper into rectangles and squares of different sizes.

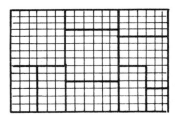

2. Draw the seven elements of design on the board.

3. Demonstrate various possibilities for designs by using these separately or by combining several. Let the children make and draw suggestions on the board.

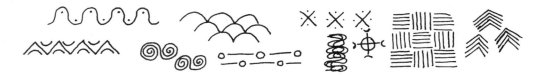

4. Make patterns and textures in each rectangle or square on the graph paper. Use many colors and try to make each pattern different. By repeating designs, one at a time, in the ¼" squares, squares within each rectangle or square, patterns and textures will be created.

Calico Animals

Technique: Linear patterns

Materials:

- (1) 9" x 12" manila or white drawing paper
- crayons
- pencil

Steps:

1. Draw a light outline of an animal on the manila or white drawing paper. Make the animal as large as possible and fairly simple in shape.

2. Divide the animal into sections or patterns.

3. Fill in section patterns of the animal, using different textures, lines, designs, and shapes with crayons. As a reminder, put the seven basic elements of design on the chalkboard.

4. Outline the animal with black crayon to distinguish the features.

Variation:

After the coloring is completed, a watercolor wash can be applied over the designs or each individual section can be painted a different color.

Pattern Handprints

Technique:
Linear patterns

Materials:
- (1) 9" x 12" white construction paper
- crayons

Steps:

1. Place one hand on the white paper and, using a black crayon, draw around the hand. Lift hand and place in another position on the paper. Draw around it with the black crayon. Repeat until the paper is filled with overlapping hands.

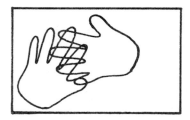

2. Fill in the spaces created by overlapping handprints with various textures and designs. Encourage children to try as many different things as they can think of using lines, dots, circles, etc.

Variation:

Draw around a familiar object such as a pair of scissors, repeating shape several times on paper and filling in with patterns.

A Border Design

Technique: Linear patterns

Materials:

- a long strip of adding machine or register tape
- crayons

Steps:

1. Fold the adding machine or register tape in half, again and again, until the tape is divided into small squares or rectangles. Open and lay flat on the desk.

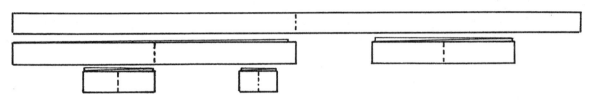

2. In the first square or rectangle, create a decorative motif or design with crayons. Remind the children of the seven basic elements of design, perhaps demonstrating the use of one or more together on the chalkboard.

(elements of design)   (variations)

3. Repeat the design or decorative motif created in the first square or rectangle in all the others.

Suggestions:

If you don't have tape, cut strip of newsprint, 3" x 24". Use the strips to make a border design on a bulletin board in the classroom.

15

A Giant Puzzle

Technique: Line drawing, linear patterns

Materials:

- a long piece of butcher's paper of the size desired for puzzle
- crayons
- watercolor paints and brush

Steps:

1. Tape the large piece of butcher's paper to the chalkboard.

2. Divide the butcher's paper into sections, using a pencil or chalk. Make sure there will be one piece for each child. Number each piece, beginning at the right and going across to the left one row at a time. This way it will be easy to put together when completed.

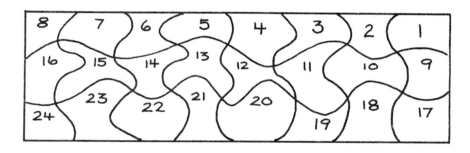

3. Cut the sections, giving each child a piece. Remind them to color on the side without a number.

4. Each child should color his piece as desired—a design, a pattern, or a picture. Color dark and thickly, leaving some white spaces.

5. When the coloring is completed, each piece can be given a watercolor wash or perhaps parts of the drawing can be filled in with watercolor.

Variations:

— The puzzle can be planned to tell a story, with each piece illustrating a particular part of the story.

— Each child can illustrate his favorite book on his or her piece and the puzzle can be displayed in the library corner.

Crayon Mosaics

Technique: Drawing

Materials:

- (1) 9" x 12" piece of graph paper, with 1" squares
- pencil
- crayons

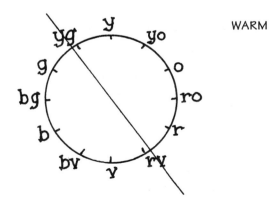

Steps:

1. With pencil draw a simple large object in the center of the graph paper. Examples: fruit, vegetables, geometric shapes.

2. Discuss warm and cool colors. Have the children divide their crayons into two piles: warm and cool.
3. Color the squares inside the design or shape either all warm or all cool colors. Remind them not to put the same colors next to each other.
4. Color the squares outside the shape the opposite, warm or cool, colors.

Hints:

Here is a color wheel showing the warm and cool colors.

COOL   WARM

y   yo
yg
g   o
bg   ro
b   r
bv   rv
v

Variation:

To make a warm/cool color fan, fold 9" x 12" graph paper into a fan using the 1" lines as a guide and color every other section warm/cool. Refer to page 108 on folding a fan.

Kaleidoscope of Color

Technique:

Linear patterns

Materials:

- (1) 9" x 12" white construction paper
- crayons

Steps:

1. Fold the 9" x 12" white construction paper in half widthwise and then lengthwise so the paper will be divided in quarters.

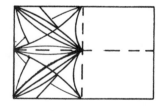

2. Using a black crayon, draw a design in one rectangle. Press very heavily with the crayon. Fold the paper in half and rub on the back of the design so the design will transfer to another rectangle. Go over the design with the black crayon so it will be dark, with a good build-up of crayon.

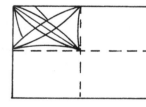 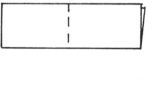

3. Fold the paper in half and rub on the back of the two rectangles with designs so they will transfer to the other two rectangles. Open the paper and go over the design with black crayon.

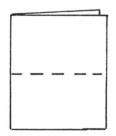 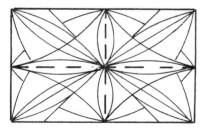

4. Color in the designs with crayons. Remember to color the same shape in each rectangle the same color.

Name Patterns

Technique: Linear patterns

Materials:

- (1) 9" x 12" white or manila paper
- crayons

Steps:

1. Fold the 9" x 12" paper in half and then in half again, widthwise.

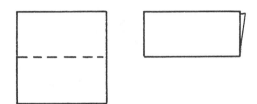

2. Open. Fold in half and in half once again, lengthwise. This will make 16 rectangles.

3. Open. Flatten out paper. Print name, one letter in each box. Do over and over, moving from left to right, across the paper.

4. Use imagination in coloring each letter a different color, solid-colored squares between words, lines, circles, and dots.

Variation:

Use numbers instead of letters:

Mirror Images

Technique: Linear design

Materials:

- (1) 9" x 12" manila or white construction paper
- crayons

Steps:

1. Fold the paper in half, lengthwise. Write or print the child's name on the folded line, very large with a dark crayon.

2. Fold and rub the paper gently with the palm of the hand. This will transfer the name to the other side of the fold line. This is much easier than attempting to write the name backwards.

3. Open the paper and go over the name with the same dark crayon very heavily.

4. Using various colored crayons, make lines following the contour of the letters to the outside edge of the paper.

Variation:

Put name in script instead of lettering.

20

Let's Take a Walk

Technique: Drawing

Materials:

- (1) 12" x 18" white drawing paper
- crayons
- large sheet of butcher's paper for illustration

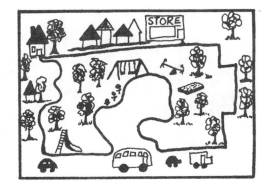

Steps:

1. Attach the piece of butcher's paper to the chalkboard with masking tape for demonstration purposes.

2. Discuss with the students how much fun can be had on a walk—seeing things, places, people, and so forth.

3. Ask them to take a walk with you on paper. With a dark crayon start in the upper left-hand corner of the paper and draw your walk. An example:

   I came down the stairs in my house and walked down the block. I saw a friend and we played a game of skipping the cracks on the sidewalk. When we came to the corner, a bus and many people were waiting for the light to change. I crossed the street and started to walk west when my hat blew off and into the playground across the street. I chased my hat into the playground. It gave me quite a chase but I finally caught it. I was so tired that I sat down on a nearby bench and watched the children playing in the playground. Some were on slides, some on the monkey bars, others were swinging, some were on the merry-go-round, and some on the seesaw. Finally I got up, recrossed the street, and continued on my way. I stopped at the store and bought bread. Then I hurried home.

   All the time the story is being told, draw a line that makes a design on the paper.

4. Now each child will draw his or her own walk around the block on paper, using a dark crayon.

5. To show what was seen on the walk, fill in with crayons, drawing the trees, houses, people, playground, and so forth.

Creative Creatures

Technique:
Line drawing

Materials:

- (1) 6″ x 12″ white drawing paper
- crayons

Steps:

1. Divide the students into groups of three.

2. Fold the 6″ x 12″ white drawing paper into three equal parts.

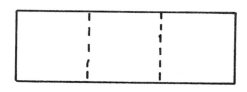

3. Open the paper flat. Starting from the left, the first person draws the head of an animal, any type of animal, on the first section only, stopping at the fold.

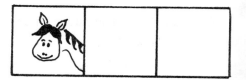

4. The first section is folded back and under, and then passed to the second person. The next person draws the body of an animal, stopping at the second fold.

5. The second section is then folded back under and passed to the third person. The third person adds a tail without knowing anything about the other two sections.

These are great for creativity as well as just for fun!

Shadows

Technique: Line drawing, cutting

Materials:

- (1) 6" x 12" piece of colored construction paper
- (1) 4 ½" x 6" piece white paper
- (1) 4 ½" x 6" piece black paper
- scissors
- crayons
- paste or glue

Steps:

1. Draw an animal, object, or self on the white paper; keep it simple.

2. Place the white paper on top of the black and cut out the figure, cutting the black shadow at the same time.
3. Fold the colored construction paper in half. Paste the drawn figure on one section and the black figure on the other so it looks like a shadow.

Variations:

— Have the students draw either their mother or father doing something at home and then cut a shadow to match. This makes a good Mother's Day or Father's Day card.

— Make a mural of students playing on the playground with all their shadows.

— Draw buildings, cities, trees, etc., with shadows.

Butterfly on a Stick

Technique:
Line drawing, cutting, folding

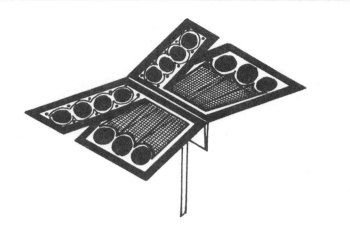

Materials:

- (1) 9" x 12" white construction paper
- crayons
- scissors
- 18" long thin stick
- masking tape or glue

Steps:

1. Fold the 9" x 12" white construction paper in half, widthwise. To make the wings, cut as illustrated.

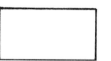 

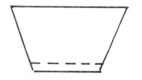 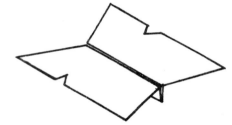

2. Fold the bottom folded edge of the butterfly shape up about one inch. This will create the "body" of the butterfly.

3. Color a design or pattern on the wings of the butterfly. Remind the children that both wings will have the same design and colors. Color both sides of each wing.

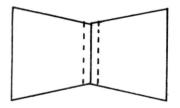

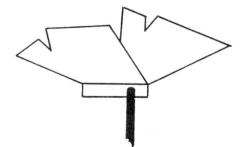

4. Using glue or masking tape, attach the stick to the body of the butterfly at the center.

Technique: Line drawing

Materials:

- 22" x 28" full sheet of newspaper, classified section
- pencil
- crayons
- scissors
- paste or glue
- newspaper for stuffing
- lightweight wire or string for inside of mouth
- masking tape

Fish Kites

Steps:

1. Discuss the characteristics of fish: color, design (pattern of gills, scales, etc.). Look at pictures of fish.

2. Fold the newspaper in half, lengthwise. Draw half a fish, making sure the back of the fish is on the folded edge. Cut out the fish shape. Do not cut along the fold.

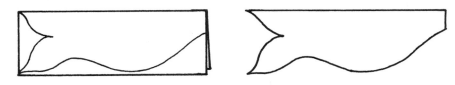

3. Open the fish shape and lay it flat. Using crayons make designs and/or patterns on the fish, drawing each side of the fish the same.

4. For mouth: To strengthen the mouth edge, fold back the paper about ¼" twice and glue down. Tape wire or string around the inside edge.

5. Fold and glue the edges of the fish shape closed. Stuff with crinkled-up newspaper, tissue paper, or plastic bags either before or after gluing edges together.

Lattice Designs

Technique: Paper cutting over crayon

Materials:

- (1) 9" x 12" white construction paper
- (1) 9" x 12" black construction paper
- crayons
- scissors
- paste or glue
- newspaper to cover desks

Steps:

1. Cover desks with newspapers.

2. Color heavily over the entire piece of white paper; use designs, stripes, etc. Make the colors dark and thick.

3. Fold the black construction paper in half, lengthwise.

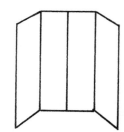

4. Fold the first section over and cut designs and shapes on the fold. Remember to leave spaces between each shape. Open. Fold the middle fold and do the same thing. Repeat on the third fold.

5. Paste or glue the cut piece of black construction paper over the top of the colored paper.

Technique: Stencil

Materials:

- (2) 4 ½" x 6" heavy bristol board or gray bogus paper
- crayons
- pencil
- scissors
- (1) 12" x 18" light-colored construction paper

Positive/Negative Stencils

Steps:

1. To make stencils: Fold a 4 ½" x 6" piece of paper in half, lengthwise or widthwise. Draw half a leaf shape, with the center on the fold. Leave a space at each end on the fold. Cut the leaf out, beginning and ending on the fold. Do not trim either piece.

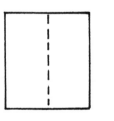  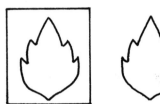

2. Fold the 12" x 18" construction paper in half, widthwise. Open and lay flat on working surface.

3. Place one 4 ½" x 6" paper with negative space out anywhere on one side of the paper. Using the end of the crayon, make short brisk strokes over the edge of the cut-out space toward the center. Go all around the edges. Repeat several times, using various colored crayons.

4. On the other half of the 12" x 18" construction paper, use the cut-out leaf as a stencil. Make short brisk strokes with the end of the crayon over the edge of the leaf onto the construction paper.

Neon Cities

Technique: Stencil

Materials:

- (1) 9" x 12" black construction paper
- crayons
- scissors
- pencil

Steps:

1. Fold the 9" x 12" black construction paper in half, lengthwise. Make a second fold about ½" below the first one on each half.

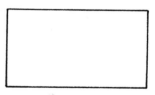 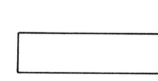 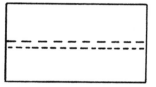

2. With a pencil sketch a silhouette of buildings or houses on the half of the paper with the extra fold. Do not go below the second fold. Cut out.

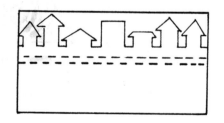 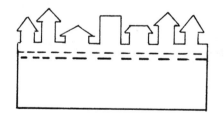

3. Fold the paper in half again on the center fold. Make short brisk strokes with the end of a crayon off the edges of the buildings and houses onto the background. Use bright-colored crayons, a different color for each building.

4. When complete, refold second fold so the buildings will stand away from the background.

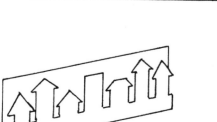

Technique: Rubbing

Materials:

- (1) piece of newsprint or copy paper
- unwrapped crayons
- leaves of various shapes and sizes with prominent veins
- newspaper to cover desks

Steps:

1. Have students collect and bring to class fresh leaves of various shapes and sizes with prominent veins. (As a variation, leaf shapes could be cut from construction paper.)

2. Cover desks with newspaper.

3. Place one leaf, vein-side up, under the piece of newsprint or copy paper. Hold down the paper firmly with one hand. Using the side of the crayon, rub over the leaf until the design of the leaf shows through.

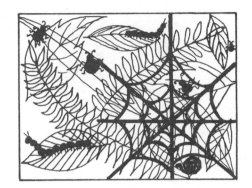

What's in the Garden?

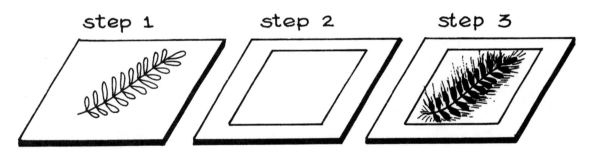

step 1   step 2   step 3

4. Repeat this a few times, moving the leaf around randomly. Use other leaves and colors until an all-over design is created.

5. With crayons, draw in insects and garden creatures one might find on leaves.

Variation:

On a background of leaf rubbings done with shades of green crayons, draw animals in the jungle.

Texture Collage

Technique: Crayon rubbing

Materials:

- (1) 12" x 18" colored newsprint
- (1) 12" x 18" colored construction paper, any color for background
- unwrapped crayons
- textured objects
- scissors and paste or glue

Steps:

1. Make a collection of flat objects with textured surfaces such as: leaves, string, fine grasses, thick paper cutouts, pieces of textured fabric, burlap, waffle-weave fabric, window screen, sandpaper, rough leather, corrugated paper, and so forth.

2. Place several of the textured objects on the working surface and place the 12" x 18" colored newsprint on top. Rub the side of the crayon back and forth or with a circular motion over the paper directly above the textured material.

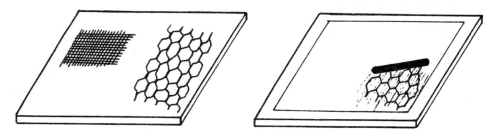

3. Move each object about or use different objects to achieve a variety of imprints of various textures.

4. A variety of effects may be achieved by using any of the following techniques:
   - Blend several shades of one color or several different colors.
   - Use greater pressure on some parts of the imprint for a shaded effect.

5. Cut or tear out each impression. Arrange on construction paper in a pleasing, attractive design. Some shapes can overlap for more interesting effects.

Texture Landscapes

Technique:

Crayon rubbing

Materials:

- (1) 12" x 18" colored construction paper
- unwrapped crayons
- collection of surface-textured objects

Steps:

1. Make an outline drawing of a landscape or city street using a pencil or black crayon.

2. Apply color to the picture by placing a piece of surface-textured fabric under one part of the picture at a time and use the crayon rubbing technique. Try burlap texture for a roof, sandpaper for a distant field or sky, string for waves, corrugated paper for fences, rough leather for a mass of leaves on a tree. Experiment and remember to use blending and shading techniques.

Variations:

— Let the type of objects in a design suggest the colors to be used, such as fall colors for leaf designs, gay colors (red, yellow, blue, green) for a circus motif, and so forth.

— Use construction paper strips, with simple patterns cut in them, for all-over strips or plaid pattern.

— Paint a watercolor wash over the top of a crayon rubbing design or picture.

Figures in Motion

Technique:

Crayon rubbing

Materials:

- 3" x 4", 4 ½" x 6" tagboard, bristol board, or other heavy paper
- 9" x 12", 12" x 18", or other sizes of colored newsprint
- unwrapped crayons
- scissors

Steps:

1. Using the tagboard, cut out a figure such as a girl jumping rope or walking.

2. Place the cutout under a sheet of newsprint.

3. Rub over the figure with the side of a crayon on the newsprint. Move the figure slightly to overlap and repeat. Do this several times. After you have repeated this process a number of times, you will have a group of figures jumping. (This is also a good lesson in how to give depth to a picture by overlapping figures.)

Variations:

Experiment with a variety of shapes such as trees, flowers, animals, people in motion.

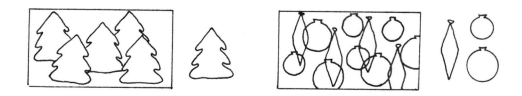

creative creations

Technique: Crayon
and watercolor

Materials:

- (1) 9" x 12" white construction paper
- crayons
- watercolor paints
- container with water
- paintbrush
- paper towel

Steps:

1. Draw an outline picture, pattern, or design using one or more colors of crayon and pressing very heavily.

2. Paint in the various parts of the picture with watercolor paints. The crayon border will keep the watercolors from running together.

Variations:

What about cities, designs, overall designs, repeat designs, etc.? This is a good "first experience" with watercolor. The children can concentrate on lightness and darkness of color and the general feel of watercolor paints.

Three-Dimensional Bouquet

Technique:
Crayon and watercolor

Materials:

- (1) 9″ x 12″ black construction paper
- (1) 4″ x 6″ construction paper, any color for vase
- (1) 9″ x 12″ white drawing paper
- crayons
- scissors
- paste or glue
- watercolor paints and paintbrush

Steps:

1. Using crayons, draw various flower shapes on the 9″ x 12″ white drawing paper. Color some parts and leave some parts white. Make them various sizes.

2. Paint a watercolor wash over each flower. Use a variety of colors.

3. When the flowers are dry, cut each one out.

4. Fold the 4″ x 6″ colored construction paper in half, lengthwise. Draw on half a vase shape with a pencil or crayon and cut out.

5. Paste or glue the vase to the lower half of the 9″ x 12″ black construction paper. Arrange the cut-out flowers above the vase and paste or glue into place.

Variations: Draw any shapes with crayons such as butterflies or ladybugs, color, and apply a watercolor wash. Paste or glue to an appropriate background.

Technique: Watercolor resist

Materials:

- (1) 9" x 12" white drawing paper
- shades of yellow and orange crayons
- black crayons
- orange, yellow, and red watercolor paints
- paintbrush

Steps:

1. Draw a happy, smiling sun face with a black crayon on the 9" x 12" white drawing paper. Make it large enough to fill the whole paper. Add facial features with black and draw the sun's rays with yellow, red, and orange crayons.

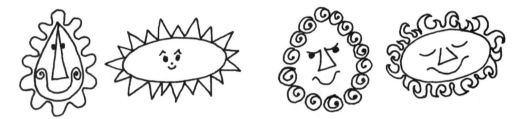

2. Paint in the sun with red, yellow, and orange watercolor paints. The crayon wax lines will keep the colors from running together. When the sun face is dry, cut it out.

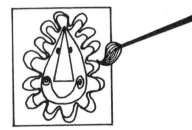

Variation:

Fill an entire sheet of paper with smiling sun faces of various sizes with yellow and orange crayons. Paint a wash over the entire paper with orange paint.

Bulletin Board:

Place the sun faces on a background of hot pink, yellow, and orange squares of tissue paper placed at angles, with the caption "Smiles Are Personal Sunshine" in black letters.

Textured Fruit

Technique: Crayon scratch

Materials:

- (1) 9" x 12" heavy paper or tagboard
- crayons
- etching tools: toothpick, nail file, paper clip, bobby pin, tapestry needle
- newspapers

Steps:

1. Cover work surface with newspaper, since this can be somewhat messy.

2. Apply bright light colors to the entire surface of the 9" x 12" heavy paper in a sort of "patchwork quilt" pattern. Press firmly with the crayons to get a good build-up of wax.

 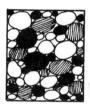

3. Pat the colored surface with some chalk dust from the chalkboard. After doing that, cover the bright colors with black crayons, thick and solid.

4. When the coloring is completed, use the etching tools to scratch out a planned picture: a bowl of fruit or one piece of fruit. Use changing pressure for medium tones and highlights and textures. Use varying widths of strokes, following the contours of the forms or masses of parallel lines to create textures. Demonstrate various techniques on the chalkboard. See samples below.

Variation:

Using a ruler as a guide, and with a scratch tool, divide the whole area into squares, then put different patterns and designs in each square.

Bright Birds

Technique: Crayon scratch

Materials:

- (3) 4 ½" x 6" tagboard or other heavy paper
- crayons
- scissors
- tempera paint, dark colors
- paintbrush
- newspapers
- liquid soap
- etching tools

Steps:

1. On each 4 ½" x 6" piece of tagboard or other heavy paper, draw the outline of a bird shape. Let the imagination run rampant. Color with bright light colors, filling in the entire shape with several layers.

2. Mix a few drops of liquid soap in the dark-colored tempera paint so that it will adhere to the crayon. Paint over the crayon surface of each bird.

3. When the paint is thoroughly dry, use the etching tools to remove some of the paint and you will be able to see the bright-colored crayon beneath. Depending on how much you remove and where you remove it, many variations are possible.

4. When the etching is completed, cut out the bird shapes. They can be suspended from a mobile if desired.

Illusions

Technique: Crayon scratch

Materials:

- (1) 9" x 12" heavy paper, bristol board, or tagboard
- crayons
- etching tools
- ruler
- newspapers

Steps:

1. Cover working surface with newspapers since this project can be quite messy.

2. Color a definite object, design, or picture heavily on the 9" x 12" heavy paper or tagboard. Color the background in a good contrasting color.

3. Paint the entire surface of the paper with a coat of black tempera paint mixed with a few drops of liquid soap. This will make the paint adhere to the crayon surface. Let dry thoroughly.

4. Using a ruler and an etching tool, divide the paper into squares. Continue using the ruler and scratch parallel lines in each division of space, changing direction of lines in adjoining areas. Make the lines close together so that an interesting effect is made when the original picture shows through.

Variation:

Using a ruler and an etching tool, divide the paper into interestingly-shaped rectangles and scratch various patterns and designs in each rectangle.

Technique: Watercolor resist

Materials:

- (1) 12" x 18" white drawing paper or butcher's paper
- crayons
- blue and green tempera (very, very thin) or watercolor paints
- paintbrush

Steps:

1. Draw and color an underwater ocean scene with all the sea life you can think of. Color over several times to get a good build-up of wax.

2. Paint over the picture with alternate lines of green and blue paint. Make sure the paint is very thin and that you do not go over the picture too many times. If you do, this will break down the crayon wax relief.

Variation: Draw a winter scene on light blue construction paper. Add snow by using white tempera paint.

Mosaic Fish

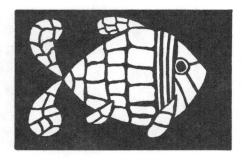

Technique: Crayon resist

Materials:

- (1) 9″ x 12″ white tagboard or other stiff paper
- crayons
- paintbrush
- thin black tempera paint
- newspaper

Steps:

1. Use a pencil to sketch lightly the outline of a fish on the 9″ x 12″ white tagboard or other stiff paper. Keep the shape large and simple, such as the fish shown here.

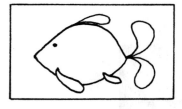  

2. Divide the shape of the fish into sections: squares, rectangles, diamonds, or any other shapes desired. Color the shapes with light bright colors. Leave a narrow space between the shapes as a mosaic. Make sure the crayon is applied heavily so there is a good build-up of wax.

3. When the drawing is completed, cover the entire piece of paper with a dark color of tempera paint. For best results, add a little water to the paint before putting it on the paper. Be sure not to go back and forth over the same place, or the paint will partly cover the wax.

Variations:

Try this technique with other familiar shapes such as fruit, vegetables, animals, flowers, or fireworks exploding in the night sky.

Crayons and Fingerpaint

Technique: Crayon and fingerpaints

Materials:

- a piece of fingerpaint paper or white butcher's paper
- bright-colored crayons (scraps are best)
- fingerpaint (powdered tempera mixed with liquid starch)
- newspaper

Steps:

1. Lay newspaper on desk and then place the white paper on top.

2. Color the entire surface of the paper with bright-colored crayons. Press firmly. Color in stripes or area blocks if you wish.

3. Cover the entire surface of the paper with fingerpaint. Use only one color and fingerpaint a picture or design over the top of the crayon.

Suggestions:

These make beautiful covers for books or folders.

"Two in One"

Technique: Chalk transfer

Materials:

- (1) 9" x 12" white construction paper or drawing paper
- piece of white or yellow chalk
- dark and light crayons
- pencil

Steps:

1. Fold paper in half.

2. Open. On one side rub lightly over the surface with chalk, covering with a light even coat of chalk.

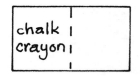

3. Over the chalk color heavily with a light crayon such as yellow or orange. Color a second layer with a dark crayon such as black or brown. Be sure to cover the light color completely.

4. Fold the paper closed. Draw a picture on the part of the paper covering the colored part with a pencil. Press heavily. When finished you will have two pictures.

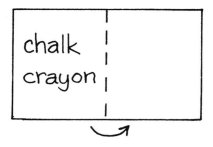

Variations:

These make marvelous Halloween pictures but can also be used in the spring for flowers, using pastel colors.

Clowns

Technique: *Crayon overlay*

Materials:

- (1) 12" x 18" black construction paper
- white tempera paint
- paintbrush
- crayons
- newspapers

Steps:

1. Look at pictures of clowns. Discuss clown make-up: exaggeration of features, hair, hats, and so forth. Draw examples on the chalkboard. Let the students draw suggestions also.

2. Using a pencil, lightly sketch the outline of the head of a clown, including his ears, hair, and hat, on the black construction paper. Paint two layers of white tempera paint, one vertical and one horizontal, within the sketch. Let dry thoroughly.

3. When the paint is completely dry, draw over it with bright-colored crayons. Outline the shape of the head, the facial features, the collar, and the hat with black crayon. Fill in the rest with bright-colored crayons. Let some white show. The black paper around the edge of the paper will frame the clown face nicely.

A Picture in Layers

Materials:

- (1) 9" x 12" or 12" x 18" stiff paper
- white tempera paint
- stiff brush
- watercolor paints
- soft brush
- container of water
- crayons
- newspaper

Steps:

1. Cover working surface with newspaper.

2. Paint the 9" x 12" or 12" x 18" stiff paper with white tempera paint, covering the entire surface with two coats, the first with the brush strokes going horizontally and the second with the brush strokes going vertically. Use a stiff brush to get finely textured lines. Dry thoroughly.

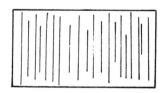

3. Draw a picture, using both the end and side of the crayon. The side of the crayon will let the textured tempera coat show through. Do not cover the entire surface with crayon.

4. Add watercolor wash to those areas of the drawing that are not heavily crayoned. The watercolor adds extra dimension to the drawing because of its transparency.

Note:

Be prepared to have this activity take several art sessions, as the white tempera paint must be thoroughly dry before applying crayon drawing.

Technique: Laminated crayons

Autumn Trees

Materials:

- (2) 9" x 12" pieces of wax paper
- crayon shavings in fall colors (brown, yellow, orange)
- (4) 2" x 9" construction paper in brown, yellow, orange
- scraps of brown construction paper
- white glue
- piece of yarn
- iron

Steps:

1. Place a piece of stiff paper on working surface. Lay one piece of 9" x 12" wax paper. Using brown construction paper scraps, tear shapes to make the trunk, limbs, and branches of a tree. Arrange on the wax paper.

2. Sprinkle crayon shavings around the branches of the construction paper tree to look like leaves. Place the second piece of wax paper on top. Place a piece of newsprint on top of that and then iron with a warm, not hot, iron. The melted crayons will hold the wax paper together completely.

3. When the wax paper is cool, glue two 2" x 9" strips of paper at the top edge and two at the bottom edge of the wax paper to make a hanging. Punch a hole in the middle of the top strips and hang with a piece of yarn.

Transparencies

Technique: Laminated crayons

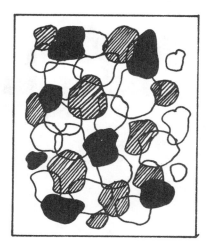

Materials:

- wax paper or plastic wrap
- newspapers
- iron
- crayon shavings

Steps:

1. Place a piece of wax paper (for a translucent effect) or plastic wrap (for a clear transparency) on a layer of newspaper. Place crayon shavings on the paper. If a lot of shavings are used, the crayon colors will run together; a few will melt but not blend together.

2. Place another piece of the same kind of paper on top so that it covers the one underneath. Cover with a piece of newspaper and press gently with a warm, not hot, iron. Use even less heat when working with the plastic wrap. The melted crayons will hold the two pieces of paper together perfectly.

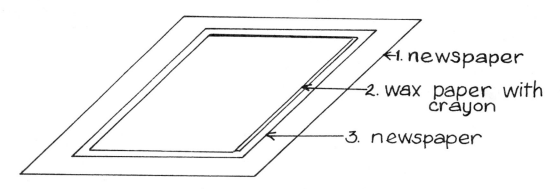

1. newspaper
2. wax paper with crayon
3. newspaper

3. Let cool.

4. The transparencies may be placed between cutouts of construction paper and hung as mobiles or individually in windows so the light will shine through.

Variation:

In addition to the crayon shavings, add bits of yarn, string, sequins, glitter, and/or construction paper cutouts for unusual effects.

Tulips in Spring

Technique:

Crayon sandpaper

Materials:

- a piece of fine-grained sandpaper, any size desired
- piece of white construction paper, same size as sandpaper
- crayons
- iron
- newspaper

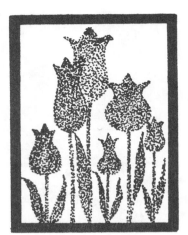

Steps:

1. Draw a picture or design on the sandpaper. Color very heavily. Remind the children that if they use printing, it must be put on the sandpaper backwards if it is to print correctly.

   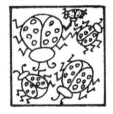

2. Lay the sandpaper on the newspaper pad with picture facing up. Cover with the white construction paper, making sure the design will be in the center.

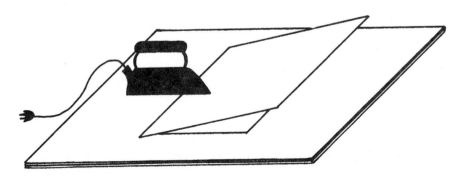

3. Preheat the iron to a medium temperature. Place on one end of the white construction paper and move gently across the paper in one direction and then back again. Lift the white paper carefully as it and the sandpaper will be very hot.

WaVe a BanNer

Technique: Crayon on fabric

Materials:

- fabric: old sheet, linen, unbleached muslin, washed to remove all traces of sizing
- crayons
- thick cardboard, Masonite™, or wood larger than fabric
- iron and damp cloth
- newspaper
- stick or dowel

Steps:

1. Use thumbtacks to attach the four corners of the fabric to a piece of cardboard, Masonite™, or wood. Sketch a design or picture directly on the fabric or make an outline of design or picture on paper with orange or red-violet crayon, and then lay the design face down on the fabric and transfer by running a warm iron over the back of the paper.

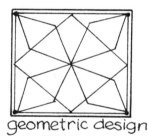

picture   simple object   geometric design

2. Color the design directly on fabric, using plenty of pressure and following the direction of the weave of the fabric.

3. Lay the fabric on the newspaper with picture facing up. Set the color on the fabric by pressing with a hot iron, using a damp cloth on the back of the fabric and a clean paper against the face of the design. (The paper will have a nice print for framing.)

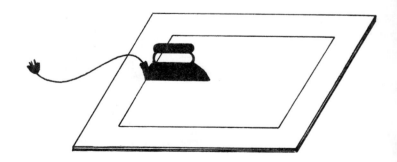

4. Pull threads around the edges to fringe and then hang from a stick or piece of ¼" doweling. Tassels can be added.

Technique: Paper batik, resist

Materials:

- 9" x 12" white or manila paper
- crayons
- brown tempera paint
- wide paintbrush
- newspaper
- running water or a large container of water in which to dip paper

Bursts of Color

Steps:

1. Lightly draw lines from one corner to the other, making an X to find the center of the paper. Draw a single shape in the center. Using contour lines, draw to the edge of the paper, filling the entire page with a design or pattern. Color with bright colors, filling in entire design.

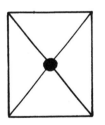

2. When the coloring is completed, put the paper under running water or in a container of water to make completely wet, and then crumple it into a tight ball so the crayon cracks. Open it up again.

3. Lay the wet paper on newspaper and paint over the entire picture with the brown tempera paint.

4. Immediately put back in the water to wash off the paint. Spread out flat on newspaper to dry. When dry it can be ironed on the back side to make it perfectly flat.

Fabric Batik

Technique: Batik, resist

Materials:

- black felt-tip pen for drawing
- fabric: old sheets, unbleached muslin
- ½" cube of paraffin, plus three crayons for each color desired
- metal juice cans
- muffin cups
- electric skillet and aluminum foil
- old brushes: small for wax and large for stain
- stain: India ink or large bottle of Rit® concentrated dye (dark)
- iron
- lots of newspaper/paper towels
- heavy cardboard or Masonite™

Preparation:

1. Combine three crayons with one cube of wax in each juice can for each color desired.

2. One can of pure paraffin should be prepared to use to clean brushes between color changes. **Caution:** Melt this slowly, for hot paraffin erupts. Stand away from the melting paraffin and take care not to get any on the skin.

3. Melt wax by placing it in juice cans in a foil-lined electric skillet (on low setting).

Steps:

1. Stretch and tack fabric to a board covered with newspaper.

2. Draw design on fabric with the felt-tip pen.

3. Paint areas formed with warm-colored wax, leaving spaces between colors. To make sure the wax penetrates the fabric, keep the heat under the crayons constant and work fairly rapidly. If the color will not penetrate the fabric, turn the fabric over and paint the melted crayon on the other side.

4. Let wax dry thoroughly. Then take the fabric between your hands and crumple gently. The extent of crumpling will determine how much the colors are "cracked" after dyeing.

5. Lay flat on newspaper and paint stain on top waxed side. If dye is used, rinse in cold water. This step is not necessary when using ink.

6. Place the cloth between sheets of paper towel on a pad of newspaper and press with a hot iron to remove wax.

Crayon on Wood

Technique: Drawing on wood

Materials:

- piece of pine wood or plywood, any size desired
- piece of white construction paper same size as wood
- crayons
- iron
- Krylon clear spray paint—matte, satin, or gloss

Steps:

1. Smooth wood with sandpaper if necessary, wipe clean.

2. Draw and color a picture or design on the piece of wood. Color heavily, building up a good coat of wax. Make strokes following the grain in the wood.

3. Place the white paper on top of the picture on the wood.

4. Iron over the top of the white paper and wood, using a medium temperature. Gently move the iron from top to bottom. Carefully remove the white paper.

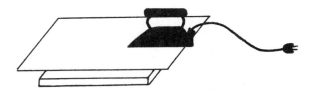

5. Often the print on paper will be quite lovely and can be mounted on construction paper or framed.

6. Spray with Krylon clear paint—matte, satin, or gloss finish.

About Paper

Paper, the most common of all art materials, is also one of the most versatile and exciting materials available for art experiences. The very presence of paper arouses interest and invites manipulation. Paper can be torn, cut, pasted, folded, curled, twisted, pleated, crushed, bent, scored, and creased. Experimentation will reveal that you can do with paper only what its qualities permit: Tissue paper can't hold weight; stiff cardboard won't easily be rolled and will crack when folded. Experimenting always leads to surprises and presents challenges which in turn motivate further experiments. With repeated opportunities to work with paper, to select, to discard, to combine colors and textures, students develop a sensitivity to the qualities of paper and the ability to manipulate it with ease.

The tool used most often with paper is the scissors. With the use of scissors, paper changes its appearance almost magically. A pair of scissors is a fascinating tool and it is important to be able to use it with confidence—to control and cut with ease, to know and understand all its possibilities and limitations. Any time spent on the basic cutting techniques is well worthwhile.

The activities in this section are really just the beginning steps on the "yellow brick road" into the world of paper. Many of the activities involve learning basic techniques with paper and scissors which can develop skill, hopefully limit initial frustrations, and provide experience on which creativity is built.

Techniques With Paper

With a fundamental, working knowledge of the following basic techniques with paper, anyone should be able to design and create in paper, manipulate and form paper into aesthetically satisfying forms, and communicate an idea to others by means of a paper form.

Tearing

Hold the paper between the thumbs and forefingers, tearing a bit and then moving the fingers and thumbs down before continuing to tear for complete control of the direction in which the paper tears.

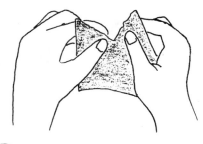

cutting

For basic geometric shapes, symmetrical shapes, on the fold, five-point and eight-point stars, snowflakes cut with the scissors, refer to pages 67–72.

- *Fringing:* slitting the paper by means of parallel cuts to desired depth to make a stringy edge.

- *A spring:* a long continuous cut in a circular or square pattern; resulting segmented paper can be pulled or twisted into exciting forms.

- *Slashing:* a long continuous eccentric cut into a flat piece of paper allows the paper to be turned, twisted, rolled, and shaped into all sorts of eccentric forms.

- *Slashing:* long eccentric cuts made inward from a folded edge allow paper to be pulled in or out into odd-shaped forms.

Folding

- Folds made in the same direction produce a form that tends to turn into itself and that encloses space. The volume enclosed will vary depending upon the number of folds and the space between them.

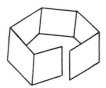

- Accordion pleats: made up of a series of back and forth folds that are of equal widths.
- Parallel folds, unequally spaced, produce rooflike forms of varying height that seem to move onward through space.

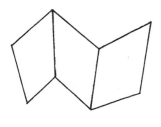

Rolling

- Cylinders: made from a rectangular-shaped piece of paper.
- Cones: made from a whole circle or a pie-shaped section of a circle.

Bending-Twisting

Strips of paper can be looped, rolled, twisted, and bent into all sorts of shapes; they stay in shape if ends are attached to each other as in the tear shape or if ends are attached to other surfaces.

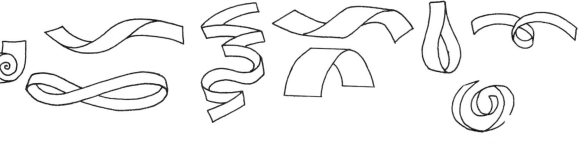

Curling

Wrapping or pulling strips of paper around a pencil, closed blades of scissors, or a dowel.

Fastening

- Use of white glue or paste, stapler, needle and thread, slits through which a strip or tab may be pushed and pasted into place, string or yarn for tying parts together.
- Self-fastening can be achieved by slitting and inserting the ends, one into another.
- Mounting objects on a cardboard base helps them to stand.

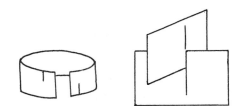

Materials

The following materials will be needed to do the activities in this book. All paper sizes used can be cut from 12" by 18" standard-sized paper to eliminate the overflowing scrap box which eventually ends up in the trash. However, there will be many activities in the book that will call for scraps so do have a box or drawer of paper scraps of all kinds.

Kinds of Paper

- **newsprint:** thin paper such as that on which newspapers are printed; comes in pastel colors and beige; is weak and flimsy, tears easily, and soaks up much water under pressure.

- **gray bogus:** an inexpensive paper which comes in bundles; absorbent, heavyweight, fibrous; good as background for collage and other activities needing fairly stiff background.

- **manila:** similar in weight to construction paper; comes in light creamy color; works well with all media; comes in large (18" x 24") and small (9" x 12") sizes.

- **construction paper:** strong paper; comes in a rainbow of colors, both pastel and vivid tones; most universally used of all papers; applies itself well to the majority of the activities in this book.

- **drawing paper:** white in color (some colored paper does come in this weight); lighter in weight than construction paper.

- **"kraft" wrapping:** also called shelf paper, comes in large rolls 20" or 36" wide; usually white or brown but is now more commonly available in eight basic colors; for the tight budget it can be substituted for construction paper in many activities.

- **tagboard:** mediumweight, fairly stiff paper; hard surface; creamy color or some pastel colors; good for collages, etc.

- **chipboard:** gray in color, comes in a variety of weights or thicknesses; if available can be used instead of cardboard.

- **tissue paper:** lightweight, versatile paper in bright vivid colors as well as variegated colors; even printed with holiday patterns, etc.; usual sizes are 12" x 18" or 15" x 30".

- **"collectible, found, free-for-the-asking" paper:**

metallic papers	newspaper	shelf paper
magazines	colored cardboard	textured papers

    used wrapping paper or gift paper

    tissue paper used in "gift bags"

    corrugated paper from cardboard boxes

    paper packing materials

    decorative papers from greeting cards, envelopes

    wallpaper—leftover ends from rolls, sample books

Additional Materials

scissors   pencils   paper punch

paste or white glue   crayons   needle and thread

rubber cement (if desired)   stapler   paper clips

cardboard   yarn   brads

lids of gift boxes or shoe boxes

- A part of the "learning to see" process can be making a collection of a variety of papers that are interesting in color, texture, or design.

- Keep different kinds of paper separated and stored in boxes; detergent boxes with the tops cut off make good paper files; for small pieces use shoe boxes.

- Keep on hand a box of pre-cut squares and rectangles of paper of various colors, 2", 3", and so forth; you never know when they may come in handy.

- When cutting 12" x 18" paper on the paper cutter, the following sizes are easily cut, cutting the solid lines first, the dotted lines second:

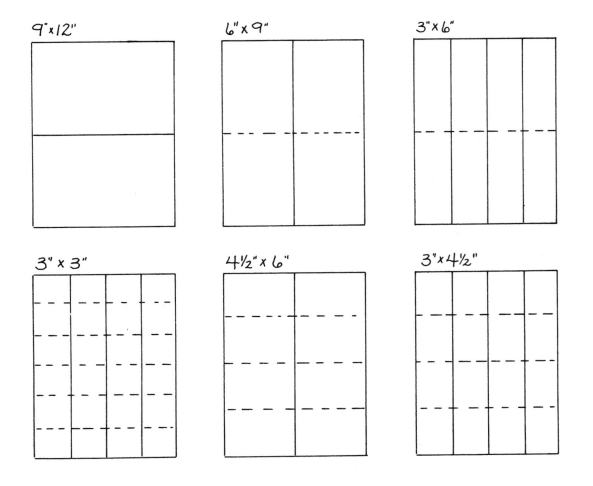

9"x12"   6"x 9"   3"x 6"

3" x 3"   4½" x 6"   3"x4½"

Torn-Paper Mosaics

Materials:

- (1) 9" x 12" or 12" x 18" colored construction paper or other heavy paper for background—dark colors with a light background or light colors with a dark background
- scraps of all colors of construction paper and/or any other kind of paper, plain or printed
- crayons, to accent shapes
- white glue or paste
- pencil

Steps:

1. Using the pencil, lightly sketch the outline of a simple object on the 9" x 12" or 12" x 18" background paper. Keep it fairly simple and large so that it will be easy to fill in with the small paper pieces.

2. Tear the various pieces of paper into small square and rectangular shapes. When tearing, hold the paper between the thumbs and forefingers, tearing a bit and then moving the fingers and thumbs down before continuing, so you have complete control of the direction in which the paper tears.

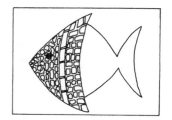

3. Fill in the outlined shape with the bits of torn paper, using glue or paste to secure in position, Leave a space between each shape so the background paper will show through.

58

Autumn Trees

Technique: Tearing

Materials:

- (1) 9" x 12" light blue or tan construction paper
- scraps of green, yellow, orange, red, and purple construction paper
- brown crayon
- white glue or paste

Steps:

1. Begin by drawing a trunk for the tree on the lower portion of the 9" x 12" construction paper with the brown crayon. Remember that it's not just a stick; all branches come out from a V shape as illustrated. Look at real trees! (The trunk can be made from brown construction paper if desired.)

2. Tear the colored construction paper scraps into small pieces. When tearing, hold the paper between the thumbs and forefingers, tearing a bit and then moving the fingers and thumbs down before continuing, so you have complete control of the direction in which the paper tears.

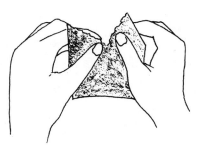

3. Paste or glue the torn-paper leaves onto the branches of the tree. They may be placed solid or with spaces between them so the branches will show. Some might be placed at the base of the tree.

Variation:

Make trees for other seasons of the year, using the tearing technique.

Turkey Cups

Technique: Tearing

Materials:

- (1) ⅓-quart milk carton
- scraps of brown construction paper
- (1) 1" x 8" strip of brown construction paper
- (8–12) 2" x 4" strips of construction paper for feathers: red, yellow, orange, tan strips
- white glue or paste
- scissors
- black crayon

Steps:

1. Cut the milk carton in half as illustrated. Use a pointed scissors or a serrated knife. Cover the bottom half of the carton with the scraps of brown construction paper torn in small pieces. Use white glue to attach the pieces to the waxy surface of the milk carton.

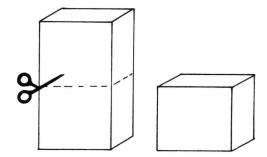

2. Roll the top of the 1" x 8" strip of brown paper and glue or paste to make the head. Using black crayon, add eyes and make red wattles from scraps. Attach the neck to one portion of the carton.

3. Fold the 2" x 4" strips of construction paper in half, lengthwise. Trim off the open corners to make the feather shape. Cut slits along the open edges. Paste or glue to the side of the milk carton opposite the neck and head to make the tail.

Variations:

— These can be made with any size milk carton and used to hold nuts, fruit, winter squash, or dried flowers.

— Decorate with all kinds of paper and use as a vase. (Can be used to hold real flowers as the container is waterproof.)

Technique:

Tearing, cutting

Torn-Paper Pictures

Materials:

- (1) 9" x 12" or 12" x 18" light blue or dark blue construction paper for background
- scraps of all colors of construction paper and/or any other kind of paper, plain or printed
- white glue or paste
- crayons

Steps:

Snow Pictures

1. Tear scraps of white paper into mound shapes for the snow on the ground. Tear small pieces for falling snow. Paste or glue the mounds of snow to the bottom of the paper (used vertically or horizontally).

2. All the other things in the picture should be torn from the paper scraps of all colors. Some things can be made from geometric shapes and pieced or overlapped. Some ideas:

3. Glue or paste all the pieces on the large background paper. Add the small white pieces of paper for falling snow.

Flowers

1. Tear various shapes such as circles, triangles, and others from scraps of various colors of construction paper and printed papers to make the flowers such as those below.

2. Use shades of green construction paper scraps to make the leaves and stems.

3. Glue or paste into position on light blue construction paper. Details may be added with crayon if desired.

Variations:

— butterflies   — cities

— landscapes   — animals

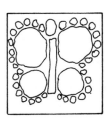

Holiday Pictures

Technique: Tearing

Materials:

- (1) 9" x 12" or 12" x 18" construction paper for background
- (1) 9" x 12" or 12" x 18" black (or complementary color) construction paper for frame
- scraps of all colors of construction paper and/or any other kind of paper, plain or printed
- white glue or paste

Steps:

The following will show how to make the Native American Chief step by step. Additional illustrations will show the shapes needed for the other holiday symbols.

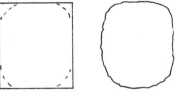

1. Tear away the edges of a piece of yellow or tan paper to make the oval shape for the face.

2. Use scraps of black or brown paper to make the hair. All colors of paper may be used to make the feathers and headband. The facial features can be torn from paper or added with crayons.

3. Apply paste or glue to the individual pieces and attach to the background paper. Begin with the neck, then the face, adding the hair and finally the feathers and headband.

 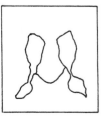 

4. When all the pieces are in place, black crayon may be used to outline and/or accent various shapes.

62

Other Holiday Symbols:

Wreath

Santa

candle/holly

turkey

Witch

Making the Frame:

Fold the 9" x 12" or 12" x 18" construction paper in half, lengthwise. Tear out the center section as shown, leaving a 1" border. Glue or paste into position on top of the completed project.

A Collage

Technique: Tearing

Collage means "collection," an artistic combination of overlapping pieces. It is a seeing and feeling design. Infinite variety may be obtained with the use of all kinds of paper such as foil, sandpaper, corrugated paper, wallpaper, tissue paper, and printed papers from magazines, catalogs, etc.

Warm and Cool Colors

Materials:

- (1) 12" x 18" fairly heavy paper such as gray bogus, tagboard, or other lightweight cardboard
- old magazines
- white glue or paste

Steps:

1. Go through old magazines and tear out sections of color. Tear out only what is needed, not the whole page, thus eliminating excess paper for clean-up. Look for solid colors, pictures of things that are warm or cool such as water, trees, fruit, sun, etc.

2. Divide papers into two piles, one with warm colors and one with cool colors. (Refer to the Tempera section, pages 168–171 for additional information on color.)

3. Fold the 12" x 18" paper in half widthwise.

4. Using white glue or paste, put all the cool colors on one side of the paper and all the warm colors on the other side of the paper. Be sure to overlap edges so no background paper is showing.

5. Label each side with crayon if desired.

A Christmas Tree

Materials:

- (1) 9" x 12" or 12" x 18" colored construction paper
- scraps of all kinds of paper, printed or plain
- pencil
- white glue or paste

Steps:

1. Pencil in the shape of a Christmas tree on the large sheet of colored construction paper.

2. Tear scraps of all kinds of paper, printed or plain, into small pieces. Use the fronts of old Christmas cards for additional visual interest.

3. Fill in the shape of the Christmas tree with the small torn paper pieces, overlapping the edges, securing in place with white glue or paste.

Variations: Try creating other holiday symbols for different times of the year; an Easter egg, a valentine heart, a shamrock, a flag.

An Abstract

Materials:

- all kinds of paper, printed or plain; a variety of sizes
- (1) 9" x 12" or 12" x 18" construction or other mediumweight paper for background
- white glue or paste

Steps:

1. From all kinds of paper, tear pieces of various shapes and sizes. Try using colors of paper to create a particular color scheme or mood. Use textured papers.

2. Arrange the pieces of torn paper on the background paper. Experiment with various arrangements before gluing or pasting into position.

Wallpaper Pictures

Materials:

- (1) 9" x 12" gray bogus or other heavy paper
- (1) 9" x 12" newsprint
- crayons and a pencil
- pieces of wallpaper or an old sample wallpaper book
- scissors, if desired
- white glue or paste

Steps:

1. Use the 9" x 12" piece of newsprint to draw a simple picture or object. This can be cut up to use a pattern when tearing or cutting the wallpaper if desired.

2. The picture is built up from the back. As an example, in the illustration, suitable colored wallpaper is cut or torn to shape and pasted into position for the sky. Clouds are added next; then the sea, the boat, and the sails are added in that order. Finally the flag and the wave curling away from the bow of the boat are added.

Scissors and Paper

Many people, children and adults alike, have a great difficulty controlling scissors properly and cutting with ease. Most resort to tearing the paper in sheer frustration. The following are suggestions for holding the scissors and paper for best control and results.

Holding the Scissors

1. Hold up the hand that will hold the scissors.

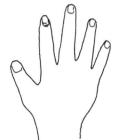

2. Holding the closed blades of the scissors in the other hand, place the thumb halfway through the first hole of the scissors and the second or "middle" finger through the second hole.

3. Rest the first finger on the bridge of the scissors to aid in the control of the scissors as well as in pushing up and down to help cut through thick paper and fabric.

4. For very young children it will probably be necessary to place two fingers in the bottom hole in the beginning because their fingers are small.

Holding the Paper

1. The paper does the moving, guided by the other hand. It is important to hold the paper in a manner which will give the greatest control. When it is held either at the bottom or the side, the fingers are out of the way of the scissors and it is easier to see what the scissors is cutting. The illustration show the position of the thumb of the paper-holding hand and the scissors.

2. When cutting an object whose center is the folded edge, always hold the folded edge. Then that edge will not be cut by mistake, making two pieces.

Note: Throughout this book the position of the thumb in the illustrations will show the best way to hold the paper to be cut.

Exercises in Cutting

The scissors is a fascinating tool when its many possibilities are explored. An introduction to the basic techniques of cutting will open a world of endless exploration of the magic of the combination of scissors and paper. Any time spent on the following exercises will be well worth it as well as fun.

Materials:

- squares and rectangles of any kind of paper: newspaper, newsprint, construction, manila, drawing, sheets torn from magazines, wallpaper, etc.
- scissors

Geometric Shapes

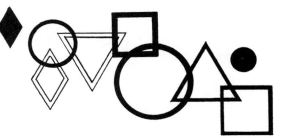

So often when constructing projects of paper, many begin with geometric shapes. With a little practice and know-how, these shapes can be cut from any size paper.

SQUARE: Use any size rectangular piece of paper. Fold one corner over diagonally to the opposite edge. Trim off the excess paper, using the edge of the paper as a guide.

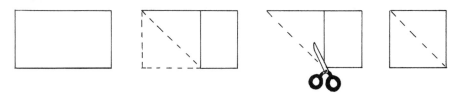

SQUARE RINGS: Fold the square in half. Holding the fold, cut half a square within the first. Begin at the folded edge, leaving a ¼" to ½" margin, and cut to the folded edge. For more square rings, repeat the process.

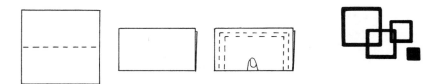

CIRCLE: Fold one square of paper in half. Hold the middle of the fold, open edges up. Trim off the top, open corners.

Begin at the middle of the side, cut to the middle of the top.

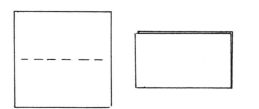

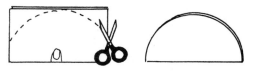

CIRCLE RINGS: While still holding the folded circle, cut half a circle within the first. Begin at the folded edge, leaving a ¼" to ½" margin, and cut around to the folded edge. For more circle rings, repeat the process.

TRIANGLE: Fold a square of paper in half. Holding the folded edge, cut from one open corner diagonally across the paper to the opposite folded corner.

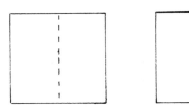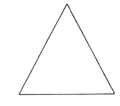

TRIANGLE RINGS: Turn the folded triangle shape so the top open edges are up. Leaving a ¼" to ½" margin, cut from the fold up to the corner; turn and cut to the folded edge. For more rings, repeat the process.

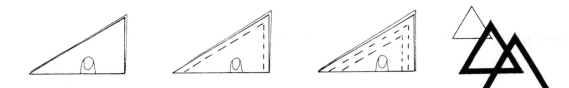

DIAMOND: Fold a square of paper in half. Hold the middle of the fold. Begin by cutting from one corner to the middle of the top open edges. Then cut from the middle of the top to the other folded corner.

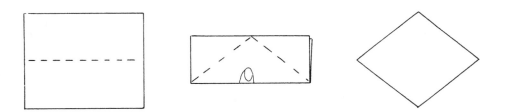

DIAMOND RINGS: Holding the folded edge of the diamond shape, cut another diamond shape within the first, cutting up from the fold to the top, turning and cutting down to the fold. Leave a ¼" to ½" margin.

Symmetrical Shapes

Any symmetrical shape, both halves the same, can be cut on the fold of the paper.

Fold the paper in half. Draw half a shape on the folded edge of the paper, keeping the center of the shape on the fold. Cut out, holding the paper on the folded edge. In the illustrations here, those areas shaded are cut away.

Other examples: the possibilities are endless!

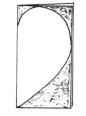  

Designs on the Fold

Fold the (9" x 12") paper in half vertically. Pencil in shapes along the folded edge of the paper. Leave spaces between each shape. Cut shapes out, holding the open edges of the paper.

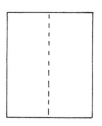  

Cut-out Panels

Fold the (9" x 12") paper in half and then in half again, vertically. Pencil in shapes along the folded edges, leaving spaces between each shape. Cut out shapes. Open paper carefully.

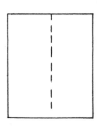 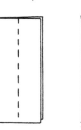  

These cut-out panels can be glued over crayon designs, tissue paper, etc.

Other examples: shapes, objects, symbols.

A Spring

Fold a square of paper in half. Trim the open corners to make a circle. Open. Beginning at the edge, cut in and around to the middle of the circle. Cut about ½" from the edge.

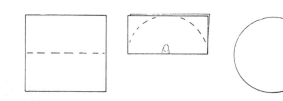

cutting a series

"Series cutting" is just making a string or row of figures or objects.

1. Place strip of paper on flat surface.

5. Continue until the entire paper has been folded.

4. Turn paper over and repeat.

3. Turn over. Fold up same amount again.

2. Fold up bottom edge about 3–4 inches.

open edges

folds

folds

open edges

6. Place paper so folded edges are on the sides.

Draw a simple figure or object on the top square. Remember to make the shape go all the way to the edge. In the illustrations below, notice the arrows which point to areas of fold that will be left. These will hold the figures or shapes together. Shaded area is cut away.

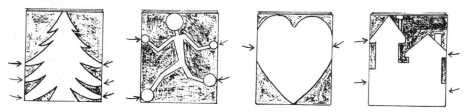

A Five-Point Star

1. To make a five-point star, fold a 9" x 12" lightweight paper as illustrated, folding in the direction of the arrows.

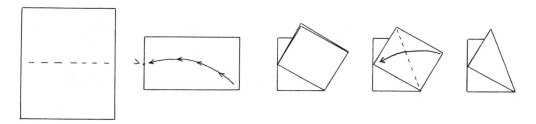

2. Fold the lower section behind.

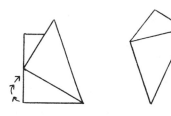

3. The closer to the bottom the cut is made, the sharper the points will be.

With practice, it will be possible to make stars with any size rectangle.

An Eight-Point Star

1. To make an eight-point star, fold a 9" x 12" lightweight paper as illustrated, folding in the direction the arrows indicate.

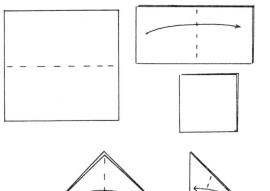

2. Turn the paper so the open edges are up and the closed edges are at the bottom.

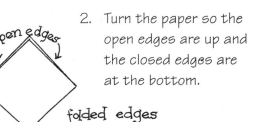

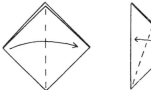

3. The closer to the bottom the cut is made, the sharper the points will be.

Snowflakes

Use a square, at least 6", of any lightweight paper such as tissue, copy, or typing paper.

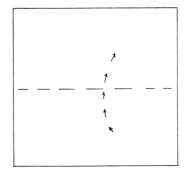

1. Fold the square in half.

2. Fold in half again.

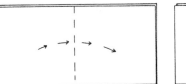

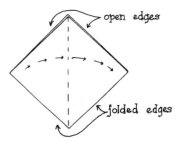

3. Turn the paper so the folded edges are at the bottom and the open edges are at the top.

4. Fold in half diagonally.

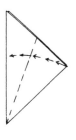

5. Fold in half, diagonally, a second time.

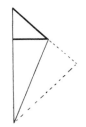

6. Trim off the top edges (shaded).

7. Pencil in shapes along both folded edges. Remember to leave a space between each shape. Cut out.

8. Complete, before opening.

Technique: Cutting

Materials:

- (2) 9" x 12" construction paper: two different colors
- pencil
- paper punch
- 8–12" piece of yarn
- scissors
- white glue or paste

Line Movement

Steps:

1. Draw a moving line diagonally across one piece of 9" x 12" construction paper with a pencil, pressing very lightly.

 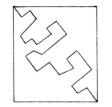  

2. Cut the paper into two pieces, cutting carefully on the pencil-drawn diagonal line. Remember to turn the paper while cutting, keeping the scissors directly in front of the body. Do not trim the edges of either piece.

3. Glue or paste one half of the design on one side of the second sheet of construction paper. Turn the paper over and glue or paste the other half of the design on the other side, back to back. Be sure to glue the edges down on both sides.

4. Punch a hole in the center of the top of the completed design with a paper punch. String yarn through the hole and tie. This way, when hung, both sides of the design will be visible.

Variations:

— Try combining one piece of plain paper and one piece of printed paper, such as wallpaper or a page from a magazine.

— Combine black construction paper and classified ad section of the newspaper.

Positive-Negative Panels

Two Panels

Materials:

- (1) 9" x 12" white construction paper
- (1) 6" x 9" construction paper, any color
- scissors and pencil
- white glue or paste

Steps:

1. Fold the 6" x 9" colored construction paper in half, lengthwise. Holding the open edges, cut shapes along the folded edge, leaving a space between each shape. (These may be penciled first.) After cutting, open. Save the small shapes cut out.

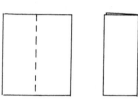

2. Fold the 9" x 12" white construction paper in half, widthwise. Open and lay flat. Place the piece with cut-out shapes on one half and glue or paste into position. Glue or paste the cut-out shapes on the other panel, down the middle, in the same order.

Four Panels

Materials:

- (2) 3" x 9" pieces of colored construction paper
- scissors
- (1) 9" x 12" white construction paper
- white glue or paste

Steps:

1. Fold the 9" x 12" white construction paper in half, widthwise, and then in half again. This will make four 3" x 9" panels. Open and lay flat.

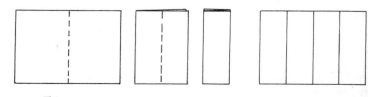

2. Fold the two 3" x 9" pieces of colored construction paper in half, lengthwise, together. Cut out various shapes on the folded edge. Remember to leave a space between each shape and save all the pieces.

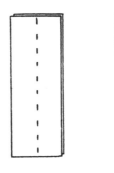

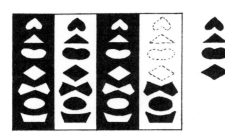

3. Paste or glue the two pieces of colored construction paper to the white paper in alternate panels. Match the small cut-out pieces to the corresponding holes and glue or paste into the other white panels. Watch spacing. It is a good idea to place the pieces in order on the work surface before beginning to glue or paste.

Cut-out Panels

Materials:

- (1) 9" x 12" colored construction paper
- (2) 3" x 9" white or contrasting color construction paper
- scissors
- white glue or paste

Steps:

1. Fold the colored construction paper in half lengthwise and then in half again. Pencil shapes on all three folded edges, leaving spaces between the shapes. Cut out the shapes; set aside.

2. Open the cut panel and glue or paste the cut paper onto the 9" x 12" sheet of construction paper. The pieces can be used to create a design on the other side of the paper or on a second sheet of construction paper. Try duplicating the cut design or experimenting with a new design.

Transparent Hang-ups

1. Fold two 9″ x 12″ papers in half, lengthwise, together. Cut out a single shape such as the Christmas tree illustrated. Save the cut-out trees. Glue the two cut papers together with a piece of tissue between so when hung the light will shine through.

2. Fold and cut a 9″ x 12″ paper into a four-panel design. Glue or paste tissue to one side. Bend ends around, tissue inside, overlap, and glue together to make a lantern.

Flags

Materials:

- 3″ x 3″, 4 ½″ x 6″, and 6″ x 9″ squares and rectangles of red and white construction paper
- sticks or strips of black construction paper for poles
- scissors
- white glue or paste

Steps:

1. Use the squares and rectangles for the shape of the flag as well as the designs for the flags. Use the techniques for cutting positive-negative panels as well as cutting on the fold.

2. Use this same technique for making flags for other occasions such as butterflies for spring, leaves for fall, jack-o'-lanterns for Halloween, and so forth.

Technique: Cutting

Materials:

- squares of all colors of construction paper or any other kind of paper, plain or printed
- pencil
- scissors
- white glue or paste

Flowers

Steps:

Colored paper flowers will brighten any dull corner, enhance a folder, make a lovely gift, and at the same time develop skill in manipulating the scissors. The more you make, the more ideas you will have.

A circle

Fold a square of paper in half. Holding the fold, cut off the top open corners to make a circle. Use scraps to make other circles; combine various circles to create any number of different flowers.

Freehand

Begin with a square of paper. The shape to be cut can be penciled on first or created while cutting. See illustrations below; shaded area is cut away.

 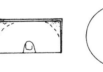

On the Fold

Fold a square of paper in half. Cut half a flower shape, holding the fold. The corners can be trimmed off to make a half-circle shape before beginning to cut the petals of the flowers.

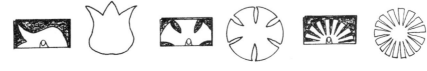

Folded

Fold a square of paper in half and then in half again in the opposite direction. Turn and hold the folded edges with the open edges up.

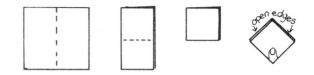

The following show three ways to trim edges of folded square to make three different shapes. Add a center of paper to each.

Fold a square of paper in half and then in half again in the opposite direction. Open. Cut almost to the center on each fold line. Then cut off the four corners. To give a 3-D look, fold the sides of each petal together as illustrated by the fold lines in the illustration. Add a bright yellow circle center.

Leaves

simple: Fold a square of green paper in half diagonally. Holding the fold, trim off the top corners of the triangle shape. Open.

complex: Fold a square of green paper in half. Holding the fold, cut a leaf shape along the open edges. Then cut a vein section along the folded edge, remembering to leave a space at the top and bottom of the leaf.

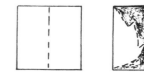

Experiment with all the kinds of flowers that can be made from parts of a circle: whole, half, or quarter.

Technique: Cutting

Three ideas for things to make with flowers . . . only a beginning of the many that are possible.

Fun with Flowers

Basket of Flowers

Materials:

- (1) 9″ x 9″ construction paper, any color, for basket
- (1) 1″ x 12″ construction paper, same color as basket, for handle
- (8–12) ½″ x 6″ strips of construction paper
- scissors
- scraps and small pieces of all colors of construction paper for flowers, green for leaves
- white glue or paste

Steps:

1. Fold the two opposite corners of the 9″ x 9″ construction paper to the center, overlapping in the center as illustrated.

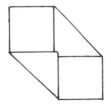

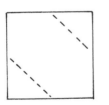

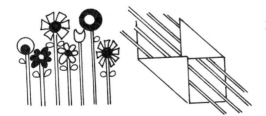

2. Cut flowers and leaves from the scraps and pieces of all colors of construction paper. Paste or glue the flowers to the green stems. Add leaves. Attach stems of flowers to the inside of the basket.

3. Fold the construction paper with the flowers in half. Attach the handle in the center between the folds or to the two top points or corners with glue or paste. Put a little glue or paste in the center to hold the two parts of the basket together.

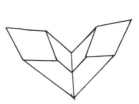

A Wreath of Flowers

Materials:

- (1) 12″ x 12″ green construction paper for wreath
- 2″ and 3″ squares of all colors of construction paper for flowers and leaves
- scissors, white glue or paste

Steps:

1. Fold the 12″ x 12″ green construction paper in half. Trim off the top, open corners. Cut a center section, as illustrated, so that you will have a ring—the base of the flower wreath.

2. Using the 2″ and 3″ squares of all colors of construction paper, make leaves and flowers. These can be cut freehand with the paper open or folded as on pages 77 and 78.

3. Paste or glue the flowers and leaves to the green ring. If you glue or paste only the centers of the flowers and the base or end of the leaves, they can be bent and folded to give a three-dimensional effect.

A Special Card

Materials:

- (1) 9″ x 12″ colored construction paper (card)
- (1) 6″ x 9″ green construction paper (stems)
- (1) 4 ½″ x 6″ colored construction paper (vase)
- scraps of colored construction paper (flowers)
- white glue or paste
- scissors and pencil

Steps:

1. Fold the 9" x 12" paper in half, widthwise, to make the base of the card.

2. Fold the 4 ½" x 6" colored construction paper in half, widthwise. Holding the fold, cut a vase or pot (see illustration). Put paste around the sides and bottom edge of the vase and attach to the lower portion of the card.

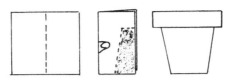

3. Cut out stems with leaves and make flowers to glue or paste on each stem. Write a job to be done on each of the stems to be placed in the flower pot or vase.

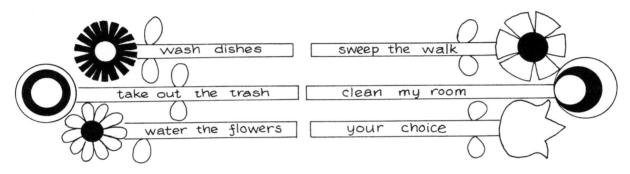

4. Write the following verse on the pot or inside the card:

    Pick a flower and
    You will see
    The job you'll pick
    This week for me.

Caption: Mother's Day, Father's Day, Valentine's Day

A Nosegay

Technique: Cutting, folding

Materials:

- (1) 9" x 12" green construction paper
- (1) 9" x 12" colored construction paper
- 2" x 2" pieces of construction paper, all colors, for flowers (or scraps)
- 1" x 1" pieces of yellow or other construction paper for centers of flowers (or scraps)
- scissors
- white glue or paste
- stapler

Steps:

1. Fold both 9" x 12" pieces of construction paper in half, together, lengthwise. Mark a line 1" from the open edges. Cut strips ½" to ¾" wide, from the folded edge up to the pencil line.

2. Separate folded, cut papers. Push one edge 1" up from the other and glue, paste, or staple. This will cause the strips to loop. Do this to both pieces of paper.

3. Roll the colored strip up and staple bottom to hold shape. Roll the green strip around this and staple all together. This will be the base. The flowers will be glued or pasted to the ends of the strips of the colored section in the middle of the rolled paper.

4. Use the 2" x 2" squares of colored construction paper (or scraps) to make flowers and 1" x 1" squares of paper (or scraps) to make centers. Glue or paste the completed flowers to the looped strips in the middle.

5. Ribbons may be tied around the base for added decoration.

Variations:

— Make all the flowers of nothing but circles.

— Adapt to different times of the year, such as Valentine's Day.

Technique: Cutting

Materials:

- (1) 12" x 12" colored construction paper
- one of the following:
  - (1) 9" x 9" colored construction paper, a complementary color
    or
  - (4) 5" squares of construction paper in complementary colors or white or a variety of squares of colored construction paper from which to cut a number of circles
- scraps of all colors of construction paper or any other paper, plain or printed
- scissors
- white glue or paste

Disc Designs

Steps:

1. The 12" x 12" piece of construction paper is the background paper on which the disc will be placed or discs arranged.

2. Fold the square or squares of paper in half. Holding the fold, trim the top, open corners to make circles/discs.

3. If using more than one disc, arrange in a design or pattern on the background paper.

4. Using the scraps of paper, cut a shape for each disc. Cut one large shape for the single disc. For ideas, refer to exercises in cutting pages 67–72, or cutting flowers, pages 77–78. After cutting, glue or paste into position.

Variations:

— Use black construction paper for the background. Fold into thirds so there are nine squares. Put a disc with a design in each square.

— Cut a snowflake of tissue paper for each disc; refer to page 72 for snowflakes.

Finger Puppets

Technique: Cutting, folding

Materials:

- strip of paper or felt for the body, approximately 2" x 3 ½"
- scraps of construction paper and/or felt
- bits and pieces of yarn, cotton, buttons, feathers, etc.
- scissors
- crayons and/or felt-tip pens
- white glue or paste

Steps:

1. Wrap the 2" x 3 ½" strip of paper or felt around a finger, overlapping ends of the strip to fit. Use a small piece of tape to hold, or make a pencil mark where the ends overlap. Remove and glue or paste the overlapped edges to make a tube.

2. Press the tube flat, making sure the overlapped section is underneath (the back); this makes it easier to decorate. If desired, glue or paste the top of the tube closed, leaving the bottom open so it can be slipped onto finger.

front   back   flat

3. Decorate with crayons, felt-tip pens, scraps of construction paper and felt, bits and pieces such as yarn, cotton, buttons, feathers, etc. Secure with glue or paste. The following are just a few of the possibilities.

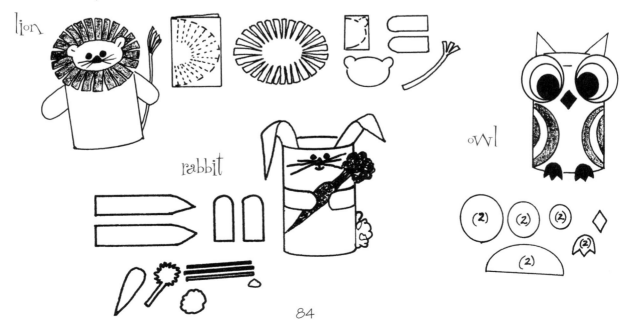

lion

rabbit

owl

84

dog

(2)

(1)

Native American

cat

(2)

Santa

Pilgrim

2

bear

chief

Variation:

To represent a large number of puppets on stage, attach a finger puppet to each finger. The five puppets on one hand might be a choir, a family, or a tribe of Native Americans like those illustrated. If one of the puppets speaks, move him forward and from side to side slightly so the audience knows which character is talking.

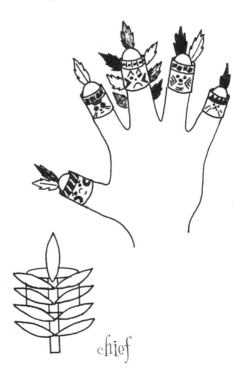

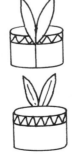

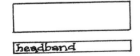

headband

A Paper Cylinder

Variations of this simple-to-make puppet are endless. The following materials are for a duck. Additional variations and paper sizes are listed on the following pages.

Technique: Cutting, folding

Materials:

- (1) 9" x 12" yellow construction paper
- (2) 3" x 3" orange construction paper
- (2) 3" x 6" yellow construction paper
- white glue or paste
- (1) 2" x 4" orange construction paper
- scraps of black construction paper or black crayon for eyes
- scissors

Steps:

1. Put paste or white glue along one 9" edge of the 9" x 12" yellow construction paper (shaded area). Roll paper into a tube, overlapping edges, and hold firmly until glue or paste is set. (Gently rub inside tube with palm of hand.)

2. On the inside of the tube, put paste or glue about two inches down and pinch the top together, making sure the overlapped edges are in the center back. With scissors, round off the top corners to make the head.

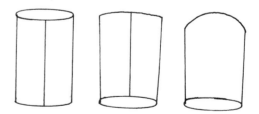

3. Place the two 3" x 6" pieces of yellow construction paper together and trim off the corners as illustrated to make the wings. Glue or paste to the tube in the middle of the back.

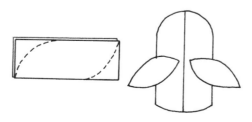

4. Fold and cut both pieces of the 3" x 3" orange construction paper as illustrated to make the feet. Fold the top part of each foot down about one inch. Put glue or paste on the flap and attach to the inside front of the tube.

5. Fold the 2″ x 4″ orange construction paper and round off the open edge corners. Fold again next to the first fold to make a flat surface, and paste or glue to the front of the duck. Use crayons or black construction paper to make the eyes.

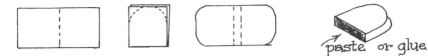

paste or glue

Variations:

The following are just a few of the many variations possible. Sizes given are for 9″ x 12″ cylinders. Colors are optional. Try using printed papers such as wallpaper or plain paper and coloring patterns such as calico designs.

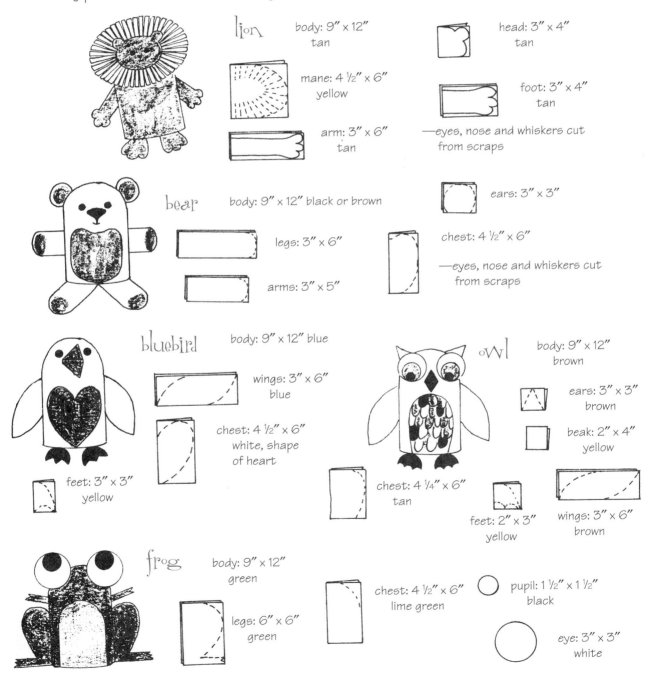

lion
body: 9″ x 12″
tan

mane: 4 ½″ x 6″
yellow

arm: 3″ x 6″
tan

head: 3″ x 4″
tan

foot: 3″ x 4″
tan

—eyes, nose and whiskers cut from scraps

bear
body: 9″ x 12″ black or brown

legs: 3″ x 6″

arms: 3″ x 5″

ears: 3″ x 3″

chest: 4 ½″ x 6″

—eyes, nose and whiskers cut from scraps

bluebird
body: 9″ x 12″ blue

wings: 3″ x 6″
blue

chest: 4 ½″ x 6″
white, shape of heart

feet: 3″ x 3″
yellow

owl
body: 9″ x 12″
brown

ears: 3″ x 3″
brown

beak: 2″ x 4″
yellow

chest: 4 ¼″ x 6″
tan

feet: 2″ x 3″
yellow

wings: 3″ x 6″
brown

frog
body: 9″ x 12″
green

legs: 6″ x 6″
green

chest: 4 ½″ x 6″
lime green

pupil: 1 ½″ x 1 ½″
black

eye: 3″ x 3″
white

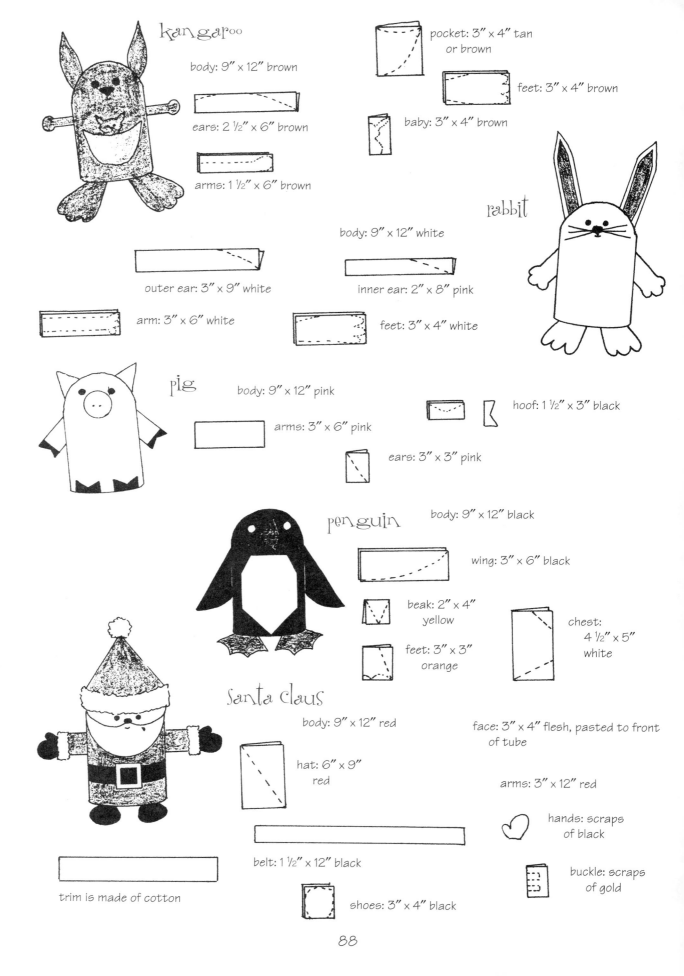

kangaroo

body: 9" x 12" brown

ears: 2 ½" x 6" brown

arms: 1 ½" x 6" brown

pocket: 3" x 4" tan or brown

feet: 3" x 4" brown

baby: 3" x 4" brown

rabbit

body: 9" x 12" white

outer ear: 3" x 9" white

inner ear: 2" x 8" pink

arm: 3" x 6" white

feet: 3" x 4" white

pig

body: 9" x 12" pink

arms: 3" x 6" pink

ears: 3" x 3" pink

hoof: 1 ½" x 3" black

penguin

body: 9" x 12" black

wing: 3" x 6" black

beak: 2" x 4" yellow

feet: 3" x 3" orange

chest: 4 ½" x 5" white

Santa Claus

body: 9" x 12" red

hat: 6" x 9" red

belt: 1 ½" x 12" black

trim is made of cotton

shoes: 3" x 4" black

face: 3" x 4" flesh, pasted to front of tube

arms: 3" x 12" red

hands: scraps of black

buckle: scraps of gold

Technique:
Cutting, folding

Standing Animals

Materials:

- (1) 9" x 12" colored construction paper for body
- (1) 6" x 9" colored construction paper for head
- scraps of construction paper, all colors, for facial features, etc.
- scraps of yarn, string
- crayons and scissors
- white glue or paste

(Additional materials for each individual animal are listed below.)

Steps:

1. BODY: Fold the 9" x 12" colored construction paper in half, widthwise. Cut out half-oval from the center of the open edges as illustrated.

2. Open the 9" x 12" paper and lay flat. Cut a slit 1" long on the center fold, from the edge.

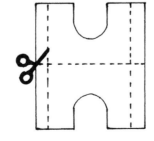

3. Fold back 1" of the paper along each side to make the legs. Stand up.

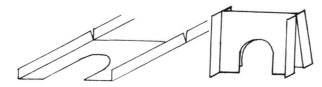

4. HEAD: The basic shape is cut from the 6" x 9" colored construction paper, folded either lengthwise or widthwise. The following will show how to cut the head and list additional materials needed for each animal.

horse

- 6" x 9" folded lengthwise

Cut half the shape of a horse's head. A mane and tail can be added with yarn.

lion

- 6" x 9" yellow paper for mane
- 3" x 4" tan paper for face

1. Fold both pieces in half, widthwise, and cut as illustrated.

2. Tail may be added with yellow or tan yarn.

pig

- 6" x 9" pink paper for head
- 2" x 6" strip for nose
- 3" square for tail

1. Make a tail by cutting a spring from the 3" square.

2. Cut the strip as illustrated for the nose.

elephant

- 6" x 9" gray paper for head
- (2) 3" x 4" gray paper for ears
- scraps of gray for tail, trunk

When cutting ears, make a tab by cutting a portion of the ear to attach to head.

giraffe

- 2" x 9" strip for neck
- 3" x 4" for head

< ears

cats

- 6" x 9" scraps for ears, whiskers

1. Make from gray bogus paper.

2. Color designs with crayons.

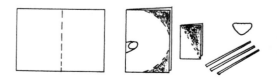

Faces

Technique: Cutting

Materials:

- face: (1) 6" x 9" flesh-colored construction paper
- hair: (1) 4 ½" x 6" or 6" x 9" construction paper, any color desired
- scissors
- white glue or paste

Steps:

1. FACE: Either trim off two bottom corners or fold the flesh-colored paper in half lengthwise and trim off the open corners as illustrated.

 or

2. GIRL'S HAIR:
   — Slash the paper at ½" intervals the length of the paper, leaving a 1" border at the top; cut away some of the strips to make bangs. The strips can be curled by rolling each strip on a pencil.

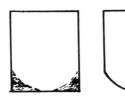

— Trace the head shape on the paper and trim edges to shape hair, using scraps for additional fullness.

3. BOY'S HAIR:
   — Slash the 4 ½" x 6" paper at ½" intervals the width of the paper, leaving a 1" border at the top; trim to shape hair to face.
   — Trace head shape on paper and trim edges at the top; trim to shape hair to face.

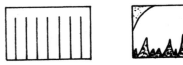

4. Attach hair to heads. Use scraps of construction paper or crayons to add facial features.

Pilgrims

Additional Materials:

- (1) 3" x 6" white construction paper for collar
- (1) 4 ½" x 6" colored construction paper for hat
- (1) 2" x 6" colored construction paper for band of hat

Hat: Round off top corners for the girl's hat and cut off the top corners diagonally for the boy's hat.

Add band along bottom to complete the hat. A buckle of yellow or gold paper may be added to the boy's hat.

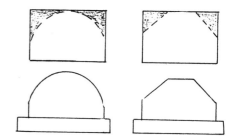

Collar: Fold the 3" x 6" white paper in half, widthwise, and trim off one open corner and one folded corner as illustrated by the shaded areas. Attach by gluing or pasting to the backside of chin area.

Santa

Additional Materials:

- 6" x 6" red paper for hat
- cotton for beard and hat trim
- scraps of construction paper for facial features and for head

Cover Your Sneeze

Additional Materials:

- 6" x 6" flesh-colored paper
- piece of facial tissue

Native American

Additional Materials:

- scraps of construction paper to make headband and feathers

Technique: Cutting, folding

Materials:

People in Motion

- flesh-colored construction paper cut to the following sizes:
  (2) 2″ x 2″   (2) 1″ x 12″
  (1) 3″ x 3″   (1) 1″ x 8″
- (1) 12″ x 18″ colored construction paper for background (light blue works very well)
- scissors
- white glue or paste
- scraps of construction paper, plain or printed papers, yarn, string, or anything else desired for clothes, hair, facial features
- crayons

Steps:

1. Fold each of the two 2″ x 2″ and one 3″ x 3″ squares of construction paper in half. Holding the folded edge, trim the top open corners to make circles.

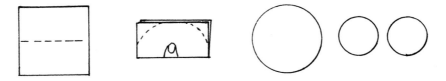

2. Fold the two 1″ x 12″ strips of paper in half and then in half again, widthwise. Open and cut into parts using the fold lines as a guide. There will be eight pieces. Curve the corners off each piece (two at a time).

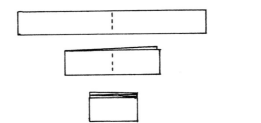
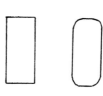

3. Fold the one 1″ x 8″ strip of paper in half and then in half again, widthwise. Open and cut into parts, using the fold lines as a guide. There will be four pieces. Curve the corners off each (two at a time).

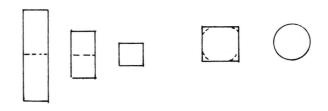

93

4. Place the pieces in the correct order (as illustrated) on the 12″ x 18″ piece of construction paper. Use a small scrap to make the neck.

Move the parts around until the figure shows some type of action. Experiment! The illustrations below show just a few of the many possibilities. When in position desired, glue or paste to paper, doing one piece at a time.

(This is also a good technique for a drawing lesson of the human figure.)

  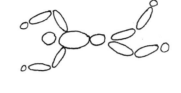

clothes

Use 3″ x 4″ pieces of paper, any kind.

Pants: Fold the 3″ x 4″ paper in half, lengthwise. Cut as illustrated.

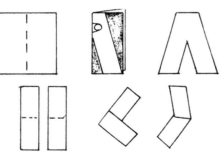

Shirts: Fold the paper in half, lengthwise, and cut as illustrated or use strips.

Skirts: Fold the 4 ½″ x 6″ paper in half, widthwise.

A Puppet

Cut two sets of pieces. Lay the pieces in order on a flat surface. Glue or paste string as shown on one set. Glue or paste the second set of pieces over the first to cover the string.

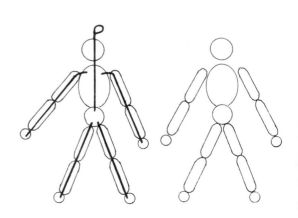

94

Technique: Cutting

Materials:

Words, Words, Words

- scraps of any kind of paper for the words
- paper for the background, plain or printed
- the lid of a box such as a shoe or gift box
- scissors
- pencil
- crayons
- white glue or paste

Steps:

1. Prepare the lid first. Either the inside or the bottom of the box lid may be used—the inside to give the effect of a frame, the bottom to stand away from the wall.

2. Use plain paper for the background if the letters are made from printed paper or vice versa. Cut a piece of paper the same size as the lid and glue or paste into position. (The lids could also be painted with tempera paint if desired.)

3. Select a word to be illustrated in a creative way. The following are a few examples. Once begun, the list of words that can be used is endless. The easiest way to make the letters is to pencil them on the paper to be used and then cut out. Glue or paste to the background.

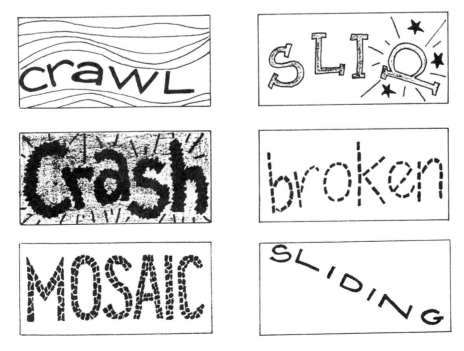

Crayons may be used to outline or accent the letters of the word.

95

Pull-Aparts

Materials:

- (1) 6″ x 9″ or 9″ x 12″ construction paper, color of object to be made
- (1) 9″ x 12″ construction paper for background, any color desired
- scissors
- white glue or paste
- a pencil

Steps:

The following will show how to make a pull-apart shamrock step by step. The other ideas illustrated are made in the same manner.

1. To make the shamrock, fold a 6″ x 9″ or 9″ x 12″ piece of green construction paper in half, widthwise. Pencil in half a shamrock. Another way is to draw three circles on a flat piece of paper and add a stem. Cut out.

2. The other shapes illustrated are cut out in the following manner:

3. Cut the shamrock into many pieces like a puzzle. As each piece is cut, place it in correct order on the 9″ x 12″ background paper, making sure the pieces do not get out of order or it will seem almost impossible to put them back together.

4. When all the pieces are in place, glue or paste into position, leaving a small space between each piece so the shape gives a "cracked" appearance.

Technique: Cutting

Materials:

Rabbit:

- white construction paper: (2) 3″ x 9″; (2) 9″ x 9″
- narrow strips for whiskers
- pink construction paper: (2) 2″ x 8″; (2) 2″ x 2″
- scraps of light blue and black construction paper for eyes

Black Cat:

- black construction paper: (1) 9″ x 9″; (2) 3″ x 3″
- narrow strips for whiskers
- scraps of green and black construction paper for eyes

For Both:

- scissors
- white glue

Steps:

1. Fold the 9″ x 9″ construction paper, white or black, in half. Holding the fold, trim the open corners to make a circle. Punch a hole on each side for strings to hold the mask on.

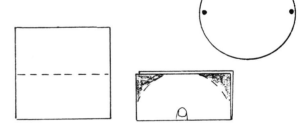

2. *Rabbit ears:* Fold the two 3″ x 9″ white and two 2″ x 8″ pink construction paper strips in half, lengthwise, each two together. Trim the open corners on one end to make the pointed ears. Paste or glue the pink inside the white.

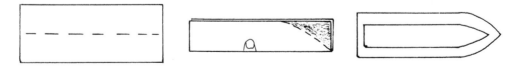

3. *Cat ears:* Fold the two 3″ x 3″ black construction paper in half, together. Holding the fold, cut diagonally from one open corner to one folded corner.

4. *Eyes:* Trim the corners of the 2″ squares and 1″ squares of paper to make circles. Glue or paste the small circles inside the large circles. Remember—the position of the small circles will show which way the animal is looking.

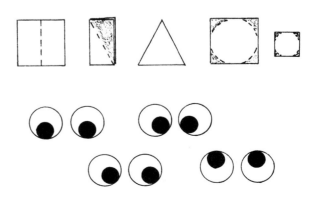

5. Open the large circle made from the 9″ square paper and lay flat. In the very center put some paste or glue and lay on strips of paper for the whiskers and then the nose. Attach the eyes and ears.

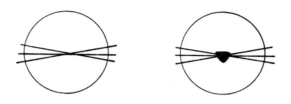

6. Cut a slit from the bottom of the circle up the fold to the nose. Pull one edge over the other and glue or paste into position so the mask will curve around the face.

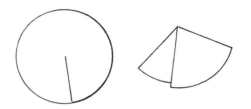

7. Add strings to the holes punched on each side of the mask.

Technique: Cutting

Materials:

A Very Special Egg

- (1) 9" x 12" white construction paper
- (1) 4 ½" x 6" yellow construction paper
- scraps of construction paper in all colors (or 2" and 3" squares)
- a brad
- white glue or paste
- (1) 12" x 18" white or colored construction paper to mount egg on

Steps:

1. Fold the 9" x 12" white construction paper in half, lengthwise. Hold the fold and curve the corners on the open edges to make an egg shape.

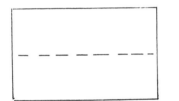 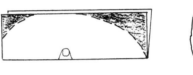 

2. Using scraps of construction paper (or 2" and 3" squares), cut any kind of shapes such as those illustrated to decorate the egg. Refer to pages 67–72 for other ideas. Paste or glue the shapes all over the egg. Overlap some. Be sure all the edges of each shape are secure.

   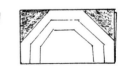

3. Fold the 4 ½" x 6" piece of construction paper in half, lengthwise. Cut half a chicken shape, holding the fold. You may wish to draw this first. Think of the letter B, which is the basic shape.

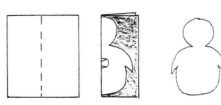

4. Cut a zigzag line across the width of the decorated egg, in the middle. Paste or glue the bottom half of the chick to the back of the lower part of the egg. Put glue or paste around the edge of the egg and attach to the 12" x 18" white or colored paper as illustrated.

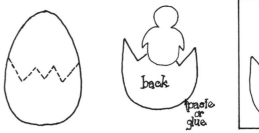

5. Attach the top half of the egg to the background paper with a brad placed in the lower left-hand edge. This will make the top movable, covering or revealing the chick inside.

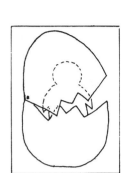

Variations:

This decorating technique can be used to create a Christmas tree, a butterfly, decorate a folder, a card, a kite, or anything desired.

Christmas Tree

Made from white or green construction paper 9" x 12" or 12" x 18", folded lengthwise. Add glitter and sequins as well as using some metallic papers for the shapes to create an exciting tree.

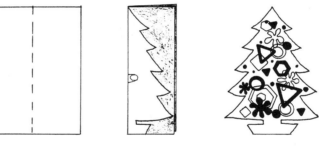

— This same tree made 3–4 feet high can be used to decorate a door at Christmas. Make of butcher paper and found papers.

Butterfly

Made of 9" x 12" white or colored construction paper, folded widthwise. Refer to the *Crayon* section, page 24, for how to mount butterflies on sticks.

Technique: Cutting

Materials:

- (1) 9" x 12" gray bogus paper
- (1) 9" x 12" black construction paper
- white tissue paper scraps
- scraps of orange and yellow tissue paper
- scissors
- white glue or paste

Steps:

1. Have a collection of pictures of houses showing different styles of architecture for the students to look at and discuss. Try to include pictures of old mansions. Talk about the building materials used to build the houses, such as lumber, bricks, stones, cement blocks, etc.

2. Fold the 9" x 12" black construction paper in half, widthwise. Cut in half, using the fold line as a guide. Cut pieces of lumber with one half and bricks, stones, etc., with the other half.

3. Use the scraps of white tissue paper to make ghosts, blowing curtains, clouds, and so forth.

4. Build a house from the foundation up, using the materials cut. Arrange the pieces first and then glue or paste into position, lifting one piece at a time.

5. Using the scraps of construction paper, add jack-o'-lanterns, black cats, witches, a moon, etc.

Lantern People

Technique: Folding, cutting

Materials:

- (1) 9″ x 12″ brown construction paper
- (1) 9″ x 12″ black construction paper
- (1) 2″ x 4″ colored construction paper for feathers
- (1) 2″ x 12″ orange or yellow construction paper for headband
- scraps of construction paper for facial features
- scissors and crayons
- white glue or paste

Steps:

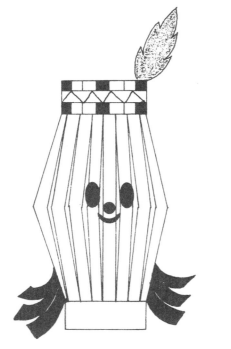

1. Fold the 9″ x 12″ brown construction paper in half, lengthwise. Cut strips, beginning at the fold and cutting to within 1″ of the top open edges.

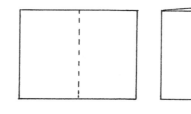

2. After cutting, open the paper. Roll, like a cylinder, overlapping the side edges, and glue or paste.

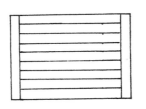

3. Hair: Draw a line 1″ from the top of the 9″ edge of the black construction paper. Cut strips from the bottom of the paper up to the pencil line. Glue or paste around the top edge of the lantern. Strips of hair can be curled by individually rolling each strip on a pencil.

4. Feathers: Fold each 2″ x 4″ strip of paper in half, lengthwise. Holding the fold, trim the open edges to make a feather shape. Slits can be cut along the edges.

5. Decorate the headband with crayons or scraps of paper. Paste or glue the feathers to the back of the hair and then attach the headband, covering the top of the hair and the ends of the feathers. Add eyes, mouth, etc., made from scraps of construction paper.

Technique: Folding, cutting

Materials:

- (1) 12" x 18" light blue construction paper
- (1) 9" x 9" white copy or typing paper
- (1) 7" x 7" white copy or typing paper
- (1) 5" x 5" white copy or typing paper
- scraps of all colors of construction paper or scraps of fabric
- white crayon
- scissors
- white glue or paste

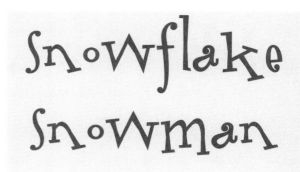

Steps:

1. Using the three pieces of white copy paper, fold and cut snowflakes following the instructions on page 72.

2. Hat: Fold a 3" square of construction paper in half and cut as illustrated. This can be any color of paper or made from fabric or pieces of wallpaper.

3. Collar: Use small scraps of paper or fabric and cut as illustrated.

4. To assemble, begin by placing the snowflakes on the 12" x 18" light blue construction paper. Begin with the largest snowflake at the bottom, the medium one in the middle, and the small one on top for the head. Add the hat and scarf as well as facial features cut from scraps of paper. Small twigs can be used for the arms. Falling snowflakes can be made with the white crayon.

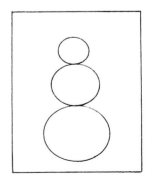

Variation:

For other projects using snowflakes, refer to the Tissue section of this book.

A Wreath

Technique: Cutting

Materials:

- (1) 9" x 12" or 12" x 18" green construction paper
- (1) 6" x 9" red construction paper
- white glue or paste
- scissors

Steps:

1. Fold the green construction paper in half, lengthwise. Fold in half again. Open to the first fold. Cut strips like a lantern, about 1" wide, from the bottom fold line up to the center fold.

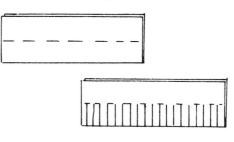

2. Open. Fold the uncut portions over each other and glue or paste. Then curve the paper around, fit one end inside the other, and glue, paste, or staple.

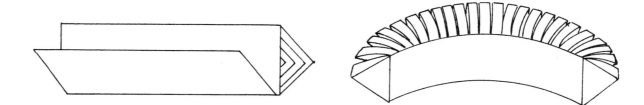

3. To cut the bow fold the 6" x 9" red construction paper in half, widthwise. Using a pencil, draw on half a bow and cut out. Also cut berries (round circles) from the scraps. Glue or paste onto the wreath.

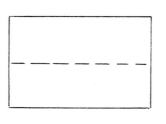

Variations:

— Make a flower wreath, covering the green wreath with bright spring flowers like those made on pages 77–78.

— Make a wreath of tan-colored paper and cover with autumn-colored leaves. Refer to page 78 for how to cut leaves.

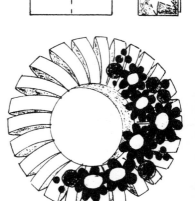

Technique: Folding, cutting

Materials:

- (1) 8″ square of construction paper or (2) 8″ squares of construction paper of complementary colors
- (1) 1″ x 12″ strip of construction paper for handle
- scissors
- white glue or paste

Steps:

This basket may be made with either one or two 8″ squares of construction paper. If using two, fold each separately and then place one inside the other before beginning to assemble.

1. Fold the 8″ square of construction paper as illustrated, folding in the direction of the arrows.

—Fold in half and then open.

—Fold outside edges to middle fold line.

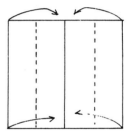

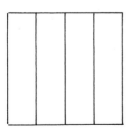

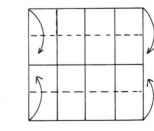

—Turn the paper and repeat the same process in the opposite direction. Open.

2. Cut away the four outside squares.

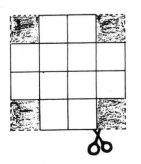

3. Overlap the corners of two squares and glue or paste.

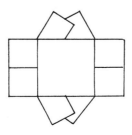

4. Add handle.

5. Decorate with flowers, etc.

Paper Building

Technique: Cutting, folding, bending, twisting, curling

Materials:

- strips of construction paper, 12" long, varying in widths: 1/4", 1/2", 1" and 1 1/2"; in complementary colors, or shades of a color
- (1) 9" x 12" or 12" x 18" colored construction paper for background
- white glue or paste
- scissors

Steps:

1. Place the 9" x 12" or 12" x 18" colored construction paper on the work surface. Arrange various strips on the paper to make a flat background design. Use plaids, or horizontal or vertical designs; discourage putting X's across the paper. When arrangement is complete (try several), glue or paste down.

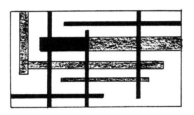 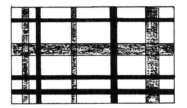

2. Experiment with various ways to curl, fold, bend, twist, and fringe the strips of paper. Remember to fold down a small piece at each end of the strips to make tabs for attaching to the background paper on top of the stripe design. A few ideas:

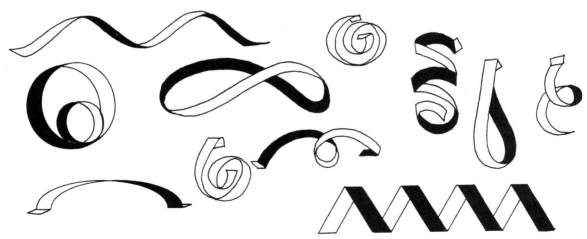

Variation:

Use red, white, and blue paper. When complete, add large gold stars cut from metallic paper. To cut 5-point stars, refer to page 71.

Technique: Cutting, rolling

Materials:

Paper Fruit

- assorted colors of construction paper, cut into 1″ x 12″ strips for fruit
- white glue or paste
- scissors
- *leaves:* scraps of green construction paper or pieces cut 2″ x 3″ and 3″ x 4″
- *cornucopia:* 9″ x 12″ brown construction paper

Steps:

1. Using one or more of the 1″ x 12″ strips of construction paper, glue or paste ends together to make the shape of a fruit. Apples, lemons, and oranges usually need only one strip. A banana takes two strips and grapes do not need a beginning shape. The rings will not stay in exact shape until they are filled with paper rolls.

2. Each shape will be filled with a number of rolled paper strips. To begin each roll, fold about ⅛″ of one end of the strip down and then roll the strip so it looks like a tight spring. Glue or paste the end of the strip to the roll.

3. Make enough paper rolls to fill the shape of the fruit. Place them in the shape to test how many are needed. Then take out the rolls, put paste or glue around the edge of each roll, and put back in the shape, sticking all together.

4. LEAVES: Fold scraps or rectangles of green construction paper in half. Cut out half a leaf. To create a three-dimensional effect, cut out parts in the center as illustrated. Glue or paste on fruit.

5. CORNUCOPIA: Fold the 9″ x 12″ brown construction paper in half, widthwise. Cut like a lantern. Open. Bring two diagonal corners together and overlap. Glue or staple.

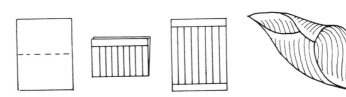

107

Accordion Pleats

Technique: Folding evenly without the use of ruler and pencil

Materials:

Materials are listed below with each idea.

Steps:

1. To fold a fan evenly, fold the 9" x 12" or 12" x 18" paper as follows, folding in direction of arrows.

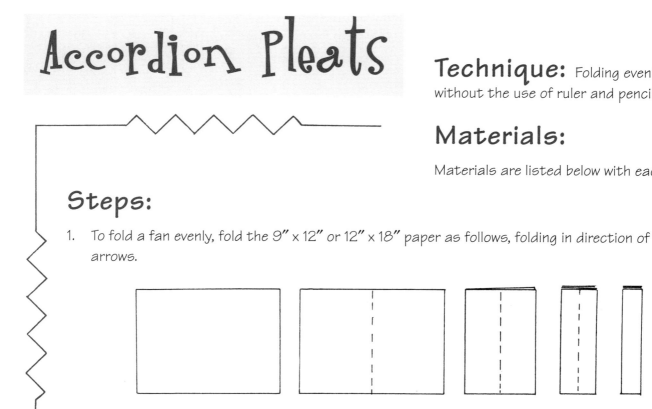

2. Now open and place flat on work surface. Using the fold lines as a guide, fold up on one side, turn the paper over and fold up again, repeating to the end of the paper.

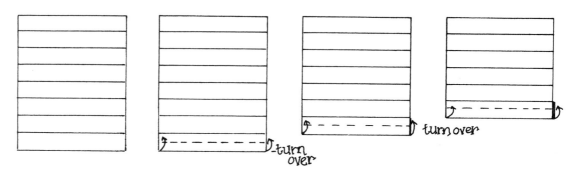

A Christmas Tree

Materials:

- (1) 9" x 12" green construction paper
- scraps of all kinds of paper
- scissors and white glue or paste
- stapler

Steps:

1. Fold the green construction paper into a fan, lengthwise. Staple all the folds together at one end.

2. Cut slits at an angle along one side of the folds, cutting from the bottom toward the top of the tree. Keep the slits unevenly spaced so ornaments can be placed all over the tree.

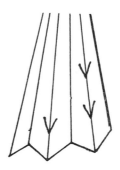

3. Cut small circles and other shapes from all kinds of paper. Try to use some metallic papers to make the trees more sparkly.

4. Put a little paste or glue on each ornament and slide it into place under a slit. After all the ornaments are on, a star may be added at the top. Refer to page 71 for how to cut a star.

Santa Claus

Materials:

- (1) 12″ x 18″ red construction paper
- (1) 9″ x 12″ white construction paper
- (1) 9″ x 12″ red construction paper
- scraps of blue, black and red construction paper
- scissors and white glue or paste
- a pencil and crayons

Steps:

1. Fold the 12″ x 18″ red construction paper into a fan, lengthwise. Staple the folds together at one end.

2. Fold the 9″ x 12″ white construction paper in half, widthwise. Holding the folds, trim the open corners to make a half-circle. Then scallop the edges of the circle.

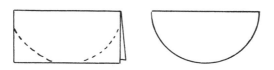

3. Fold the 9″ x 12″ red construction paper in half, widthwise, and cut a hat. This can be any shape, as illustrated.

4. Glue or paste the hat onto the white collar on the folded edge. Using the scraps of paper, add facial features.

5. With the leftover white paper, cut out a circle for the top of the hat and two hands. Attach to Santa, over stapled section of fan.

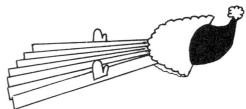

A Medallion

Materials:

- a square of lightweight paper:
  9" x 9", 10" x 10", or 12" x 12"

- 12" string or heavy thread

- glue or paste

Steps:

1. Fold the paper into a fan, lengthwise. Round off the corners of folds on both ends of one edge.

2. Along both folded edges cut out shapes as you would for a snowflake. Cut a V-shape from each side at the center.

3. Tie a string or heavy thread around all the folds in the center where the two V-shapes are. Then bring edges together and glue or paste together.

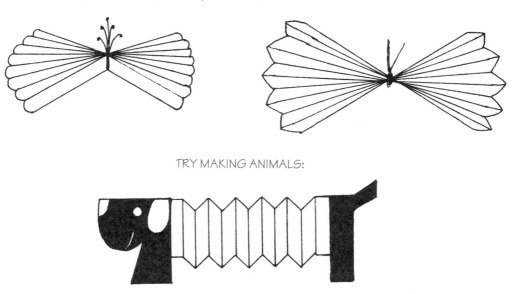

TRY MAKING ANIMALS:

Technique: Folding, cutting

Materials:

- (1) 9" x 12" construction paper
- white glue or paste
- scissors
- pencil

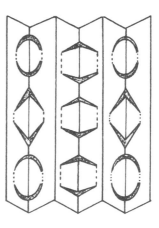

Steps:

1. Fold the 9" x 12" construction paper as illustrated, following the direction of the arrows.

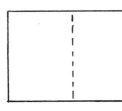 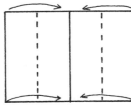

3. Open the paper so it is only folded in half. Make similar cuts along the center fold.

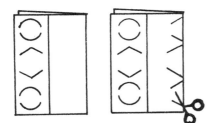

2. When the paper is folded as illustrated, make an equal number of cuts along the two folded edges as if cutting out shapes, but do not completely cut out the shape.

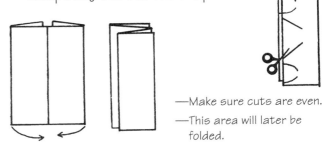

—Make sure cuts are even.
—This area will later be folded.

4. Open up the cut and folded paper. Let it lie like a fan on the desk. The cut portions are now pushed in the opposite direction so they will stand out. Experimentation is the best explanation at this point. Once learned, the effect is great.

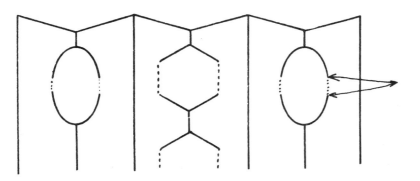

When the shape is pushed in the opposite direction and folded here, the shape will stand away from the paper.

Variation: Refer to the Mobiles section, a sculpture of paper, page 341.

Folded Paper Animals

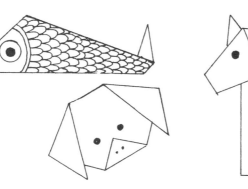

Materials:

- (1) 6" square of mediumweight paper such as fadeless, newsprint, copy, etc., for each animal
- scissors
- pencil
- crayons
- white glue or paste

Steps:

All the animals are made from 6" squares. Each animal illustrated may be made by folding as follows, always folding in the direction of the arrow.

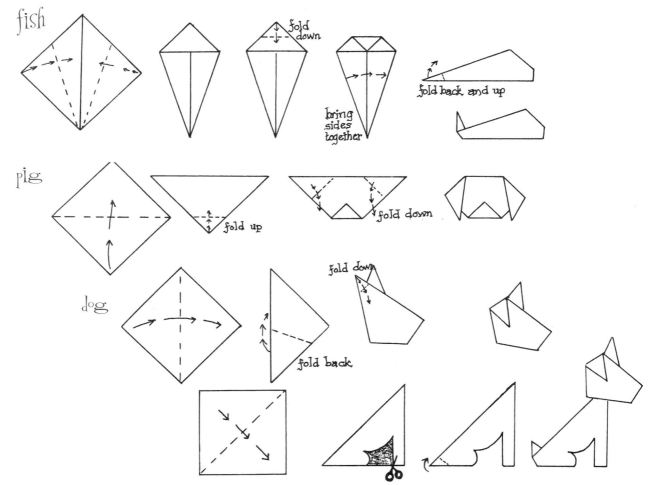

Bodies, such as the dog has, may be added to the other animals using the same technique. Details may be added with crayons.

About Tissue

Hurray for tissue, that gossamer, brilliantly hued material that seems to come from the very land of enchantment. So many wonderful experiences can evolve from this exciting medium. Tissue is vivid, translucent, light in weight, durable, and flexible. There are also the wonderful printed tissues we are surrounded with at holidays and on special occasions in the "gift bag." Collect all you can. Persons of all age levels work with it with great enthusiasm and success. It can be pasted, glued, starched, crumpled, stuffed, torn, wet, and cut. Overlapping can be done successfully because of its great translucent quality and amazing new colors can be achieved. The magic of blending and creating different hues and values inspires the imagination of children. Since tissue is so very lightweight and easy to manipulate, crumpling and pasting the tissue can provide two- and three-dimensional effects. It lends itself to many different techniques and combines well with other media.

We will explore the many exciting possibilities in the world of tissue, from very simple experiences such as overlapping colors and creating secondary colors to making wall plaques. Sometimes there will be several variations of the same technique, each involving a little more skill and coordination, while other projects will only have one example with suggestions for variations. There has been no attempt to dictate how or what one is to draw. Tissue provides endless opportunities to create.

Techniques With Tissue

The following techniques will be used in the tissue activities in this section. Here is a brief summary of each:

tearing   Do several pieces at one time as tissue paper is very lightweight; it will be easier to control.

cutting   free-form, symmetrical shapes on the fold

applying tissue to other surface   *liquid starch*—Easiest and least expensive to use as an adhesive, adheres to most surfaces; apply with use of soft bristle paintbrush, putting starch underneath and on top of each piece of tissue.

     white glue—Provides a durable, glossy, hard finish to completed project; expensive, sometimes too thick to work with.

     white glue mixture—Consists of two parts white glue to one part water; gives a hard, waterproof, fairly glossy surface to completed project.

tissue transparencies   Tissue paper between two layers of cut-out construction paper; hung or placed so the light can shine through the tissue paper.

laminated tissue   Torn or cut pieces of tissue paper placed between two layers of wax paper and ironed with a warm iron; the wax melts and bonds all together.

layered tissue   Cut or torn pieces of tissue paper are applied to a piece of wax paper with liquid starch, each piece overlapping, several layers thick. When dry, the wax paper is peeled away and the pieces of tissue paper adhere, creating one sheet of paper.

It is often desirable to add a protective durable finish to a completed project. The following materials can be used:

polymer gloss medium   Gives a hard, durable, waterproof surface to finished project; clean-up is easy as brushes can be cleaned with water. It looks like white glue but dries to a clear finish.

Krylon clear spray paint   Gives a matte, satin, or gloss finish to completed project; easiest to use, dries quickly.

clear plastic spray   Quick and easy to use, especially nice for flatwork projects; doesn't give a real high gloss to project, just a protective covering.

Materials

The following materials are needed to do the activities in this section:

tissue paper, all colors	crayons
construction paper, all colors	marking pens
white drawing paper	scissors
cardboard or chipboard	#6, #10, and #12 watercolor paintbrushes
aluminum foil	iron
wax paper	balloons
newspapers	paper towels
liquid starch	needle and thread
small containers	yarn, jute string
(milk cartons are best)	sequins, glitter
coat hangars	dried flowers, weeds
liquid bleach	pieces of wood for wall plaques
Q-tips (cotton swabs)	paste
white glue	

To give your projects a protective surface or covering, use a clear spray such as Krylon—matte, satin, or gloss finish.

Additional Materials

- Make a collection of things that have textured surfaces for crayon rubbings such as:

leaves	string	fine grasses	cutouts
burlap	sandpaper	textured fabric	waffle-weave fabric
cheese grater	window screen	corrugated paper	rough leather

- Save all the tissue scraps! They are marvelous for layered tissue projects as well as free-form collages and other projects.

- Be prepared to have the colors of tissue bleed; when a project is completed, go over the surface with a wide brush, making the strokes all one way. This will even out the color and when dry give the background a "watercolor" look.

- White glue and water mixtures will work well for adhering tissue to other surfaces, but be sure to wash brushes thoroughly when through.

- Milk cartons are excellent for individual containers for starch as they are easy to get, and do not tip over easily.

- Keep a box with 3" and 5" squares of tissue paper of all colors on hand. Many activities call for this size tissue and in an emergency will be waiting.

- Collect all those beautiful, printed tissue papers that come with "gift bags" at birthdays and holidays. (I never let a piece be put in the trash.) You get a reputation but who cares if it enhances an art project.

Creating Colors

Technique: Cutting, applying tissue to paper

Materials:

- 3″ square of tissue, 3 pieces each of red, blue, and yellow
- (1) 12″ x 18″ white construction paper
- liquid starch in a small container
- soft bristle brush and scissors
- newspaper for working surface

Steps:

1. Fold the 3″ squares of tissue paper in half, all 3 pieces of a color together. Trim off the open corners to make circles.

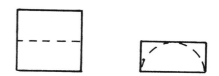

2. Fold the 12″ x 18″ white construction paper in half, widthwise.

3. On one half of the white construction paper, place the primary colors, red, yellow, and blue; one circle of each color in the order shown. Put a circle of starch on the white paper with the paintbrush, lay on the tissue circles, and then cover the tissue with starch.

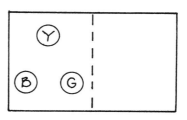

4. In the spaces between the primary colors, put the other tissue circles in the order shown below to produce the secondary colors, orange, violet, and green.

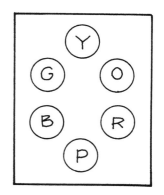

between:	red and yellow:	starch, red, and then yellow
	blue and red:	starch, blue, and then red
	yellow and blue:	starch, blue, and then yellow

Be sure to put starch under and over each piece of tissue.

5. On the other half of the white construction paper, use the tissue scraps to make a design. Paint the paper with starch and lay on the tissue pieces, overlapping colors to make the secondary colors. Put starch over and under each piece of tissue.

Tissue Bottles

Technique: Cutting, applying tissue to an object

Materials:

- (1) 9" x 12" white construction paper
- (1) 6" x 6" square of tissue paper of each color: red, yellow, blue
- liquid starch in a small container
- scissors, paintbrush, black crayon
- newspaper for working surface

Steps:

1. Cut each of the three pieces of tissue paper into a different shape bottle. The tissue paper can be folded as illustrated and the shape cut on the fold.

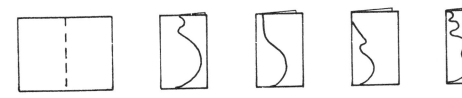

2. Using the paintbrush, cover the entire piece of white paper with liquid starch.

3. Arrange the tissue bottles on the white paper in the following order so that the secondary contrasts will show through the translucence of the bottles:
   - red
   - yellow overlapping red
   - blue overlapping yellow and red

   As each shape is placed on the white paper, apply a coat of starch, making sure not to go over the edges.

4. When the tissue bottles are dry, outline the shapes with black crayon.

Variation:

Cut the 6" squares into various geometric shapes; put on white paper with starch, overlapping shapes and colors to create the secondary colors. When dry, outline with black crayon.

Tissue Plaids

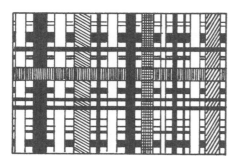

Technique: Cutting, applying tissue to paper

Materials:

- (1) 9" x 12" white construction paper
- pre-cut strips of tissue paper of various widths
- liquid starch in a small container
- paintbrush, scissors
- newspaper for working surface

Preparation:

Place three or four different color sheets of tissue paper in a single stack. Using the paper cutter, cut into ½", ¼", ¾", 1", and 1 ½" strips.

Steps:

1. Place the white construction paper on newspaper. Paint the entire surface with a coat of liquid starch.

2. Lay on horizontal strips, three or more of each color. Vary widths and spaces between the strips. Let the ends stick over the edge. Fill the brush with starch and paint the entire surface horizontally.

3. Lay on the vertical strips, three or more of each color. Vary the widths of the strips and the spaces between. Let the ends stick over the edge. Fill the brush with starch and paint the entire surface vertically.

4. When dry, trim off the ends of the tissue paper.

Suggestions:

These make beautiful cards, book or folder covers, and also are very striking when mounted on paper of a complementary color.

Technique: Tearing, collage

Materials:

Autumn Leaves

- (1) 9″ x 12″ white construction paper
- (2 each) 5″ squares of red, yellow, orange, and tan tissue paper
- liquid starch in a small container
- soft bristle brush and scissors
- pencil, 4 ½″ x 6″ pieces of newsprint

Steps:

1. Tear or cut the tissue paper squares into small pieces.

2. Paint the entire surface of the white drawing paper with liquid starch. Place small pieces of tissue paper on the white paper, one at a time. Paint over each piece with liquid starch. Mix the colors, overlapping pieces. Cover entire paper. Let dry.

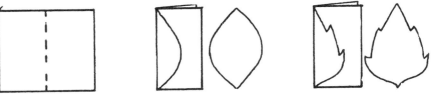

3. Fold the pieces of newsprint and on each draw half a leaf centered on the fold. Cut out. These will be used as patterns.

4. When the tissue paper is dry, lay the leaf patterns on the paper and draw around them with the pencil. Cut out. Make as many as possible different sizes. Scraps may be used for letters for captions, etc.

5. The leaves can be glued to a dried branch, put on the bulletin board, or hung as a mobile.

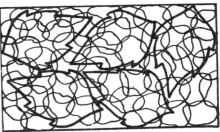

Variation:

Can also be done on wax paper for transparent leaves to hang in windows.

Action People

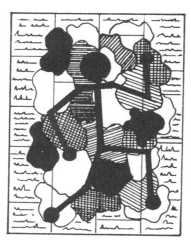

Technique: Tearing, layering tissue

Materials:

- 12" x 18" or 9" x 12" piece of the classified section of newspaper
- tissue paper, any colors desired
- liquid starch in a small container
- wide brush
- black crayon

Steps:

1. Tear tissue paper into medium-size pieces.

2. Paint the newspaper with liquid starch and lay on pieces of tissue paper. As you put down each piece of tissue paper, cover it with a coat of starch. Remind the students that they don't need to cover every bit of the newspaper with tissue paper.

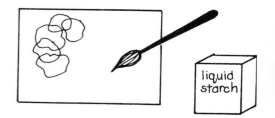

3. Let dry. (This will be a two-day or two-part project.)

4. Using the black crayon, make five dots on the paper far apart. Make stick figures running, jumping, skipping, and so forth: Make one dot the head, draw hands and feet at the other dots, then connect with lines for the body.

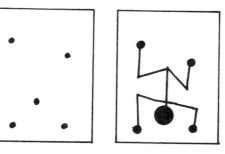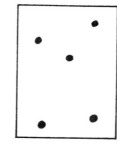

Variations:

Geometric shapes, snowflakes, patterns, or cut letters all made of tissue look delightful with the classified sections of the newspaper as background.

Tissue People

Technique: *Tearing, arranging*

Materials:

- 9" x 12" light orange tissue (for parts of body)
- all sizes of scraps of bright-colored tissue for clothes
- liquid starch in small container
- soft bristle brush
- 9" x 12" white construction paper

Steps:

1. Using the light orange tissue paper, tear out the parts of the body.

2. Cover the white construction paper with liquid starch using the paintbrush. Lay on the parts of the body, placing the head and torso first, and then putting on the arms and legs so that they show action.

3. Put a coat of starch on top of each part of the body.

4. Using the colored tissue paper, tear out clothes, hair, and any other details. Lay over the parts of the body and cover with starch.

5. The following illustrations show easy ways to cut clothes.

Technique:

Tearing, arranging

Materials:

- (1) 9" x 12" white drawing paper
- (1) 4 ½" x 6" yellow or tan tissue
- (1) 4 ½" x 6" brown tissue paper
- tissue scraps, all colors
- soft bristle brush
- liquid starch in a small container
- (1) 9" x 12" black construction paper

Native American Chief

Steps:

1. Tear away edges of the yellow or tan tissue paper to create the face. Use the 4 ½" x 6" brown tissue paper to make hair.

2. Using the scraps of tissue paper, tear out facial features and feathers for the headdress. Use many colors for the feathers.

3. Using the paintbrush, cover the entire surface of the white paper with liquid starch. Place the face shape in the middle or just below the middle of the paper. Cover with starch. Add the hair and facial features. Add feathers, remembering to overlap to create new colors.

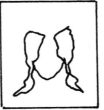

4. When the project is dry, black crayon can be used to outline and/or accent the various shapes.

Making the Frame:

Fold the 9″ x 12″ black construction paper in half lengthwise. Tear out the center section as shown, leaving a one-inch border.

Technique: Cutting,
applying tissue to paper

Cascading Shapes

Materials:

- (6) 5" x 5" squares of colored tissue paper, 2 each of three colors
- scissors
- soft bristle brush
- liquid starch in small container
- (1) 6" x 18" white drawing paper

Steps:

1. Fold the tissue pieces of each color together and cut out half-a-shape on the fold. These can be lightly penciled on the tissue paper before cutting if desired. Some suggested shapes:

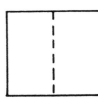  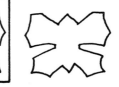

2. Arrange the shapes on the white paper; experiment with different arrangements, turn them at all angles, some overlapping. Tissue scraps can be added as well.

3. Remove pieces from white paper. Using the soft bristle paintbrush, cover the white paper with a coat of liquid starch. Lay shapes on one at a time, covering each piece separately with starch before adding another.

4. When all the shapes are on, fill the brush with starch and go over the whole paper with straight, even strokes, going from edge to edge either horizontally or vertically. This will spread out and even up any color that has bled from the tissue paper and creates a very interesting effect.

125

Over and Over

Technique: Cutting, applying tissue to other surfaces with a brush

Materials:

- 12" x 18" gray bogus paper
- 4" x 4" squares of tissue paper, 10 pieces each of three colors
- liquid starch
- small container for starch
- paintbrush
- scissors
- black crayon

Steps:

1. Fold the 4" x 4" tissue squares in half. Do several at one time. Cut out many sizes and shapes on the fold.

2. Using the paintbrush, apply liquid starch to the grey bogus paper. Lay tissue shapes on, covering each with liquid starch. Remember to overlap the shapes.

3. When dry, outline the shapes with black crayon, add lines, dots, etc.

Variation:

Calico Designs—Cut various size squares and rectangles; overlap shapes when applying to white paper. Add details with black crayon.

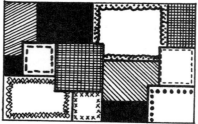

Misty May Gardens

Technique:
Tearing, cutting, collage

Materials:

- (4) 5" x 5" squares of light green and yellow tissue paper
- (2) 5" x 5" squares of dark-colored tissue paper (for flowers)
- (2) 5" x 5" squares of dark green tissue paper
- scissors
- liquid starch and paintbrush
- 9" x 12" lime green construction paper

Steps:

1. Tear the light green and yellow tissue into small pieces.

2. Put a coat of starch over the lime green construction paper with the paintbrush. Then put the light green and yellow pieces of tissue paper all over the green paper. Cover each piece of tissue paper with starch. This will make the background for the garden.

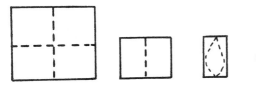

3. Cut one dark green square into thin strips for stems. Fold the other piece into fourths and then fold once more. Cut out a leaf shape. This will make 8 leaves.

4. Lay stems and leaves on the background while it is still wet. Lay some of the stems at angles so that the flowers look like they are moving. Then, using the tip of the brush, carefully apply starch to these, just on the tissue so the color doesn't run.

5. Cut out flowers all at the same time by folding both pieces of tissue together in fourths.

6. Put the flowers on top of the stems and cover carefully with starch.

Busy Cities

Technique: Tearing, cutting, arranging, layering

Materials:

- (1) 5" x 5" square of dark blue tissue paper
- (3) 5" x 5" squares of white tissue paper
- (4) 5" x 5" squares of tissue paper of different colors
- scissors
- liquid starch
- 9" x 12" light blue construction paper

Steps:

1. Tear the white and dark blue tissue into pieces.

2. Put a little starch all over the light blue construction paper and then lay the white and dark blue tissue on, one piece at a time, overlapping and covering each with starch. This will make sky and background.

3. Cut the colored squares of tissue into different sizes of squares, rectangles, triangles, and circles. Put them together to make houses and buildings. Lay them out along the top of the working surface.

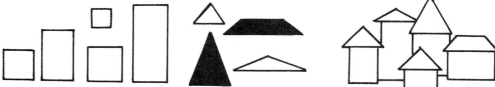

4. Place the houses over the background on the construction paper. This will still be wet, so lay each piece carefully and then cover with starch before adding another. Put starch just on the pieces so the colors don't run.

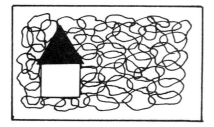

5. The following day when it is dry, use crayon to outline the buildings. Add details such as T.V. antennae, tiny people, cars, and so forth.

Technique: Tearing, cutting, applying tissue to other surfaces

Materials:

- (1) 9" x 12" black construction paper
- (1) 12" x 18" white construction paper
- tissue paper, bright colors, torn into medium-size pieces
- small container of liquid starch
- paintbrush and paper towel
- scissors and pencil

Positive–Negative Shapes

Steps:

1. Lay the 12" x 18" piece of white construction paper on top of newspaper. Using the paintbrush, cover the entire surface of the paper with liquid starch. Lay on the torn pieces of tissue paper, one at a time, and cover with starch. Cover the entire paper with tissue. Let dry overnight in a flat area.

2. Fold the 9" x 12" black construction paper in half, lengthwise. Draw half a butterfly on the fold. The older the students are, the more detailed this can be.

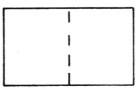

3. Cut out the butterfly. Remind the students to keep the butterfly in one piece. Follow the pencil line and cut carefully.

4. Fold the tissue-covered paper in half, widthwise. Paste or glue the cut-out butterfly on one half and the outline on the other side of the paper. This creates a positive-negative picture.

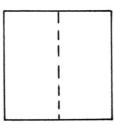 

Variations:

Any symmetrical shape cut on the fold can be used to create positive-negative designs as shown in these examples.

 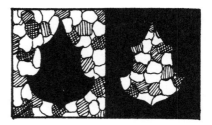

Create images of fall using orange, brown, and yellow tissue with cutouts of brown construction paper.

Technique: Cutting, applying tissue to other surfaces with brush, arranging

Materials:

- tissue paper: brown, purple, red, blue, green, orange, yellow
- (1) 9" x 12" newsprint
- (1) 9" x 12" white construction paper
- small container of liquid starch
- paintbrush, scissors, and pencil

Steps:

1. Cut cornucopia out of brown tissue paper and cut various fruit shapes from the other colors of tissue paper.

2. Arrange the design on the 9" x 12" piece of newsprint.

3. Paint the white construction paper with liquid starch. Move the arrangement from the newsprint to the white paper, one piece at a time. Go over the top of each piece lightly with starch. Be careful not to go over the edges so the colors won't run.

4. Outline the shapes of the fruit and cornucopia with black crayon after it is dry. The colors of the tissue may have run just a bit and this makes it more interesting; just outline the original shape of the fruit.

Variations:

This technique is applicable to any picture. After doing this activity, so the process is understood, put all sorts of tissue scraps and paper out to create seasonal pictures, still lifes, and designs. The following are examples:

Landscapes

Technique: Cutting, applying tissue to other surfaces with brush, arranging

Materials:

- (1) 9" x 12" white drawing paper
- small container of liquid starch
- (1 each) 6" x 6" squares of tissue paper: lavender, light green, dark green, light blue, turquoise, and purple
- scissors
- soft bristle paintbrush

Steps:

1. Cut the 6" tissue squares into the following shapes:

   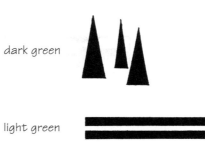

   light blue

   turquoise

   dark green

   light green

   lavender and purple

2. Cover the entire surface of the white construction paper with a coat of liquid starch, using the soft bristle paintbrush.

3. Apply the shapes to the white paper in the following sequence, covering each piece of tissue paper with liquid starch, overlapping pieces:

   light blue—sky

   lavender, purple—mountains

   light green—grass
   (leave room for lake)

   turquoise—lake

   dark green—trees

132

Technique: Tearing, cutting, applying tissue to other surfaces

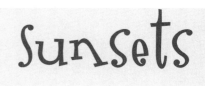

Materials:

- (3 each) 5" x 10" pieces of red, yellow, and orange tissue paper
- (1) 5" x 10" purple tissue paper
- (1) 9" x 12" white drawing paper
- liquid starch in a small container
- soft bristle brush
- (1) 6" x 9" black construction paper
- glue or paste

Steps:

1. Tear the 5" x 10" strips of purple, red, yellow, and orange tissue paper into various width strips. Tear several pieces at one time.

2. Brush the entire surface of the white paper with liquid starch. Apply the strips of tissue paper, overlapping edges of each strip horizontally in the following sequence:

purple

red

orange

yellow

red, orange, yellow

3. While the paper is drying, cut out silhouettes using the black construction paper and scissors.

   Suggestions: trees, buildings, cactus, sailboats, birds, people

4. Paste or glue the black construction paper silhouettes on top of the tissue paper sunset.

   Variation: The black silhouettes placed on top of the tissue paper sunset can be made with black ink or tempera paint.

Painting With Paper: still Lifes

Materials:

- tissue paper, all colors and sizes
- heavy white paper such as tagboard, or illustration board cut to desired size
- newsprint, same size as white paper
- scissors
- liquid starch in a small container
- newsprint for working surface

Steps:

1. Begin with a little pre-planning, sketching some ideas on newsprint with crayon. Show how small sketches can be made on newsprint, trying colors, shapes, and arrangements. Then select the still life liked best.

2. Using the various colors and sizes of tissue paper, cut out the shapes desired for the still life. Remember to use scraps whenever possible and to cut on the fold.

3. Arrange the shapes on the piece of newsprint which is the same size as the white paper, remembering to overlap pieces until the arrangement is pleasing.

4. Put starch over the entire surface of the white paper. Transfer the tissue pieces, one at a time, to the white paper, covering each with a layer of starch before adding another. If you don't want the colors to bleed, keep the starch on the tissue only and don't go over the edges.

5. If the colors do bleed when the picture is completed, while still wet, go over the entire surface with a brush full of starch. Paint from edge to edge, making the brush strokes all in one direction.

6. For a glossy finish, spray the finished picture with clear plastic, varnish, or shellac, or paint on a coat of gloss medium.

Technique: Rubbing, tearing, applying tissue to other surfaces

Crayon/Tissue Rubbings

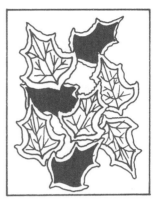

Materials:

- 5" squares of tissue paper in autumn colors
- fresh leaves with prominent veins
- pieces of brown crayon
- (1) 9" x 12" white construction paper
- liquid starch in a small container
- paintbrush and paper towel

Steps:

1. Put a leaf on the table with the vein side up. Place a single piece of tissue paper on top of the leaf and rub over the top of the leaf with the side of the crayon. This will pick up the leaf pattern.

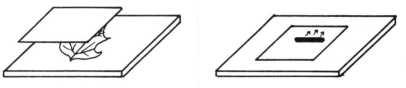

2. Do this many times on different colors of tissue paper. Then tear out the leaf shape rubbing on each piece of paper, following the basic shape of the leaf.

3. Using the paintbrush, cover the 9" x 12" white construction paper with liquid starch. Then, one at a time, lay the tissue leaves on the paper, covering each piece with liquid starch before adding another.

Seasonal Symbols in 3-D

Technique: Cutting, applying tissue to other surfaces—3-dimensional effect

Materials:

- 1 ½" squares of tissue paper in desired colors
- 9" x 12" construction paper in appropriate color for shape
- paste or glue and scissors
- pencil
- scraps of construction paper for details

Steps:

1. Cut the shape desired out of the colored construction paper. Fold the paper in half widthwise or lengthwise if a symmetrical shape is used. The following are a few suggestions for different seasons of the year:

2. Put some paste or glue in a flat container or on a piece of thick paper.

3. Place the forefinger or end of the pencil in the center of a tissue square and pinch up the sides. Dip the end of the tissue in paste or glue and then place on the construction paper shape. Repeat this step, placing each tissue square close together, until the entire shape is covered. Create designs by using different colors in patterns.

4. When the entire shape is covered with tissue, details can be added with pieces of construction paper, yarn, sequins, glitter, and so forth.

A Tree for All Seasons

Painting, tearing, applying tissue to other surfaces

Materials:

- (1) 9" x 12" construction paper in seasonal color—tan, light blue
- thin black or brown tempera paint
- a straw
- 1 ½" squares of tissue, seasonal colors
- scissors
- paste or glue

Steps:

1. To create the tree and branches, put a few drops of the very thin tempera paint on the 9" x 12" background paper, near the bottom. Blow lightly at the paint with the straw. Move the paper and change the direction in which you blow several different times. Add more paint if necessary. Let dry.

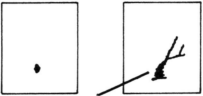

2. When the paint is dry, use the tissue paper squares to add the seasonal touches to the tree. Place the forefinger or end of the pencil in the center of a tissue square and pinch up the sides. Dip the end of the tissue in paste or glue and then place on the tree. The following are some suggestions for various times of the year.

Fall Tree

Background: tan
Tissue: brown, gold, yellow, rust, orange, red

Cherry Tree

Background: white or pink
Tissue: white, pink
Construction paper for cherries

Spring Tree

Background: light blue
Tissue: white, pink–blossoms, green–leaves

Summer Tree

Background: light blue
Tissue: shades of green

Technique: Cutting, applying tissue to other surfaces

Tissue Fantasies

Materials:

- (1) 12″ x 18″ white drawing paper
- (1 or 2) 12″ x 18″ tissue paper, light color
- crayons, scissors, paintbrush
- sequins, glitter, yarn, string
- tissue scraps
- liquid starch in a small container
- newspaper

Steps:

1. Draw a simple shape in a large pattern on the 12″ x 18″ white drawing paper. Any design or object can be drawn but preferably something with an inner pattern—birds, flowers, butterflies, or seasonal objects such as Easter eggs or Christmas ornaments. Complete the design with strong crayon outlines.

  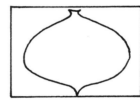 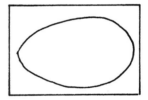

2. Lay a piece of tissue paper about the same size on top of the drawing so that the drawing may be used as a guide.

3. Place long lengths of string in liquid starch and squeeze out excess starch with the fingers. Place the string on the tissue along the outlines of the drawing underneath. When the outline is complete, set aside to dry.

 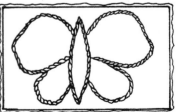

4. Add individual touches and decorations with glitter, yarn, sequins, tempera paints, and pieces of tissue paper, attaching with glue or starch.

5. To create a laminated effect, another piece of tissue may be placed on top, covering the surface with starch and putting the second sheet of tissue on top. Put another coat of starch on the second sheet of tissue. Allow to dry thoroughly. Trim away the extra paper around the shape, leaving a small edge next to the string or yarn.

Snowflakes

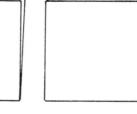

Technique: Cutting

Materials:

- (1) 9″ x 9″ square of tissue paper
- scissors

Steps:

1. Fold the paper in half.

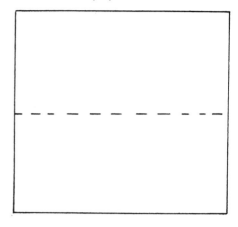

2. Fold in half again so it is 4 ½″ x 4 ½″ square.

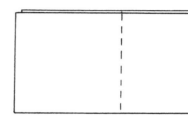

3. Turn so open edges are at the top. Fold in half diagonally.

4. Fold in half a second time, diagonally.

5. Trim off top edges.

6. Pencil in shapes along folded edges.

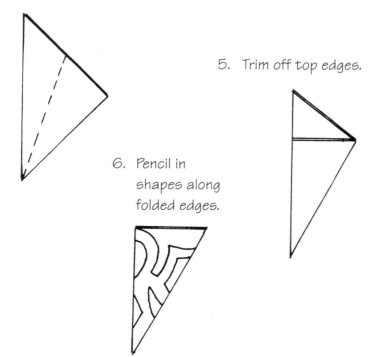

7. Cut out shapes so it looks like this. Open carefully.

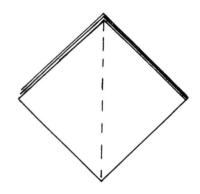

A Snowflake Collage

Technique: Cutting, applying tissue to other surfaces

Materials:

- (6–8) 5″ squares of tissue paper in assorted colors
- (1) 12″ x 18″ white construction paper
- scissors, paintbrush
- liquid starch in a small container
- newspaper for working surface

Steps:

1. Fold and cut the 5″ tissue squares into snowflakes of various sizes and shapes. See page 140 for instructions on how to cut snowflakes.

2. Place the 12″ x 18″ white construction paper on top of a piece of newspaper.

3. Paint the entire surface of the white construction paper with a layer of liquid starch. Then place the tissue snowflakes on the white paper, one at a time, in a pleasing arrangement. Overlap edges of the flakes. Cover each snowflake with a coat of starch before adding another.

4. Since some tissue paper colors bleed, fill the brush with starch and go over the entire surface of the collage, while wet, painting in only one direction to even out the colors and to make more attractive.

Variation:

Try cutting other shapes and applying to different kinds of background papers such as wallpaper or newspaper for interesting effects.

Hanging Snowflakes

Technique: Cutting, layered tissue

Materials:

- (3) 9" x 9" squares of tissue paper, all the same or different colors
- piece of wax paper
- liquid starch in a small container
- scissors, paintbrush
- string or thread

Steps:

1. Fold each square of tissue paper in the following manner to prepare for cutting snowflakes (refer to page 140):

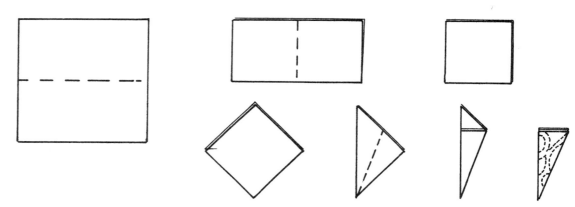

2. Place the piece of wax paper on top of a piece of newspaper.

3. Paint the wax paper with a coat of starch. Place one snowflake on this. Cover with starch. Place the second snowflake on top of the first and cover with starch. Place the third snowflake on top and cover it with starch. Paint carefully, gently as the snowflakes are fragile.

4. Let the tissue dry thoroughly, overnight if possible. When the tissue is dry, the wax paper will peel away, leaving a stiff layered tissue snowflake. String with thread to hang.

Technique:

Cutting or tearing, layered tissue

Translucent Mobiles

Materials:

- scraps of tissue paper, assorted colors
- liquid starch in a small container
- scissors, paintbrush
- large piece of wax paper
- string or thread, needle
- lump of clay, coat hanger
- newspaper

Steps:

1. Cover working surface with newspaper. Place the piece of wax paper on the center. Cut or tear the scraps of tissue into pieces of all sizes and shapes.

2. Using the paintbrush, cover the wax paper with a coat of starch. It will not cover evenly but this will be remedied when the tissue is applied.

3. Place one piece of tissue paper at a time on the wax paper and cover with starch. The pieces can be picked up with the tip of the brush. Overlap the pieces of tissue paper, and continue until the entire piece of wax paper has two or three layers of tissue paper.

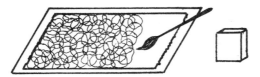

4. Let dry thoroughly, overnight at least. When the tissue paper is dry, the wax paper will peel away, leaving a sheet of tissue collage.

5. Stretch the coat hanger and bend into a curved shape. Place one end in a lump of clay for a base.

6. Cut the tissue collage into shapes: butterflies, fish, flowers, etc. Using the needle and thread, add a string to each shape, making sure it is long enough to leave room to tie to the wire.

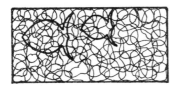

Rice Paper

Technique: Cutting or tearing, tissue transparency with dried flowers

Materials:

- 1 piece of 2-ply facial tissue
- piece of wax paper, larger than facial tissue
- colored tissue paper scraps
- flat dried weeds (or flowers, ferns)
- scissors and soft bristle paintbrush
- liquid starch in a small container
- newspaper for working surface

Steps:

1. Spread newspaper on working surface. Place the piece of wax paper on the center of the newspaper.

2. Paint the surface of the wax paper with liquid starch. Arrange cut or torn pieces of colored tissue paper on the wax paper in any manner desired, covering each piece with liquid starch. Arrange the dried weeds on top of the tissue paper design. Cover the weeds with starch.

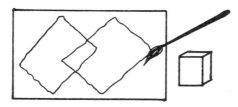

3. Separate the 2-ply tissue into two single pieces. Place one piece on the top of the design on wax paper, putting one edge of the facial tissue along the top of the wax paper, securing with starch. Pull the opposite edge until it is taut. Go over the design and press down. Use a brush or sponge to cover the surface of the facial tissue with starch.

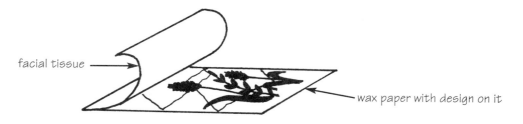

facial tissue ⟶   ⟵ wax paper with design on it

4. If one piece of facial tissue is not big enough, add the second piece, overlapping ¼" where they meet.

5. Let dry thoroughly. Coat front with protective covering, any desired.

Technique: Tearing, tissue transparency

Parchment Paper

Materials:

- 1 piece of 2-ply facial tissue
- piece of wax paper, a little larger than facial tissue
- colored tissue paper scraps
- scissors and paintbrush
- small container of liquid starch
- newspapers

Steps:

1. Spread newspaper on working surface. Place piece of wax paper on center of newspaper.

2. Paint the surface of the wax paper with liquid starch. Separate the 2-ply facial tissue into two pieces. Lay one piece on the starch-coated wax paper. Cover the piece of facial tissue with liquid starch, painting from the middle to the outside edges.

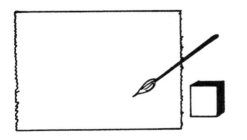

3. Place the torn tissue paper shapes on top of the starch-coated piece of facial tissue. Paint starch carefully on the tissue shapes.

4. Place the second piece of facial tissue on top of the tissue design and paint over with starch, again painting from the middle to the outside edges.

5. When the paper is dry, peel away the piece of wax paper. Mount on construction paper or simply trim edges and hang in window so the light will shine through.

Laminated Panels

Materials:

- tissue paper, assorted colors
- 2 pieces of wax paper, same size
- (2) 2" x 12" pieces of construction paper for trim
- (1) piece of construction paper, same size as wax paper
- warm iron, newspaper to iron on
- 1 piece of yarn

Steps:

1. Place one piece of wax paper on top of the piece of construction paper. The construction paper will give support to the wax paper when moving it from the working surface to where it will be ironed.

2. Create a picture or design on the wax paper with torn pieces of tissue paper. Do not use scissors.

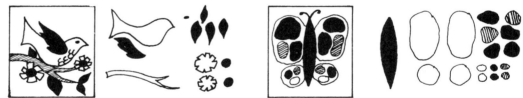

3. When the design or picture is completed, place the second piece of wax paper on top of the tissue paper. Place on a pad of newspapers and lay a single sheet of newspaper on top of the wax paper. Iron over the top, using a low or medium temperature. This will seal the tissue paper between the layers of wax paper.

4. Trim the top and bottom edges of the transparencies with 2" wide strips of construction paper and hang with yarn if desired. They look great hung in the windows so that the light shines through.

146

Technique:
Cutting, laminated tissue

Laminated Banners

Materials:

- good quality wax paper
- wax crayons
- old iron
- tissue paper, all colors
- assorted string, sequins, glitter
- scissors and white glue
- construction paper
- newspapers

Steps:

1. Place a sheet of wax paper the size desired on several thick layers of newspaper.

2. Cut out tissue shapes and lay on the wax paper.

3. Add other items such as sequins, glitter, pieces of scraped crayon, sprinkling over tissue.

4. Place a second sheet of wax paper on top of the arrangement.

5. Iron the entire design only once or twice with a medium-hot iron. Too much ironing can remove so much of the wax that there will not be enough left to seal the transparency.

6. Cools instantly. Add border at top and bottom using construction paper, yarn, braid, etc.

7. Display where the light will shine through.

Suggestions:

— A pile of newspaper thick enough so the heat won't penetrate to the surface below makes a fine ironing surface.

— Because of the size and length, make the banner where it can be ironed without moving.

147

Magic Gift Wrapping

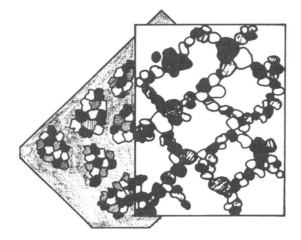

Technique: laminated tissue
(using crayon shavings)

Materials:

- (2) 20" x 30" white or light color tissue paper
- old crayons
- vegetable grater
- newspapers
- cardboard
- warm iron

Steps:

1. Using the vegetable grater, make shavings with the old crayons. Use only one or two colors.

2. Sprinkle the crayon shavings on one piece of tissue paper. These can be sprinkled in particular areas, patterns, or designs if desired or scattered all over the paper.

3. Place the tissue on a thick pad of newspapers.

4. Place the second sheet of tissue paper on top of the crayon shavings. Put a single sheet of newspaper on top of the tissue paper. This will help the iron slide easily and hold the tissue paper still. Iron with a warm iron—just long enough to melt the wax without making the colors muddy.

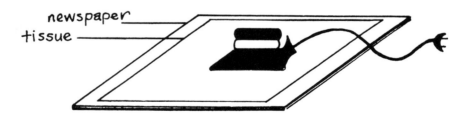

newspaper
tissue

5. Remove the newspaper. Take the two pieces of tissue paper and quickly pull apart. If the melted crayon gets cold and hard, it is possible that areas of melted crayon may pull apart entirely from one sheet or the other.

Suggestions:

— Use a piece of cardboard under the tissue paper when carrying it to the ironing area.

— Both pieces of tissue paper may be the same color or each may be a different color.

— Try using two colors of crayons that will produce a third color when they melt together: red and yellow, blue and yellow, or red and blue.

Technique:

Cutting, tissue transparencies

Stained-Glass Mobiles

Materials:

- 4 ½" x 6" black construction paper, 2 for each object
- colored tissue paper
- needle and thread
- paste or glue and scissors
- reeds, straws, or sticks on which to suspend objects

Steps:

1. Fold two pieces of the black construction paper in half, lengthwise. Cut out half the shape of a butterfly. (You may wish to pencil the shape in before cutting.)

2. While the shape is still folded, sketch in inner shapes. Then cut into the wing shapes and cut out.

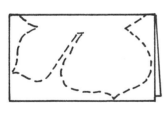

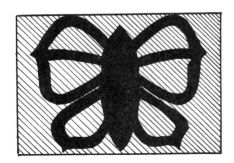

3. Unfold the shapes, paste or glue one side of one shape and lay it on the tissue paper. Put paste or glue on the other shape and attach to the other side of the tissue paper right behind the other shape so that they match exactly, back to back.

4. Trim the extra tissue paper away when the paste or glue is dry.

5. Using the needle and thread, attach the shapes to the sticks. You can use more than three shapes, making the mobile as simple or complex as desired.

6. It is possible to make many other mobile shapes with tissue paper in-between, following the same steps.

- Fold two pieces of construction paper the same size and cut out a shape.

- Cut into the shape and cut the center out while it is still folded.

- Open shapes, put on paste, and place back to back, one on each side of the tissue paper.

- Trim away the excess tissue paper when the paste is dry.

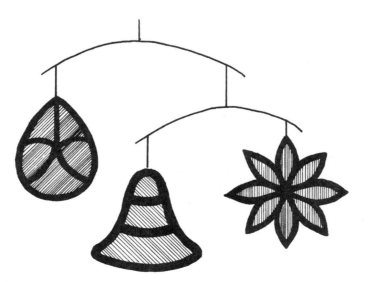 

Technique: Cutting,
tissue transparencies

Materials:

- (1) 9" x 12" black construction paper
- pieces of colored construction paper
- tissue paper, assorted colors
- scissors
- pencil
- white glue or paste

Steps:

1. Fold the black construction paper in half, lengthwise. Draw a ½" border around the open edges.

2. Draw a Christmas tree (or any shape) inside the border and a triangle inside each branch section. Join each branch section to the ½" border with a double line.

3. Leaving the paper folded, cut out all the spaces around the double-lined design.

4. Open out the design and fill in the open spaces with colored tissue paper. Lay a piece of tissue paper on top of the hole to be covered and draw around the space, leaving a small border for gluing. Keep the design symmetrical by gluing the same color tissue in the matching spaces.

Window Transparencies

A Bouquet

Technique: Cutting, folding, arranging

Materials:

- 5" x 5" squares of tissue, 3 squares of 3 colors each
- 3 pieces of string
- scraps of green tissue for leaves
- 1 pipe cleaner
- scissors and paste or glue
- (1) 9" paper doily
- ribbon or yarn

Steps:

1. Separate the tissue squares into three stacks containing three squares of tissue, three different colors.

2. Fold each stack of tissue together, accordion style, like a fan. Tie a piece of string around the middle of each fan. *Do not tie too tightly or gather the tissue.*

3. Round off the corners and spread out like a fan.

4. Carefully separate each layer of tissue by pulling up gently to the string, fluff out.

5. Attach a pipe cleaner to the string holding the flower together. Cut leaves from the green tissue scraps and paste or glue to the stem near the flower.

6. Put a hole in the center of the paper doily. Put stems through holes. Secure doily to stems with tape. Add ribbon.

Technique: Cutting, applying tissue to other surfaces

A Bleached Design

Materials:

- (1) 9″ x 12″ white construction paper
- (1) 9″ x 12″ tissue paper, any color
- small pieces of tissue paper, many colors
- scissors
- paintbrush
- liquid starch in a small container
- Q-tips (cotton swabs)
- small amount of liquid bleach in a sturdy container

Steps:

1. Place the 9″ x 12″ colored tissue paper on a layer of newspaper. Dip the end of the Q-tip in liquid bleach. Draw on the tissue paper with the Q-tip; dip in the bleach whenever necessary. Draw designs, patterns, shapes. The bleach will take the color out of the tissue paper. (**Caution:** Handle the bleach with care. Do not breathe in the fumes.)

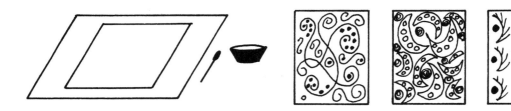

2. While the tissue paper with the bleach is drying, apply the small piece of tissue paper to the 9″ x 12″ white construction paper. Paint the white paper with a layer of starch. Place the small pieces of tissue on the paper, leaving parts of the white paper showing. Cover each piece with starch.

3. Place the tissue paper with the bleached design on top of the white paper with the tissue pieces, carefully lowering into place, patting gently. Cover the entire design with a coat of starch. Let dry thoroughly.

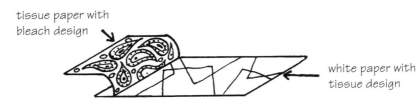

tissue paper with bleach design

white paper with tissue design

Tissue and Weeds Collage

Technique: Tearing, applying tissue and dried flowers

Materials:

- dried weeds—long, thin, feathery
- 4" x 4" squares of tissue paper: light blue, shades of green, browns, and yellows
- white glue and water mixture
- paintbrush
- 9" x 12" heavy white paper

Steps:

1. Tear the squares of tissue paper into pieces of various sizes. Make a mixture of equal amounts of the glue and water.

2. Paint the 9" x 12" heavy white paper with a coat of the glue mixture. Then put on some of the pieces of tissue paper, covering each piece with a coat of the glue mixture. (Keep in mind a landscape, putting the blue tissue at the top of the paper for sky and the other colors lower to give the impression of land, etc.)

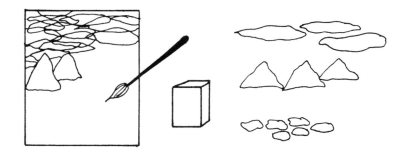

3. Make sure the entire paper has a good coat of the glue mixture and then arrange the dried weeds in a desired pattern over the tissue.

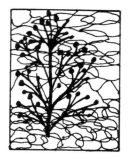

4. Cover additional pieces of tissue paper with the glue mixture and place over the dried weeds. Put on several layers of tissue.

Technique: Cutting, folding, gluing

Wire Creatures

Materials:

- (1) wire coat hanger
- (2) 15" squares of tissue paper, any color for creature to be made
- scraps of construction paper to decorate
- scissors and paste or glue

Steps:

1. Holding the top of the hanger with one hand, pull the bottom of the hanger with the other hand to make a diamond shape. Pull around edges to shape the wire into a circular shape.

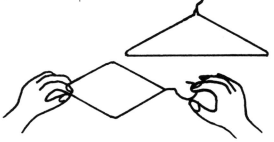

2. Place one sheet of 15" square tissue on the working surface. Place the hanger shape on top. Trace around the outside of the wire with a pencil onto the tissue paper.

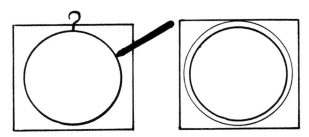

3. Place the second sheet underneath and cut out the shape, leaving a one-inch border.

4. Put paste or glue all around the edge of one piece of tissue paper. Then lay the hanger on top and put the second sheet of tissue on top. Press the edges gently, all the way around, sealing the hanger between the two pieces of tissue.

5. Using construction paper, cut features and other items to be placed on face of creatures. The following illustrations will provide some ideas:

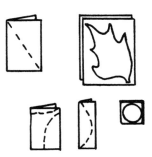 

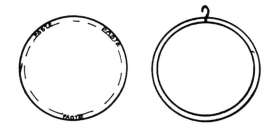

Flying Kites

Technique: Cutting, gluing, arranging, assembling

Materials:

- 20" x 30" tissue paper
- white glue, scissors
- liquid starch, paintbrush
- string
- thin strips of wood, reeds, or the bamboo strips from an old bamboo shade
- scraps of cloth for tail

Steps:

1. Depending on the number of equal-length sticks used, a great variety of shapes can be created for the framework of the kite. The following illustrations will provide ideas for two-stick and three-stick kites.

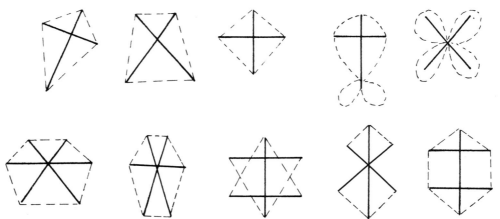

2. After deciding on the basic shape, glue and bind the sticks together. Notch (cut slits) the ends of the sticks and bind the ends with string for strength. Attach the string frame.

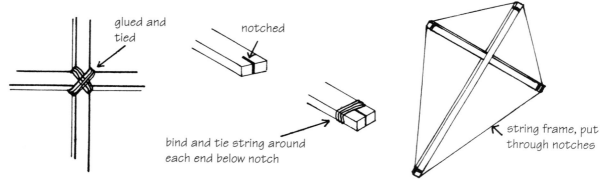

glued and tied

notched

bind and tie string around each end below notch

string frame, put through notches

3. Lay the kite frame on a piece of tissue paper and draw lightly around it with a pencil. Cut out, allowing a one-inch border all the way around. Cut out the corners as shown.

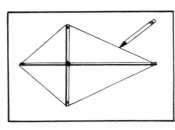 

4. Decorate the tissue covering with other pieces of tissue using liquid starch and a paintbrush. Add details with crayons or tempera paint.

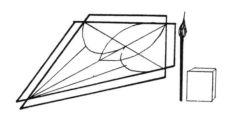 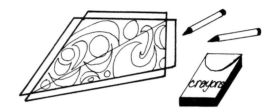

5. Place the kite frame on the dry tissue covering. Put glue or paste on the 1" border and fold over the string fame. Make sure all edges are securely pasted down.

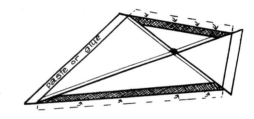

6. Attach the bow string across the width of the back of the kite as shown. Attach the string bridle across the front of the kite as shown, as well as the flying string.

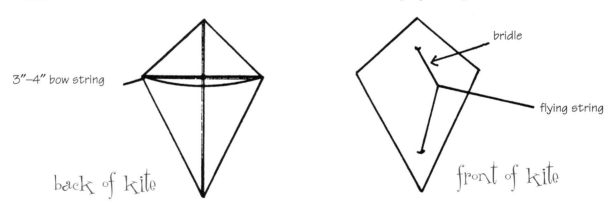

7. The tail for the kite can be made with scraps of cloth. The tail helps to keep the bottom of the kite at the bottom by acting as a balance. It is necessary to experiment with the length of the tail, so start with a long tail and cut to the length that gives the best results.

Suggestions:

Try using wrapping paper, large thin sheets of plastic, and other materials for the covering of the kite.

Tissue on Foil

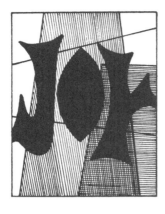

Technique: Tearing and/or cutting, applying tissue to other surfaces

Materials:

- 1 piece of cardboard or chipboard of desired size
- piece of aluminum foil, larger than cardboard
- scraps of tissue paper
- small container
- scissors and masking tape
- white glue and water mixture

Steps:

1. Lay the foil on the table, shiny side down. Place the cardboard in the center. Fold the corners of the foil over and secure with tape. Then fold the side and end edges over and secure with tape. Turn over.

2. Make a mixture of glue and water in the small container, two parts glue to one part water. Paint the entire surface of the foil with the glue mixture. Add tissue shapes, designs, or patterns, painting some of the glue mixture on top of each as it is put in place.

3. Finish by painting the entire surface of the decorated foil with a coat of the glue mixture. Let dry.

Suggestions:

— These make beautiful covers for notebooks.

— Try cutting Christmas ornament shapes from thin cardboard, covering with foil, and decorating with tissue—absolutely beautiful.

Technique: *Tearing, applying tissue to other surfaces*

Materials:

- a balloon, any size desired
- tissue paper, assorted colors
- liquid starch in a small container
- small container to rest balloon on while applying tissue
- #12 watercolor paintbrush
- decorating materials for inside and outside of egg: yarn, green grass, etc.
- white glue
- yarn, scissors

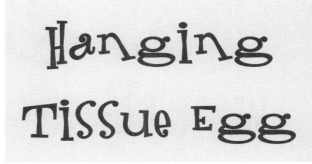

Hanging Tissue Egg

Steps:

1. Blow up balloon and *tie securely.*

2. Tear tissue into pieces that are small to medium in size. Pieces too large will wrinkle and be difficult to apply to balloon.

3. Using the paintbrush, apply a coat of starch to an area of the balloon surface. Pick up pieces of tissue with the tip of the paintbrush and put on the balloon. Cover each piece with liquid starch. Continue, covering the entire surface or the balloon several times, all pieces of tissue overlapping. Put many layers of tissue around the neck of the balloon as this will support the hanging egg. Let dry overnight or several days.

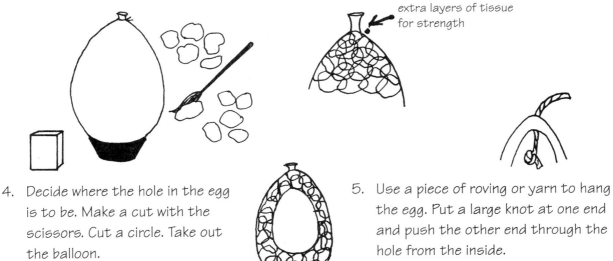

extra layers of tissue for strength

4. Decide where the hole in the egg is to be. Make a cut with the scissors. Cut a circle. Take out the balloon.

5. Use a piece of roving or yarn to hang the egg. Put a large knot at one end and push the other end through the hole from the inside.

6. Decorate the outside of the egg; yarn, ribbon, rickrack, etc., can be glued around the hole in the egg and all over the surface. Sequins, felt flowers, or anything else desired can be added.

159

Tissue and Wood Plaques

Technique: Cutting, applying tissue to other surfaces

Materials:

- tissue paper, assorted colors and various sizes (scraps too)
- white glue and water mixture
- small container, scissors, paintbrush
- ¼" to ⅝" thick piece of wood*
- grosgrain ribbon, Krylon clear spray paint—matte, satin, or gloss, black marking pen or paint
- picture hook or ring

Steps:

1. Using the various pieces of tissue paper, cut out simple shapes. Experiment by arranging the shapes on a piece of paper the same size as the piece of wood. The background can be left plain or covered with pieces of tissue paper.

2. Make a mixture of 2 parts glue to 1 part of water in a small container.

3. Paint the surface of the wood with the glue mixture. Transfer the tissue pieces one at a time, from the paper to the wood, covering each piece with the glue mixture after it is placed on the wood. Let dry.

4. When the picture is dry, add details and accents with black marking pens or black paint.

5. To finish, spray the surface of the plaque with Krylon clear spray paint. If black marking pens have been used to add details, then spray, don't paint, so they won't smear.

6. Grosgrain ribbon can be glued to the outside edge of the wood and a picture hook or ring can be added for hanging.

---

*Before applying the tissue designs, the surface of the wood can be finished by using one of the following techniques:

- Paint entire plaque with water or oil-based paint, by hand or using spray paint.
- Rub the surface of the wood with paste shoe polish to give an antique look, or use a water-soluble stain.
- Leave it the natural color, sanded very smoothly.

Technique: Cutting, applying tissue to other surfaces

Bottles and Seeds

Materials:

- tissue paper, assorted colors
- white glue and water mixture
- small container, scissors, paintbrush
- piece of wood*
- dried seeds, beans, cereals
- ribbon, Krylon clear spray paint—matte, satin, or gloss
- picture hook or ring

Steps:

1. Cut bottle shapes from tissue paper. Each bottle can be a different shape or different size of the same shape. Arrange on a piece of newsprint to get an idea of placement, etc. More pieces of tissue can be added to create interest and to tie the composition together.

2. Make a mixture of 2 parts glue to 1 part water in the small container.

3. Paint the surface of the wood with the glue mixture. Transfer the tissue pieces, one at a time, from the newsprint to the wood, covering each piece with the glue mixture after it is placed on the wood. Let dry thoroughly.

4. Using straight white glue, add dried beans, peas, seeds, or cereals on the bottle shapes, giving the impression of partially filled bottles.

5. To finish, spray the surface of the plaque with Krylon clear spray paint. Ribbon can be glued to the outside edge and a picture hook or ring can be added for hanging.

---

*Before applying the tissue bottles, the surface of the wood can be finished using one of several techniques:
- Paint entire plaque with water or oil-based paint, by brush or with spray paint.
- Rub the surface of the wood with paste shoe polish to give an antique look, or use a water-soluble stain.
- Leave it the natural color, especially if using scrap paneling.

Pretty and useful

Materials:

- scraps of tissue paper or pieces cut into various shapes
- liquid starch in a small container
- bottle, box, tin can or jar
- paintbrush, scissors
- gesso or latex paint
- Krylon clear spray paint— matte, satin, or gloss

Steps:

1. Select a bottle, jar, box, or tin can. If the container has printing on it, first apply a coat of gesso or latex paint and let dry. This will provide an opaque surface.

2. Tear or cut the tissue paper into small pieces.

3. Apply pieces of tissue paper to chosen container, using the liquid starch and paintbrush. Paint a small portion of the surface of the container with starch, put on pieces of tissue, and cover with starch. Cover the entire surface in this manner.

4. After the tissue and starch have dried, the container can be decorated with yarn or string, secured with white glue.

5. To make durable and waterproof, spray the entire surface with Krylon clear spray paint.

Suggestions:

This is a marvelous quick fun way to make unsightly objects useful and pretty. Boxes can be used for files, storage, personal objects. Flowers can be added to the bottles. The tin cans can be used as pencil holders, for scissors, paintbrushes, or anything else you can think of.

About Tempera

Ours is a world of color. So long as there is light to see by, we encounter color in our surroundings—an ever-changing, shifting world of color. The colors we see affect our moods and influence our actions. Color can play a decisive role in the experience of a work of art. An awareness of the infinite flow of colors around us can be developed by encouraging observation. At an early age students should be familiar with colors and their combinations and variations. Older students should gain some knowledge of how colors may be selected and used in a composition in terms of hue, value, and intensity. Experiments in mixing color are essential to understanding it.

Tempera is one of the best art media for use in exploring color. Its free-flowing quality and its vivid colors make it delightful to use. Available in a dry, powdered form or in liquid, it is water-soluble, easily controlled, and so opaque that it covers its own mistakes. Tempera may be applied in a thick or a thin coat, will allow light colors to be painted over dark colors, may be brushed, stippled, sponged, dipped, and spattered, as well as being used in dry form. Other names for this popular media are *poster paint* and *showcard* paint.

Used for making individual or group pictures, painting constructed objects, and printing, tempera is most frequently and effectively used in a flat poster technique. There are, however, other methods of using tempera that are worth further exploration. In addition to ideas for exploring the world of color and suggestions for mixing colors, shades, and tints and developing color schemes, you'll find a variety of techniques for applying paint to paper and combining tempera with other media.

Techniques With Tempera

The following techniques will be used in the tempera activities in this section. Here is a brief summary of each:

brush The brush is used as a drawing tool to create lines, textures, symbols, and pictures of a variety of subjects.

fold prints Place drops of tempera of one or more colors on the surface of the paper; fold and rub the surface gently to blend and spread the paint. These lend themselves beautifully to animals, flowers, creatures, abstract prints; details may be added with other mediums.

finger painting A process of creating a picture or design by using fingers, hands, and parts of the arm to apply paint on a glazed or non-glazed piece of paper.

sponge painting Small sponges are clipped with clothespins and used to apply paint by dabbing, twisting, pulling, or pushing the sponge on the surface of the paper. Good for broken color or putting textures over an area, such as foliage.

resists A symbol, design, or picture is drawn on heavy paper, using the point of the crayon heavily to build up a line waxy enough to resist paint. When completed, a thin coat of tempera is brushed over the surface of the wax drawing, which will resist the water-soluble paint, and the design remains intact.

impasto Application of thick layers of paint using a variety of tools such as cardboard, forks, and spoons to apply paint and create textures and designs.

sgraffito Covering an area with a layer of paint and then cutting or carving through to expose the base color as design.

With other Media

construction projects Excellent for covering the surfaces; add a little liquid glue for better adhesion.

printing ink Mix tempera with liquid starch to a thick consistency.

with rubber cement Areas are blocked out with rubber cement; dry. Apply wash of tempera over top; when dry, rub off rubber cement to expose background paper.

overlay painting with watercolor, tempera, and crayon

mixed media with ink, chalk, pencil, and ink sketches

Materials

The following materials are needed to do the activities in this section:

Tempera Paint

Tempera paint comes in liquid or dry form. Powdered tempera is less expensive and more versatile as it can be mixed with different liquids for varying consistencies, depending on the intended use. Tempera paints are water-soluble and designed to be used in an opaque consistency.

For the most satisfactory results, the mixture of powder paint with liquid should be thin enough to flow easily from the brush and thick enough to cover the surface. When the mixture is too thin, the paint is hard to control and the colors are weak; when the mixture is too thick, it sticks to the brush, stacks up, and cracks and flakes off from the painting.

Proportions for Mixing

— easel painting: 2 ½ parts liquid, 1 part paint

— general painting: 2 parts liquid, 1 part paint

— thin tempera or a wash: 3 parts liquid, 1 part paint

Mixing and Storing

- Mix powdered tempera with pure or diluted liquid starch so it is very thick. It will be easier to control on the palette and water can be added while working.

- When mixing large amounts for easel painting and future use, add a few drops of oil of wintergreen or cinnamon to keep the paint smelling sweet.

- Store large amounts of mixed tempera in glass containers such as mayonnaise jars. Grease such as cold cream or Vaseline around the inside of the lids will keep them from sticking.

- Powdered paint will rub off to some extent after it has dried but it can be made permanent by giving the finished product several thin coats of clear varnish, lacquer, or clear plastic.

- Add a few drops of liquid soap to the paint mixture to aid in thoroughly covering waxy or printed surfaces in construction projects as well as make it easier to wash paint out of clothes.

- Recently, most liquid tempera comes in plastic squeeze bottles. This is particularly handy for distributing paint onto palettes and lends itself to several art projects. Mustard and ketchup squeeze bottles, or those in which hair solutions, liquid soap, and other products come, can be substituted. It's a clean, easy way to use and store paint.

Paint Trays, Palettes

- For individual use, plastic egg trays are ideal. The 12 small, round-bottomed cups provide space for the primary and secondary colors plus black and white, with some extra cups, as well as the lid, for mixing. They can be washed or thrown away.

- A palette that can be used repeatedly can be made from a piece of cardboard, approximately 9" x 12". Cut several pieces of wax paper the same size; stack the pieces of wax paper and staple to the piece of cardboard, once at each corner. The top piece is used as a palette and then thrown away after use.

- For small groups, 1/3-quart milk containers or frozen juice cans hold a sufficient amount of paint, do not tip easily, and can be washed and used again or disposed of. An ideal tote tray for these containers is a six-pack carton used to hold soda bottles.

A Paint Board

A piece of Masonite™, thick cardboard, cut up cardboard boxes, or 1/4" plywood can be used as a painting board. Paper is tacked or taped to this. The board may be used on the desk or rested on the back of a chair with the paints and water on the desk and the student standing in the aisle.

Paper

newsprint — thin paper such as that on which newspapers are printed; comes in pastel colors; is weak and flimsy, so it tears easily and soaks up much water under pressure, but it is good for easel painting.

gray bogus — an inexpensive gray paper that comes in bundles; absorbent, with enough body to take colors and paints easily.

manila — similar in weight to bogus paper; comes in a light creamy color; works well with all media; comes in large and small sizes.

construction — strong paper; comes in assorted colors, both pastel and vivid tones; can be used the same as manila or bogus.

drawing — white in color; lighter in weight than construction paper.

wrapping — also called shelf paper, comes in rolls; good surfaces for painting with tempera; useful for projects that need large areas such as murals or scenery.

tagboard — mediumweight, fairly stiff paper; hard surface; creamy color; good for impasto, sgraffito, and resists.

chipboard — similar to bogus paper except that it is much heavier; this is a strong cardboard and comes in a variety of weights or thicknesses.

watercolor	a special, high-quality paper made from linen rags; is handmolded and has a very tough, grainy surface—also very expensive.
fingerpaint	firm, stiff paper with a hard glossy surface.
other	printed papers such as gift wrap, wallpaper, metallic papers, sandpaper, corrugated paper.

Brushes

- Soft or stiff bristle brushes, varying in size, depending on the project.
- Small pieces of sponge are good for making broken color or putting textures over an area.
- Small rollers or brayers can be used to cover large areas with flat paint.
- Other painting tools that can be used quite successfully are pens of various shapes and sizes, a palette knife, sticks, straws, cotton swabs, and pieces of cardboard.

Additional Materials

wax crayons	wax paper	stapler
white glue or paste	clothespins	paper towels
scissors	masking tape	containers for water
sponges	old newspapers	liquid starch
tinfoil	India ink	plastic egg cartons
Tide soap	sgraffito tools	plastic forks, spoons
cotton swabs	fabric	collage materials
chalk	pencils	

Important!

paint cloths	old pieces of fabric, sheeting, or bath or kitchen towels for wiping brushes and cleaning up.
paint smock	a man's old shirt, minus sleeves, put on backwards works perfectly; also an old apron or smock.

About Color

Color is part of an orderly world and has its own rules and reasons for happening. Understanding these rules and reasons expands children's ability to put on paper or canvas the pictures they see in their mind. The best way to learn about color is not by talking about it but by using it. From looking at color, experimenting with it and using it, can come a true understanding and real feeling for it.

To Describe Color

hue   The name of the color. We see hue colors at their brightest and purest.

value   A hue can be lightened by adding white to make a tint; a hue can be darkened by adding black to make a shade.

intensity   The brightness or dullness of a color. A color is dulled by adding its complement, the color opposite it on the color wheel.

The Properties and Relationships of Color

primary colors   red, blue, yellow

secondary colors   green, orange, violet

tertiary colors   yellow-orange   blue-green
                        red-orange   red-violet
                        yellow-green   blue-violet

neutral colors   black, white, gray, brown

white   also the absence of color; it reflects color and is used to make tints

The Color Wheel

The colors are placed on a color wheel in the following order:

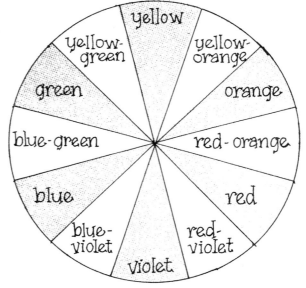

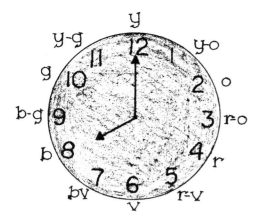

Think of the color wheel as a clock:

primary colors: 12, 4, 8 o'clock

secondary colors: 2, 6, 10 o'clock

tertiary colors: 1, 3, 5, 7, 9, and 11 o'clock

Mixing Colors

Primary Colors red, blue, yellow

These colors, at their truest hue, cannot be made by mixing other colors; but by mixing combinations of them, all the other colors on the color wheel can be produced.

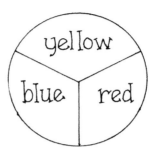

Secondary Colors

yellow and red   =   orange

yellow and blue   =   green

red and blue   =   violet

To mix: Use equal amounts of each of the primary colors.

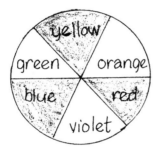

Tertiary Colors

yellow and orange   =   yellow-orange

red and orange   =   red-orange

red and violet   =   red-violet

blue and violet   =   blue-violet

blue and green   =   blue-green

yellow and green   =   yellow-green

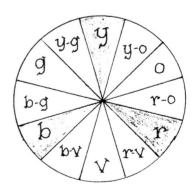

Mix at a ratio of 2 to 1. Example: 2 drops of yellow and 1 drop of orange make a good yellow-orange. When working with tempera paints, this seems to work best.

Neutral Colors black, white, brown, gray

To mix: —Equal amounts of red, yellow, and blue will make black.
—Adding more red than yellow or blue will make brown.
—Adding more blue than red or yellow will make a bluish-gray.
—Mixing two color complements will produce shades of gray.

Ways to change Colors

Hue change   Mix a related color.

Value change   Add black or white.

Tone change   Add both black and white.

Intensity change   Add complementary color.

Color Schemes

complementary colors   Those colors opposite each other on the color wheel. The amount of a complementary color added to another determines how dull or gray it becomes.

monochromatic colors   The use of one color in different values and intensities, created by adding varying amounts of either black or white to a color.

analogous colors   Those colors in a series, next to each other, on the color wheel, such as:
—yellow, yellow-orange, orange
—blue, blue-violet, violet

triad scheme   Composed of three hues an equal distance apart on the color wheel. Usually the three primary colors are avoided as a scheme.

warm colors   Colors in which red and yellow predominate:

red	red-orange	orange
yellow	yellow-orange	

cool colors   Colors in which blue and green predominate:

blue	blue-violet	violet
blue-green	green	yellow-green

Combining Colors

- No color in itself is ugly. Any color may be made more beautiful if used in the right relationship with others.

- Warm colors are more harmonious with warm colors, but more exciting if accented with cool ones.

- Cool colors are more harmonious with cool colors, but more exciting if accented with warm ones.

- Warm-colored backgrounds tend to hold things together and establish unity. Cool backgrounds tend to hold things apart.

- Sometimes colors may be made to harmonize with each other by combining a neutral such as black, white, or gray.

- It is usually a mistake to use a color only once in a scheme; but by repeating it, the color may be made to belong. It is better if repeated in large, medium, and small amounts.

- A color combination is usually more successful if bright, medium, and dull intensities are used. The "law of areas" delegates the smallest areas to the brightest colors, and as areas get successively larger, colors become successively duller.

- The use of too many colors often weakens the effect.

- Every color scheme should have some dark and some light color, but do not use them in equal quantities.

First Experiences With Color

When exploring the world of color with the very young, it is very important to use color, not just talk about it. The following activities are simple ideas for first experiences with primary colors and secondary colors. References are given for additional experiences using the same techniques.

Basic Materials

- paint cloths and/or paper towels
- paint smock or shirt
- newspaper for the working surface
- tempera paint: red, blue, yellow; powdered or liquid, in squeeze bottles or shaker containers

- liquid starch
- paper: butcher, shelf, drawing, or fingerpaint paper; large sheets
- paint applicators: brushes, sponges, straws

To Discover Color

fingerpaint   Use two primary colors, large sheets of butcher, shelf, or fingerpaint paper. Cover the surface of the paper with liquid starch and sprinkle with powdered tempera paint or several daubs of liquid tempera paint; "paint" one half of the paper with one color and the other half of the paper with a second color. Blend the two colors in some areas to create a third color (pages 198–199).

sponges   Clip small sponges with clothespins. Dip the sponge into one primary color and make large rhythmic patterns on a large sheet of paper, repeating the process with a second primary color. Overlap and blend the two colors in some areas to create a third color (page 204).

fold prints   Squeeze drops of two primary colors over half a sheet of paper; fold the paper in half and rub the top surface of the paper to blend the colors; open and dry flat (page 192).

brush   Wet the surface of the paper with a small wet sponge; spatter, drop, or flow two primary colors on the paper with a brush. Make sure the paint is mixed to a very thin consistency so the colors will flow and mingle together (page 173).

blow paintings   Using very thin tempera paint, put drops of two primary colors on a sheet of paper; blow down on the paint with or without the use of a straw to spread the paint, letting the colors meet and blend (page 177).

string   Paint a piece of thick string or yarn with two primary colors; lay it in a wavy pattern on half a sheet of paper, letting one end stick out over the edge. Fold the other half of the paper over. Place one hand on top to hold firmly (or use a book) and pull the string out with the other hand. Result: blending of colors and a colorful rhythmic design. Try two pieces of string, each painted with only one color of paint; repeat the process twice. (See *Printing* section, page 298.)

Technique: Brush

Materials:

- painting easel or paint board
- stiff-bristle brushes, one for each color of paint
- tempera paint in containers
- 18" x 24" newsprint paper, colored or white
- paint smock or shirt
- "clothesline" to hang finished paintings on

Steps:

1. *Brushes:*
   — Wipe the brush on the edge of the container so that it is not overloaded with paint.
   — Brushes should be washed when the painting is completed . . . never let brushes sit, bristles down, in the paint for a long period of time.
   — Be sure to have a brush for each color of paint.

2. *Tempera:*
   — Mix 1 ½ parts liquid (water, liquid starch, or both) to 1 part paint.
   — When mixing large amounts of paint for future use, be sure to add a few drops of oil of wintergreen or cinnamon to keep the paint smelling sweet.
   — Store paint in glass containers; put grease such as cold cream or Vaseline around the inside of the lid to keep from sticking.
   — Selection of colors will vary, depending on the subject matter:

rainy day	grayed colors
holiday	appropriate colors
harbor picture	several blues
foggy day	grayed colors, white
spring picture	yellows, greens, tints

3. *Ideas:*
   - Personal experiences, daily activities
   - Places never seen or never will see: New York City . . . Panama Canal
   - Paintings involving large groups of people such as parades, carnivals, a sports event, activities in a park or on a playground
   - Movements of nature: rain or snow storm, a windy day
   - Try illustrating words: TALL, short, big, little, "fall," water, warmth

4. A student's painting is his or her own work. Keep from painting on it. Combining your version with theirs often results in confusion and odious comparisons.

5. Hang the completed paintings on a "clothesline" to dry and also for view.

173

Murals

Technique: A mural is a *large* wall decoration that may be painted directly onto the wall or applied to some other material that is fastened to the wall.

Materials:

- butcher paper cut to fit the space for which the mural is planned
- chalk or charcoal
- tempera paint, variety of colors
- soft- and/or stiff-bristle brushes
- containers for paint and water
- sponges
- brayers for painting large areas
- newspaper for working surface
- paint smock or shirt

Steps:

1. Plan mural around a particular content area. The picture may be informative, representational, or decorative.

2. Gather background information from films and other audio-visuals, recordings, art prints, reading, and observation.

3. Develop a plan for the mural. Review ideas to be expressed and make a list of them. Make preliminary sketches using pencil or crayon on individual paper. Select ideas from individual sketches.

4. Sketch main shapes with chalk or charcoal. Light-colored chalk is less apt to show or smudge badly. Consider:
   — areas of importance to emphasize
   — rhythm, use of lines that connect one area to another
   — repetition of objects

   Remember: Distance can be shown by putting large objects lower on panel and smaller objects higher; by overlapping objects; by making close objects darker and brighter, far objects lighter and grayer.

5. Choose colors needed for mural and technique for applying paint: brush, sponge, brayer. Apply paint to background or center of interest first. Make sure that there is contrast between background and areas of interest. Repeat colors throughout picture. Allow one color or a group of colors to dominate.

6. Outline centers of interest. Overpaint, if desired, for added emphasis.

Variations:

— The background may be painted on first with a sponge. Then elements that are to appear on the mural may be painted on separate pieces of paper, cut out, and arranged. When all is satisfactory, each individual part is glued on.

— Murals can be made using colored tissue laminated with paint, mosaic-cut or torn papers, yarns and fabrics.

— **Sectional mural:** Plan mural and sketch full scale on paper. Cut into sections. Each student paints one section. Assemble and glue to background paper. (See page 16 in *Crayon section.*)

— **Block mural:** Cut mural paper into squares. Each student makes a crazy-quilt design on a block. Reassemble when all are made. Ideas for the blocks:
  - a favorite book
  - geographic design
  - particular period in history
  - holiday
  - seasonal symbols
  - individual poem and illustration

The possibilities for the block mural are endless and ever fascinating.

stripes and checks

Technique: Color

Materials:

- thick tempera paint: red, blue, and yellow
- paint palette or individual containers
- #7 or #12 soft-bristle brushes
- small container of water
- paint cloth
- paper towels
- (1) 9" x 12" or 12" x 18" white paper
- newspaper for working surface

Steps:

1. Prepare the paint palette. Cover the working surface with newspaper.

2. To create stripe and check designs, it is important to remember that the lines must run in one of three directions:

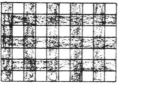      

     vertically   **horizontally**   **diagonally**

— The simplest stripe design is made up of stripes of equal width set an equal distance apart. When one stripe pattern is made to cross another, a check or plaid design is created. The chessboard is the simplest form of check design. Other patterns can be made by using diagonal stripes in conjunction with vertical and horizontal stripes of varying widths.

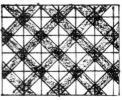   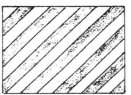

3. To paint, the stripes can first be penciled on the white paper with the use of a ruler if a more precise, finished product is desired. If you do not want the colors to run when they cross each other, paint the vertical or horizontal stripes first, let dry, and then paint the others. Encourage experimentation with a variety of patterns on newspaper first.

Technique: Color

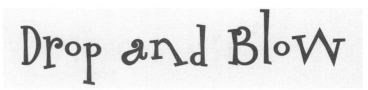

Materials:

- very thin tempera paint the consistency of ink: red, yellow, and blue
- a drinking straw
- container of water and a small sponge, if desired
- (1) 9" x 12" or 12" x 18" white paper
- newspapers for working surface

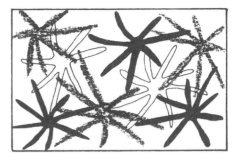

Steps:

1. Cover the working surface with newspaper and position the white paper in the middle.

2. Mix the three tempera colors in separate containers, each to a very thin consistency, using only water.

3. If it is desired that the colors run and mingle with each other, make the paper wet with a small sponge before beginning. Do not let the paints dry between applications.

4. Put two or three drops of the first color of tempera paint at random on the white paper. Blow down and also across the surface of the paint with the straw, shooting the paint in several directions. Let dry for several minutes.

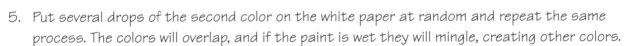

5. Put several drops of the second color on the white paper at random and repeat the same process. The colors will overlap, and if the paint is wet they will mingle, creating other colors.

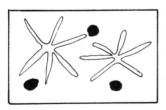

6. Repeat the same process, using the third color.

6-Part Color Wheel

Technique: Color

Materials:

- (2) 9" x 12" white paper
- thick tempera paint: red, blue, and yellow
- #7 soft-bristle brush
- container of water
- paper towels
- paint cloth
- paint palette or plastic egg carton
- white glue or paste
- scissors and pencil
- 9" circle template
- newspaper for working surface

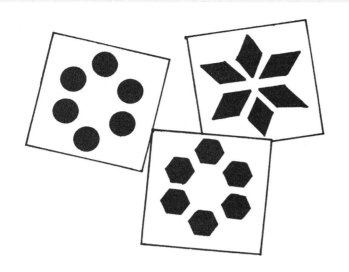

Steps:

1. Fold the 9" x 12" white paper in thirds, lengthwise. Open. Fold in half, widthwise, twice. You will have 12 rectangles.

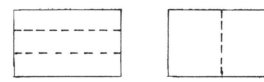

2. On the paint palette or egg carton, put approximately one tablespoon each of red, blue, and yellow tempera. It should be of a thick consistency so it will be easy to work with.

3. Using the brush, paint in one rectangle with each of the three colors: red, yellow, and blue. Leave a blank rectangle between each painted rectangle.

red		yellow	
	blue		

4. Mix the secondary colors on the palette:
   red and yellow—orange
   yellow and blue—green
   blue and red—violet
   Paint one rectangle of each color.

red		yellow	
	blue		orange
violet		green	

5. When the paint is dry, cut the paint paper into rectangles. Using one of the empty rectangles, cut a circle or a simple symmetrical shape to use as a template pattern. Trace around the template shape on the colors painted. Cut out.

6. Trace around the 9" circle template on the second sheet of white paper. Arrange the cut-out shapes in the correct order on the penciled circle and glue or paste into position.

12-Part Color Wheel

Technique: Color

Materials:

- (1) 12″ x 18″ white paper
- (1) 12″ x 12″ white paper
- ruler and pencil
- thick tempera paint: red, blue, and yellow
- #7 soft-bristle brush
- container of water
- paper towels
- paint cloth
- paint palette
- white glue or paste
- 10″ circle template
- newspaper for working surface

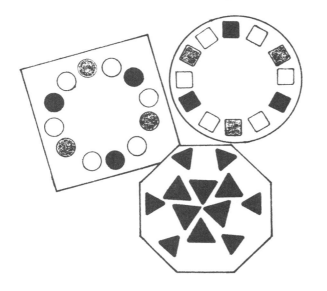

Steps:

1. Cover the working surface with newspaper.

2. Line the 12″ x 18″ white paper into 3″ x 3″ squares like a checkerboard.

3. Begin with the primary colors. Paint one square red, another blue, and a third, yellow.

4. Use only the primary colors. Paint the other nine colors. Select one secondary color—for example, orange.

5. Mix the two tertiary colors that are closest to orange: yellow-orange and red-orange.

6. Complete all the secondary and tertiary colors in the same way. Do not mix a brown, gray, or black. Don't let the colors become muddy. Change the water frequently. Dry.

red		blue	
	yellow		orange
green		violet	
	red-violet		blue-violet
yellow-green		blue-green	
	red-orange		yellow-orange

7. Using the circle template, draw a lightly penciled circle in the center of the 12″ x 12″ white paper.

template

180

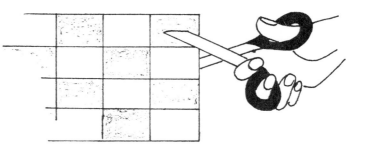

8. When the paint is dry, cut the painted paper into individual rectangles, using the fold lines as a guide.

9. Using one of the blank rectangles, cut a simple, symmetrical shape to use as a template. Below are a few examples. Trace around the shape on each of the painted rectangles. Cut out.

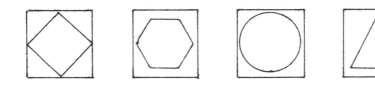

10. Arrange the cut-out colors in their correct position around the penciled circle on the 12″ x 12″ white paper. Glue or paste into position.

Variations:

Instead of using the same shape for all the colors, try using three different shapes—one for the primary colors, one for the secondary colors, and one for the tertiary colors. Experiment with various arrangements.

181

Color and Pattern

Technique:
Color, pattern

Materials:

- thick tempera paint: red, blue, and yellow
- #7 soft-bristle brush
- container of water
- paper towel
- paint cloth
- paint palette
- one page of the classified section of the newspaper
- black crayon
- newspaper for working surface

Steps:

1. Cover the working surface with newspaper. Put some of the red, blue, and yellow tempera paint on the palette.

2. Spread out a page of the classified ad section of the newspaper on the working surface. Make sure the columns are horizontal. Using the black crayon, divide the paper into squares and rectangles, using the columns as a guide. Press heavily with the crayon for a good wax build-up.

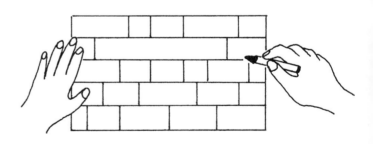

3. Mix colors on the paint palette, using the red, blue, and yellow tempera paint. Mix as many different colors as possible. Paint in the squares and rectangles marked on the classified section with crayon.

4. When dry, use a black crayon to make lines, designs, and patterns, and to create textures on the painted squares and rectangles. Keep in mind the seven elements of design; experiment with many variations.

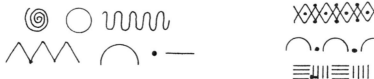

Suggestion: Frame or mount with black construction paper.

Technique: Color

Materials:

- (2) 12" x 18" white drawing paper
- thick tempera paint: red, yellow, blue, black, and white
- #2, #5, or #7 soft-bristle brush
- paint palette or plastic egg carton
- container of water
- paint cloth
- paper towels
- scissors
- pencil and ruler
- newspaper for working surface

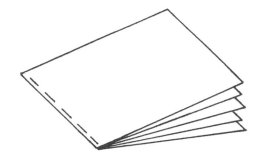

A Color Reference Book

Steps:

1. Fold the two 12" x 18" papers in half, lengthwise. Open. Fold in half, widthwise, and then in thirds. There will be twelve 3" x 6" rectangles.

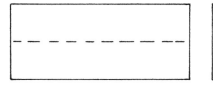

2. Cover the working surface with newspaper. Prepare the paint palette.

3. Using the primary colors, mix and paint in the rectangles on the first sheet of paper as follows:

   — Paint one rectangle for each of the three primary colors:

   red, blue, yellow

   — Paint one rectangle for each of the three secondary colors:

   violet, orange, green

   — Paint one rectangle for each of the six tertiary colors:

   red-orange, yellow-orange
   red-violet, blue-violet
   blue-green, yellow-green

red	blue
yellow	violet
orange	green
red-orange	yellow-orange
blue-green	yellow-green
red-violet	blue-violet

4. Using the primary colors, and black and white, mix and paint in the rectangles on the second sheet of paper as follows:

— Paint one rectangle for each of the four neutral colors: black, white, brown, gray.

For the following, divide the rectangles into thirds:
— An analogous scheme
— A cool color scheme
— A warm color scheme
— Two complementary colors
— A monochromatic color scheme

black	brown
white	gray
a tone (shade)	warm
cool	analogous
complementary	mono-chromatic

5. When dry, cut each color out and stack in the order painted. Cut two blank rectangles for the front and back covers. Staple at one end.

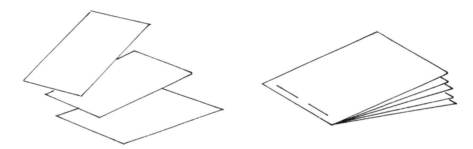

6. On the back of the page opposite, identify each color with a description. For example—A tint: white + a small amount of red = pink. This color reference book can be referred to when reviewing how to make a certain color.

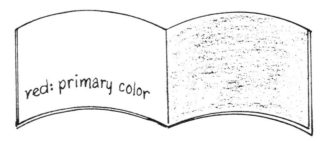

red: primary color

Technique: Color

Materials:

- tempera paint: one primary color, black, and white
- paint palette or plastic egg carton
- #7 soft-bristle brush
- container of water
- paper towel
- paint cloth
- (1) 9" x 12" white paper
- black crayon
- newspaper for working surface

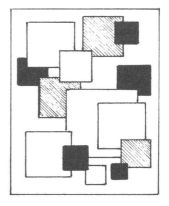

Steps:

1. Using the black crayon, draw a simple geometric shape or motif on the white paper, repeating in a variety of sizes until the paper is covered.

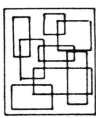 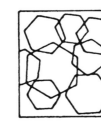  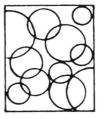

2. Cover the working surface with newspaper. Prepare the paint palette: one primary color, black, and white.

3. By mixing varying amounts of either black or white with the primary color, many shades and tints of one color can be created. As they are mixed, paint in the various shapes on the white paper. Mix a wide range of colors. *Remember:* When mixing colors, add small amounts of the darker color to the lighter color. For example, to make light blue, begin with white and add small amounts of blue until the desired tint is achieved.

Variation: Instead of shapes, mark the paper off in 2" squares; paint a different shade of tint in each square. When dry, cut and arrange in order from light to dark, creating a full range on a second sheet of paper. Glue or paste into position.

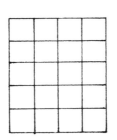

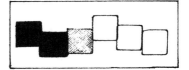

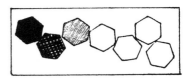

185

Complementary Colors

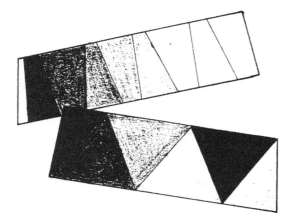

Technique: Color

Materials:

- tempera paint: two complementary colors
- paint palette or plastic egg carton
- #7 soft-bristle brush
- container of water
- (1) 6" x 18" white paper
- paper towels
- paint cloth
- optional: paper to mount on
- scissors
- white glue or paste
- newspaper for working surface

Steps:

1. Select any two colors directly opposite each other on the color wheel. These are called complementary colors. For example: red and green, orange and blue, yellow and violet.

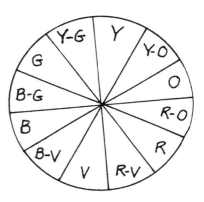

2. Make a series of folds on the 6" x 18" white paper to create a progression of unequal number shapes, rather like a fan, regular or irregular in size and shape. Some examples:

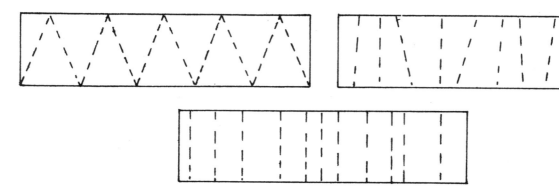

3. Cover the working surface with newspaper. Put paint (two complementary colors) on the palette.

4. On one end of the white paper, paint one shape with one of the colors and paint the shape at the other end of the paper with the other color.

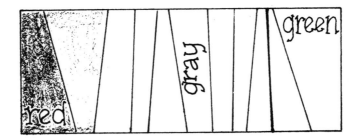

5. Mix equal parts of each color, creating gray, and paint in the center shape on the white paper.

6. *Remember:* Small amounts of a complementary color added to a pure color will dull the color and lower the intensity of that color.

    Beginning with one of the colors, add small amounts of the other color, mixing varying intensities of the color, and paint in the shapes, progressing across the white paper, to the gray. Repeat the process in reverse.

A Kaleidoscope of Complementary Colors

Technique:
Color

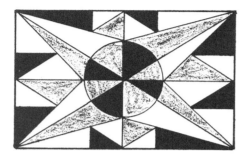

Materials:

- tempera paint: two complementary colors
- (1) 9" x 12" white paper
- paint palette
- #7 soft-bristle brush
- paint cloth
- paper towels
- container of water
- black crayon
- newspaper for the working surface

Steps:

1. Fold the 9" x 12" white paper in half widthwise and then lengthwise so the paper will be divided in quarters.

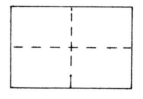
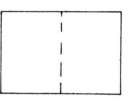

2. Using the black crayon, draw a design in one rectangle. Press very heavily with the crayon. Fold the paper in half and rub on the back of the design so it will transfer to another rectangle. Go over the transferred design with the black crayon so it will be dark, with a good build-up of wax.

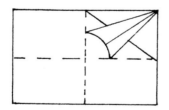
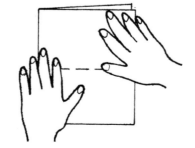
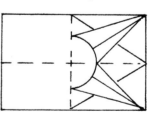

3. Fold the paper in half and rub on the back of the two rectangles with designs so they will transfer to the other two rectangles. Open the paper and go over the design with black crayon.

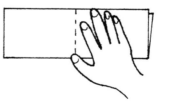
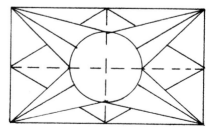

4. Using the two complementary colors of tempera paint and the various intensities of colors created by mixing the two, paint in the designs. Paint the same shape in each rectangle the same color.

Technique: Color

Materials:

- (2) 9" x 12" or 12" x 18" white paper
- tempera paint: one primary color, black, and white
- #5 or #7 soft-bristle brush
- container of water
- paint cloth
- paper towel
- (2–3) 2" x 3" tagboard or bogus paper to make a template
- scissors
- pencil
- paste or glue
- newspaper for the working surface

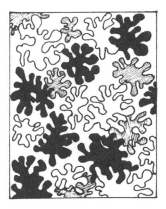

Steps:

1. Cover the working surface with newspaper. Prepare the paint palette.

2. Fold the 9" x 12" or 12" x 18" white paper in half, widthwise, and in half again. Open and fold into thirds, lengthwise.

3. Put one primary color, black, and white on the paint palette. Using only this color, mix varying amounts of black or white to make value and intensity changes in the color. Paint in the rectangles on the white paper with the different shades and tones. Let dry.

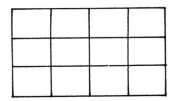

4. Draw a simple shape on the 3" x 3" rectangles of tagboard or bogus paper. Cut out. Select one to use as a template. Trace around the template on each painted rectangle. Cut out. Try enlarging the shape.

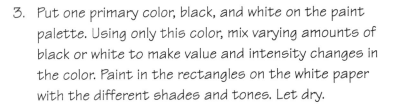

5. Arrange the painted shapes on the sheet of white drawing paper. Make some of the shapes overlap. Paste or glue the shapes into position.

Warm and Cool Color Panels

Technique: Color

Materials:

- (1) 12" x 18" white drawing paper
- tempera paint: red, blue, yellow, or assorted pre-mixed colors
- #2, #5, or #7 soft-bristle brush
- paint palette or egg carton
- container of water
- paint cloth
- paper towels
- newspaper for the working surface

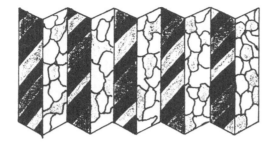

Steps:

1. Refer to page 170 for a review of the warm and cool colors.

2. Cover the working surface with newspaper and prepare the paint palette.

3. Fold the 12" x 18" white paper into a fan, widthwise. To fold a fan easily, refer to page 108. Open and spread flat on the working surface.

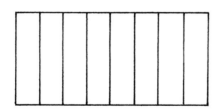

4. Paint in alternate sections of the fan with warm and cool colors. More than one color may be used in each section as long as all the colors in one section are either warm or cool. Try painting irregular sections, patterns, stripes.

5. When the paint is dry, stand the fan on a table. When looking from one side, only warm colors are visible; from the other side, only cool colors are visible.

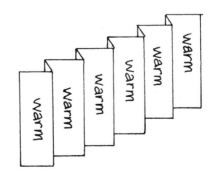

Variation: Instead of paint, this fan can be made with crayons or colored paper torn from magazines and applied to the sections of the fan with paste or glue.

Technique: *Color*

Materials:

- (2) 4" x 4" pieces of gray bogus
- ½ sheet of the classified section of the newspaper
- tempera paint: red, yellow, blue, black, and white
- #2, #5, or #7 soft-bristle brush
- paint palette
- container of water
- paint cloth
- paper towels
- scissors
- pencil or crayon
- newspaper for the working surface

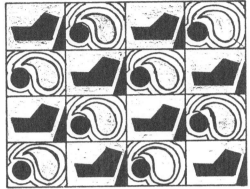

Steps:

1. Cover the working surface with newspaper. Prepare the paint palette.

2. Using the pencil or crayon, draw a different shape on each of the two pieces of gray bogus. Cut out.

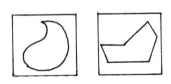

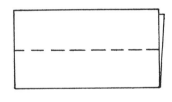 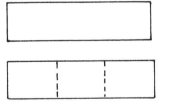

3. Fold the half-sheet of the classified section of the newspaper in half and in half again, widthwise. Then fold the long strip into thirds. This will make squares approximately 4" in size.

4. Open the newspaper and lay flat on the working surface. Using the shapes cut from gray bogus, create a repeat pattern in the 4" squares. The shapes may be in the squares, on the fold lines, overlap, and so forth.

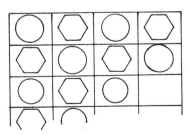

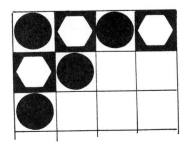

5. Use the tempera paint to link the shapes together by means of painted lines, spaces, etc. Textures can be added to give variety. Remember to let some of the newspaper show through and be a part of the design.

Experimenting with Fold Prints

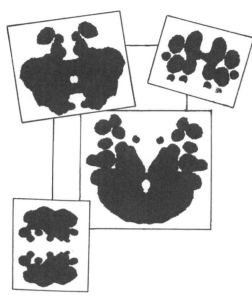

Fold Prints

Materials:

- thick tempera paint: two or three colors
- a squeeze bottle or small container
- paintbrush for each color of paint
- (1) 4 ½" x 6" or 6" x 9" paper: white drawing or construction paper, newspaper, wallpaper, shelfpaper . . . anything goes!
- newspaper for the working surface

Steps:

1. Fold prints are exciting. For the purpose of experimenting, cut paper to be used in small sizes such as 4 ½" x 6" or 6" x 9" so that it will be possible to make many different prints.

2. Cover the working surface with newspaper. Put various colors of thick tempera paint in squeeze bottles or each color in an individual container, with a paintbrush for each color of paint.

3. Fold the paper to be used in half. Open. Put drops of paint at random on half of the paper, either drops with a brush or squeeze drops from the bottle. Try using two colors of tempera paint such as blue and yellow which will create a third color, green, when blended.

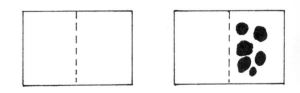

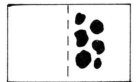 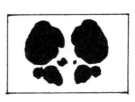

4. Fold the other half of the paper over the painted half. Rub the top surface gently and carefully with the palm of the hand to blend the colors. Open carefully and let dry.

5. Try dribbling the paint in lines or specific designs or patterns. Create flowers in a vase, leaving the lower half of the paper free for a vase or stems and leaves. When dry, add details with crayon.

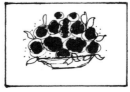 

Technique:

Fold prints

Materials:

- thick tempera paint, any colors desired
- a squeeze bottle or a small container
- paintbrush for each color of paint
- (1) 9" x 12" or 12" x 18" white construction paper
- crayons
- scissors
- glue or paste
- (1) 12" x 18" colored construction paper to mount creature on
- newspaper for the working surface

Creature Cut-outs

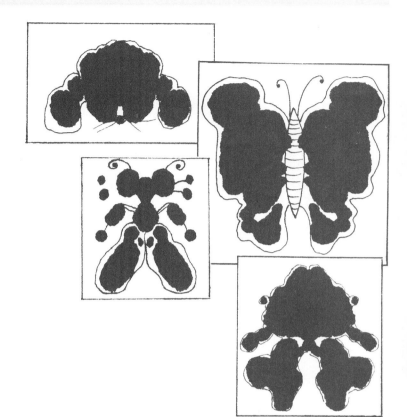

Steps:

1. Cover the working surface with newspaper. Put a small amount of tempera paint of each color in individual containers or in squeeze bottles.

2. Fold the 12" x 18" white paper in half, widthwise. Open and place in the center of the working surface. Dabble or squeeze drops of the various colors of tempera paint over one half of the paper.

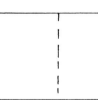 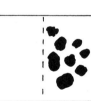

3. Fold the other half of the paper over the painted half and rub the top surface gently and carefully with the palm of the hand to blend the colors. Open carefully and let dry.

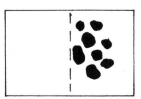 

4. Using the crayons, outline a "found" creature; this could be just the head or the entire animal. Use the crayons to add features and so forth. Cut out.

5. Glue or paste the creature onto the 12" x 18" colored construction paper. Background details may be added with the crayons if desired.

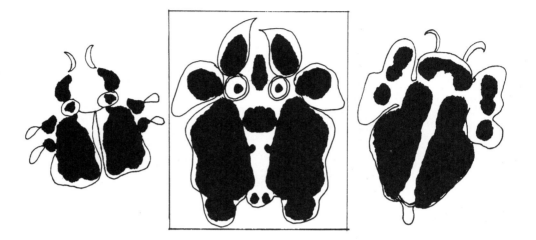

Technique: Fold prints

Materials:

- three colors of tempera paint
- squeeze bottles or individual containers
- paintbrush for each color of paint
- (1) 9" x 12" white or manila paper
- scissors
- glue or paste
- crayons and a pencil

Butterflies

Steps:

1. Cover the working surface with newspaper. Put the tempera paint in squeeze bottles or individual containers.

2. Fold the 9" x 12" white or manila paper in half, widthwise. Open. Place in the center of the working surface. Dab or squeeze the three colors of tempera paint at random over one half of the paper.

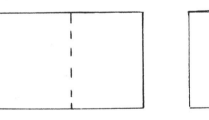

3. Fold the other half of the paper over and rub the top surface gently and carefully with the palm of the hand to blend the colors. Open carefully and let dry thoroughly.

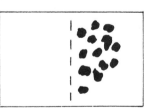 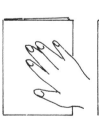 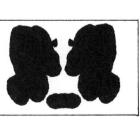

4. When the paint is dry, fold the painted paper again and draw an outline of half a butterfly, with the center of the body on the fold. Cut out.

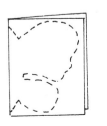 

5. Accent markings may be added on the butterfly shape with crayon. It can be glued or pasted onto a piece of colored construction paper; trim the edges of the colored paper, leaving a border around the edge of the butterfly.

Variations:

— Cut the painted paper in half, using the fold line as a guide. Fold each piece in half, lengthwise. Draw "half" butterflies, varying in size, along the fold line of each piece. Cut out. Make as many butterflies as possible.

— Tape or glue a pipe cleaner to the underside of each butterfly. Fold the long end of the pipe cleaner down so the butterfly appears to be flying. Gather all those made together and tie with a ribbon . . . a nosegay of butterflies!

— Make flowers instead of butterflies for the nosegay.
— Make just one butterfly. Staple or glue the body portion of the butterfly near the wings and fold the wings down to give the appearance of flying. Attach a stick or piece of ¼" dowling to the body with tape or glue; carry like a balloon. (See Crayon section.)

Technique: Fold prints

Materials:

- thick tempera paint, two or three colors
- a squeeze bottle or small container and paintbrush for each color of paint to be used
- paper: white or manila, any size
- piece of construction paper, a complementary color to the paint
- pencil and scissors
- glue or paste
- newspaper for the working surface

Steps:

1. Cover the working surface with newspaper. Put various colors of paint in squeeze bottles or each color in an individual container. Have a paintbrush for each color.

2. Fold the white or manila paper in half, widthwise. Open. Dabble or squeeze drops of paint at random on half the paper.

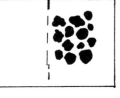

3. Fold the other half of the paper over the painted half and rub the top surface gently and carefully with the palm of the hand to blend the colors. Open carefully and let dry.

4. Fold the piece of colored construction paper in half, widthwise. Using the pencil, draw on half of an object or symbol, center on the fold. Leave a good margin of paper around the edge of the shape. Cut out, beginning and ending on the fold.

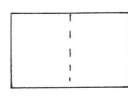

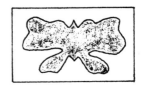

5. Open and glue or paste the silhouette on top of the painted paper; use either the outside edge (negative) or the inside piece (positive).

About Fingerpainting

Fingerpainting is a process of creating a picture or design by using fingers, hands, and parts of the arms to apply paint on a glazed or nonporous piece of paper.

The Paper

Large sheets of paper, at least 12" x 18" or 18" x 24", are best to allow for freedom of movement and large designs and patterns.

A commercial fingerpaint paper that has a special glazed surface is most often recommended but not always available. It is also more expensive. Alternative suggestions of other nonporous paper include:

— butcher paper, any color

— shelf paper

— white construction paper

— brown wrapping paper, large brown grocery bags

One Color

Materials:

- powdered tempera paint mixed with liquid starch
- commercially prepared fingerpaint

Steps:

1. Cover the working surface with newspaper. Place paint paper in the middle.

2. Pour about ¼ cup of liquid starch in the middle of the paper. Using the palm of the hand, spread the starch evenly over the surface of the paper.

3. Sprinkle the powdered tempera paint onto the starch and blend with the fingers. Spread the mixture over the entire surface of the paper.

4. Use the many parts of the hand—wrist, fingers, and fingernails—to make impressions in the paint.

5. Dry. When dry, press under a pile of books to flatten. If you find the fingerpaintings curl and buckle, use less liquid starch.

Several Colors

Materials:

- powdered tempera paint or commercially prepared fingerpaint
- liquid starch
- small containers for paint mixture
- paint cloth and/or paper towels
- wooden tongue depressors or plastic spoons

Steps:

1. Mix the powdered tempera paint with liquid starch to a thick consistency before beginning to paint. Put each color in a small separate container.

2. Place the containers on the newspaper-covered work surface within easy reach of the paint paper.

3. Spread a small amount of liquid starch over the surface of the paper to dampen it.

4. Dip one hand into one color of paint and apply areas of color to the paper. When ready for a second color, wipe hand with paint cloth. Dip hand into second color or use a plastic spoon or wooden tongue depressor to add paint to the paper.

Hints:

Fingerpainting has great possibilities. Don't make this a "one time" experience.

Always *keep one hand clean* to reach for things, open doors, turn on the water for washing hands, holding the paper, etc.

Experimenting with Fingerpaint

Technique: Fingerpaint

Materials:

- tempera paint: liquid or powdered, or commercially prepared fingerpaint
- paper to paint on
- liquid starch
- paint cloth
- paper towels
- paint smock or shirt
- newspaper for the working surface

Steps:

1. Pour ¼ cup of liquid starch in the middle of the paper. With the palm of the hand, spread the starch evenly over the entire surface of the paper.

2. Add powdered tempera paint or a small amount of liquid tempera paint and mix in with the liquid starch, spreading over the entire surface of the paper.

3. Try the following, "erasing" between experiments:
   — Using the forefinger, make one big line from the top of the paper to the bottom. Make more lines parallel to the first with space between. Put dots in rows between the lines or circles.

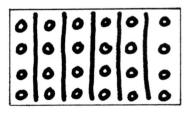
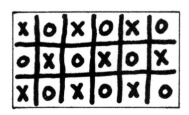

— Make parallel lines from left to right with a space between. Try putting small triangles or squares between the diagonal lines.

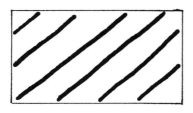 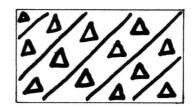

— Make concentric ovals:

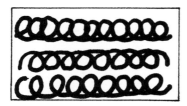

— Make "wavy" hills, peaks, and dips alternating.

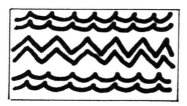

— Experiment with the seven elements of design to create repeat patterns.

Symbols of the Seasons

Technique: Fingerpaint

Materials:

- white butcher paper, any size
- colored butcher paper for mounting
- fingerpaint or tempera paint
- liquid starch
- paper towels
- paint cloth
- scissors
- glue or paste
- pencil
- paint smock or shirt
- newspaper for the working surface

Steps:

1. Cut the white butcher paper into large pieces, the size the symbol is to be.

2. Cover the working surface with newspaper. Place the piece of butcher paper in the middle.

3. Pour about ¼ cup of liquid starch in the middle of the butcher paper. Sprinkle or pour some of the tempera paint of desired color on top of the paper. Blend the paint and the starch with the palm of one hand.

4. Fingerpaint the shape of the symbol desired. Try jack-o'-lanterns, Christmas trees, snowmen, hearts, kites, birds, butterflies, etc. Add details such as facial features and decorations. Let dry.

5. Cut out the shape fingerpainted. Cut out some details so the background mounting paper will show through. Example: jack-o'-lantern—cut out the facial features.

6. To mount: Glue or paste the cut-out symbol in the middle of a piece of colored butcher paper. Trim around the edge of the shape, leaving a border of color around the outside edge.

Technique: Fingerpaint

Finger Art

Materials:

- fingerpaint or tempera paint
- liquid starch
- small container with a sponge (as a paint pad)
- wet cloth or paper towel
- paper to print on
- paint smock or shirt
- newspaper for working surface

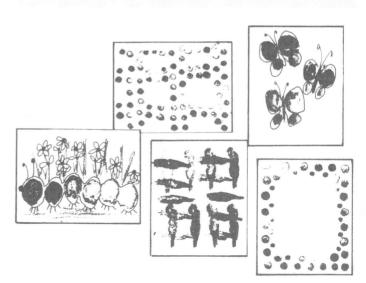

Steps

1. Cover the work surface with newspaper. Pour some of the thick tempera paint on the sponge in the small container to make a paint pad.

2. Touch the tip of one finger to the paint pad and then press against the printing paper to make a print. Try making rows of fingertips, dipping into the paint pad to pick up more paint as needed.

3. Press the underside of one finger on the paint pad and make a print. Print rows of fingers diagonally, horizontally, and vertically. Do not slide the finger on paper or the image will be blurred.

4. Try:

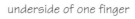

fingertips   underside of one finger   edge of hand

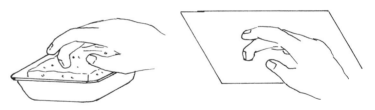

5. When the prints are dry, use black crayon to add accent lines and facial features.

— Also refer to the *Printing* section, pages 276–280.

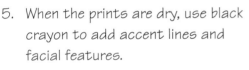

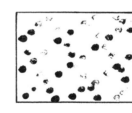

Painting with Sponges

Materials:

- a variety of small sponges in different sizes and shapes
- a clothespin for each piece of sponge to be used
- tempera paint, a variety of colors
- a small container for each color of paint, such as an egg carton or a muffin tin
- paper to paint on
- newspaper for the working surface

Steps:

1. Cover the working surface with newspaper. Clip wet sponges with clothespins, one for each color of paint to be used.

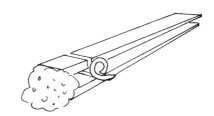

2. Prepare the paint: Pour a small amount of each color in separate small containers. To avoid many different containers, a muffin tin or a plastic egg carton may be used.

3. To paint: Dip the sponge in paint, wiping excess paint off on the edge of the paint container. Dab sponge on the paper.

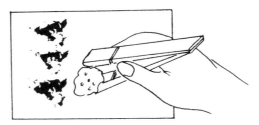

4. Try pulling, pushing, and twisting the sponge. Print one color on top of another color. Experiment on newspaper.

5. When the paint is dry, outline or add accents to the sponge shapes with crayon. The crayon lines do not need to conform to the painted shapes.

Suggestion: This technique is marvelous for creating backgrounds for murals, dioramas, or any large area such as backdrops for puppet theaters and so forth.

Technique: Sponge painting

Sponge Flowers

Materials:

- small pieces of sponge, each clipped with a clothespin
- tempera paint: any colors (try a particular color scheme)
- (1) 9" x 12" or 12" x 18" construction paper, any color, for background
- a muffin tin or individual containers, one for each color
- black crayon
- newspaper for the working surface

Steps:

1. Clip clothespins to the small pieces of sponge. Put small amounts of tempera paint in the muffin tin or in individual containers. Cover the working surface with newspaper.

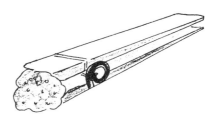

2. Place the background paper to be printed on in the middle of the work surface, positioning it either vertically or horizontally.

3. The flowers: Dip the sponge in the paint, wipe excess paint on the edge of the paint container, and dab on the construction paper. Scatter various shapes of color over the top two-thirds of the paper. When creating flower shapes, keep in mind basic floral arrangements such as those illustrated below. If desired, guiding circles can be lightly drawn on the piece of paper with a piece of chalk before beginning to paint.

      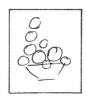

4. Leaves: Scatter dabs of green throughout the arrangement after the flowers have been made.

5. The vase: By either dabbing or pulling the sponge on the paper, make a vase shape on the lower third of the paper.

6. Draw flower and leaf shapes on top of the sponge-painted shapes with a black crayon. The crayon shapes do not need to conform to the painted shapes. Other accents may also be added.

Snowy Days

Technique: Sponge painting

Materials:

- thick white tempera paint
- small sponge clipped with a clothespin
- (1) 9″ x 12″ or 12″ x 18″ light blue or soft gray construction paper
- wax crayons
- small container for paint
- newspaper for the working surface

Steps:

1. Using the wax crayons, draw an outdoor winter scene on the light blue construction paper: in the country skiing, a city in a snow storm, etc. Press heavily with the crayon to get a good build-up of wax. Leave areas of the colored construction paper showing through.

2. Pour a small amount of the thick white tempera paint in a small container. Clip the clothespin to the small sponge.

3. Add touches of snow to the crayon drawing by dabbing on the white paint; put snow on the roofs and branches of the trees, make snowflakes, and so forth.

Resists With Crayon

The possibilities of crayon resists are endless. The following are just a few ideas. Since the technique for each is the same, the basic materials and techniques are described first and then illustrations and variations of materials for individual projects are listed. Some references will be made to other sections of this book which also have ideas for resists.

Materials:

- wax crayons
- white or colored construction paper, drawing paper, or art board
- thin tempera paint, color desired
- 1" soft-bristle brush

Steps:

1. On white or colored construction paper, drawing paper, or various weights of art board, draw a design or picture with the wax crayons, pressing heavily to build up a line waxy enough to resist the paint.

2. Mix the tempera paint to a very thin consistency, rather like skim milk.

3. Using the 1" wide soft-bristle brush, cover the entire surface of the wax design with paint, brushing freely and lightly over the design. The wax crayon resists the water-soluble paint and the design remains intact.

Variations:

design: squiggles made with a black crayon; fill in areas with bright colors or a particular color scheme

wash: a dark color

design: linear pattern with black or white crayon on colored paper

wash: a complementary color. All of these have variations in the Crayon section.

design: vertical and horizontal lines using a particular color scheme; i.e., warm or cool colors

wash: a related color

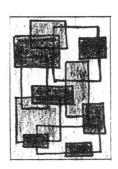

design: repeat a geometric shape in a variety of sizes over the entire paper; fill in some areas with color using a particular color scheme

wash: a complementary color

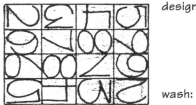

design: letters, numbers; fold paper into squares or rectangles; put a different letter or number in each rectangle; fill in areas with color

wash: a dark color

design: fold paper into squares or rectangles; fill in alternating spaces to create a repeat pattern

wash: a dark color

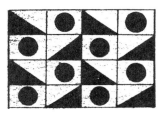

design: repeat a particular shape over and over, each within the other, filling the whole paper; use one or more colors of crayon

wash: a complementary color

design: overall pattern, repeating a particular shape or symbol over the entire paper; fill in areas with a particular color scheme

wash: a dark color

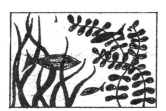

design: draw a particular scene such as "under the sea" or "in the desert"

wash: seas—blues and greens
desert—yellows and browns

design: a crayon rubbing, placing textured objects under the paper and rubbing over the surface of the paper with the side of the crayon

wash: a complementary color

Technique: Resist

Materials:

- ends of white wax candles (or white crayon)
- thin tempera paint, any color desired
- (1) 12" x 18" white or colored construction paper
- (1) 1" wide soft bristle brush
- newspaper for the working surface

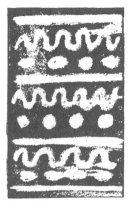

Steps:

1. Cover the working surface with newspaper. If desired, use a knife to make a point on the end of the wax candle.

2. Draw a design, picture, or pattern on the white or colored construction paper with the wax candle. Press heavily to build up a thick layer of wax. It will be somewhat difficult to see the wax candle lines so it is best not to try anything too intricate. Try:

ghost pictures

plaids

simple repeat patterns

geometric designs

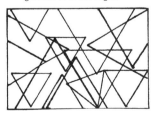

symbolic designs: letters, numbers

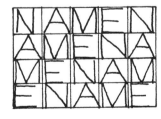

3. Using the *thin* tempera paint, any color or colors desired, brush freely, lightly, and quickly over the surface of the paper. "Magically" the design, pattern, or picture appears. If it doesn't, the paint may be too thick, there may not be enough wax built up to resist the paint, or by painting over and over, the wax was broken down and could not resist the paint. If this happens, try again.

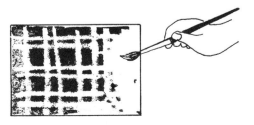

ReSiSt Plus!

Technique: Resist

Materials:

- thick tempera paint, assorted colors
- #7 and/or #12 soft-bristle brush
- heavy art board, illustration or tag, any size desired
- paint cloth
- paper towels
- container for water
- muffin tin, egg carton, or small containers for tempera paint
- India ink, black
- 1" or wider soft-bristle brush
- pencil
- newspaper for the working surface

Steps:

1. Begin with a well-thought-out design. Try several, doing the planning on newsprint the same size as the art board to be used. Plan to leave a margin or border around and between the structural areas of the design. See illustrations:

2. Transfer the chosen design onto the art board freehand or by graphite carbon (rub pencil lead over the back of the newsprint).

3. Pour small amounts of desired colors of tempera paint into small containers, muffin tins, or plastic egg carton cups. Cover the working surface with newspaper.

4. Paint in areas of design. Apply two or three layers of paint, each a different color. Let each layer dry before applying another. Make sure the paint is of a heavy, creamy consistency.

5. Let dry thoroughly.

6. Using the wide soft bristle brush, apply a layer of India ink over the entire surface of the design. Use a light touch with the brush.

7. After the ink has dried overnight or longer if necessary, the picture is ready for a bath under lukewarm water. The final color scheme can be determined by the amount of color washed off in various areas.

Impasto

Fork Designs

Materials:

- (1) 9" x 12" black construction paper or other dark paper of an equal weight
- tempera paint, mixed to a thick consistency
- liquid starch
- individual containers for paint
- plastic or metal fork
- newspaper for the working surface
- 1" wide stiff-bristle brush

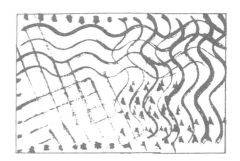

Steps:

1. Cover the working surface with newspaper.

2. Using any color of tempera paint desired, mix with liquid starch to a thick consistency rather like whipped cream.

3. Apply a thick layer of the tempera paint over the entire surface of the black construction paper. Apply evenly, keeping the brush strokes all going in the same direction.

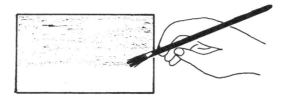

4. Draw designs across and through the paint with the plastic or metal fork. If you wish to try another design, go over the paint with the paintbrush and begin again.

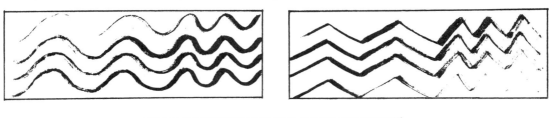

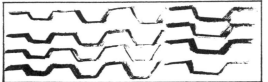

Variations: After applying the paint to the dark paper, use any object that will create textures in the surface of the paint, such as a comb, hair clip, wadded-up paper, etc.

Cardboard Patterns

Technique: Impasto

Materials:

- tempera paint, limited to red, yellow, and blue
- small containers, a muffin tin, or plastic egg carton for paint
- ½" to 2" wide pieces of cardboard, chipboard, or illustration board
- scissors
- tagboard, illustration board, or cardboard, any size
- newsprint for working surface

Steps:

1. Cover the working surface with newspaper. Mix the tempera paint to a thick consistency and put in small individual containers or sections of the muffin tin or egg carton.

2. Cut some of the edges of the pieces of cardboard to be used as paint applicators to create different textures and patterns. It is best to use a different piece of cardboard or several pieces for each color of paint. Some suggestions for notching the edges of the cardboard:

3. Begin by experimenting on a piece of newspaper to learn to apply the paint with the pieces of cardboard. Dip the edge of the piece of cardboard in the paint and then apply to the paper. Try pulling, twisting, turning, straight lines, curved or curvy lines, disconnected lines, or anything else. After experimenting, paint on the tagboard, illustration board, or cardboard.

212

Technique: Impasto

Pulled-Scraped

Materials:

- (1) 6" x 18" white or colored construction paper
- three colors of tempera paint
- individual squeeze bottles
- 3" x 7" stiff cardboard strip
- newspapers for the working surface

Steps:

1. Cover the working surface with newspaper. Put tempera paint in squeeze bottles.

2. Place the 6" x 18" paper in the center of the working surface. Squeeze the tempera paint onto the paint in "squiggly" lines and dribbles. Use two or more colors.

3. Hold the paper securely with one hand. Place the cardboard strip firmly on one end of the paper and gently pull across the paper, scraping the paint off with *one stroke*. Do not lift the cardboard strip edge off the paper until all the way to the opposite edge of the paper. Be sure to *scrape sideways, not down*, or you'll end up with a lap full of paint.

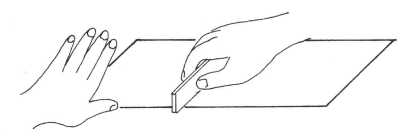

Variation:

Pull the paint across the first sheet of paper. Have another right next to it and pull the scraped paint across the second sheet of paper. Try a printed paper such as newspaper, wallpaper, or any unusual paper.

Fluff 'n stuff

Technique: Impasto

Materials:

- powdered Tide soap
- mixing bowl
- an egg beater (electric hand mixer works best)
- powdered tempera paint, any colors
- liquid starch
- piece of colored construction paper, tagboard, or chipboard
- plastic spoon, piece of cardboard, or wooden tongue depressor to apply paint
- newspaper for the working surface

Steps:

1. Cover the working surface with newspaper.

2. *To mix fluff:* Put 1 cup of Tide soap and ½ cup of liquid starch in the mixing bowl. Using the egg beater, beat constantly until the mixture is of whipped cream consistency.

3. *To add color:* Put a small amount of the fluff mixture in a small container and add a small amount of powdered tempera paint, depending on the depth of color desired, and mix thoroughly.

4. Small amounts of the fluff mixtures of different colors can be placed on a paint palette, muffin tin sections, or individual containers.

5. Apply the paint with fingers, pieces of cardboard, wooden tongue depressors, or other things such as a fork or spoon. Mix colors together or use them side by side. A myriad of textures can be created, giving a three-dimensional quality too. Allow to dry thoroughly.

Variations:

— Cut out a particular symbol such as a cornucopia, a snowman, or a window ornament; use the "fluff" mixture to decorate.

— Use for relief maps instead of salt and flour; much easier and not nearly so messy.

Technique: Impasto

Materials:

- thick tempera paint, any colors desired
- paint palette, egg carton, or small containers for each color
- 1/2" to 2" wide pieces of cardboard varying in length
- white paper to paint on, any size
- newspaper for the working surface

Flowers with Cardboard

Steps:

1. Cover the working surface with newspaper. Put a small amount of each color of tempera paint to be used on the paint palette, in egg carton cups, or individual shallow containers.

2. *To make flowers:* Use pieces of cardboard 1/2" to 2" wide. Dip the edge of the piece of cardboard in paint and then place the painted edge firmly on the paper. Move from right to left to make one petal. Add three or four more petals to form a circular-shaped flower.

3. Try:

twisting

layered for hyacinths

tulips

4. *Leaves, stems:* Use the side of longer pieces of cardboard to make the stems. By bending the cardboard, many different angles can be made. Small pieces of cardboard are used to make the leaves.

Variations: Try creating other shapes, figures, designs, creatures using only the cardboard pieces to apply the paint.

Tissue and Fingerpaint

With Other Media

Technique: Fingerpaint

Materials:

- white construction paper, butcher paper, or shelf paper, any size
- fingerpaint or powdered tempera
- 3" x 3" squares of colored tissue paper, any color or colors
- liquid starch
- scissors
- paint cloth
- paper towels
- paint smock or shirt
- newspaper for the working surface

Steps:

1. Cover the working surface with newspaper. Place the paint paper in the center.

2. Cut the tissue paper into shapes. These can be irregular shapes or the squares can be folded to cut symmetrical shapes.

3. Pour about ¼ cup of liquid starch in the middle of the paper. Sprinkle some tempera paint of desired color on top of the starch. Blend together and spread over the entire surface of the paper with the palm of the hand.

4. Fingerpaint a design, pattern, or picture.

5. When the fingerpainting is complete, *before* the paint is dry, place the tissue paper shapes on top. These can be placed to create a pattern or at random. When in place, press gently with the fingertips to make sure each piece is secure.

Variations:

— Use blue and green paint; cut bright-colored tissue into shapes of fish, underwater sea life.

— Use blue paint; cut objects for a landscape of tissue paper.

— Use any color paint; cut a single shape, varying in sizes, to make an all-over pattern.

Technique: Fingerpaint

Materials:

- white butcher paper or white construction paper, any size
- bright-colored crayons (scraps are best)
- fingerpaint or powdered tempera paint
- liquid starch
- paint cloth
- paper towels
- paint smock or shirt
- newspaper for working surface

Crayon and Fingerpaint

Steps:

1. Cover the working surface with newspaper. Place paint paper in the middle.

2. Color the entire surface of the paint paper with bright-colored crayons. Press firmly, applying a good layer of wax. Apply color in blocks, stripes, or any other way.

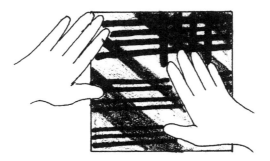

3. Apply liquid starch and tempera or fingerpaint to the crayon surface. Use only one color, preferably dark. Fingerpaint a design over the surface of the crayon surface.

Variation:

After fingerpaint is completed, before the paint is dry, place another piece of paper on top and rub gently with the palm of the hand to make a print of the fingerpaint design. To do this use a plain colored paper or any previously printed paper such as newspaper or wallpaper.

Paste, Paint, Paper

Technique:
Color, cutting

Materials:

- (1) 12″ x 18″ manila or colored construction paper
- scraps of colored construction paper, "found" papers such as wrapping paper and wallpaper
- white glue or paste
- scissors
- tempera paint, assorted colors
- individual containers for each color of paint or paint palette
- container of water
- paper towels
- paint cloth
- newspaper for the working surface

Steps:

1. Cover the working surface with newspaper. Prepare paints, assemble other materials.

2. Use the scraps of paper and scissors to create building shapes and other shapes such as cars, signs, people. Symmetrical shapes can be cut on folded paper.

3. Paste or glue the cut-out shapes onto the 12″ x 18″ paper to be used as the background, in any arrangement desired, using the paper vertically or horizontally.

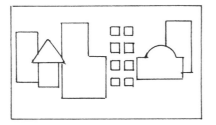

4. Using the tempera paint, brush in areas of color which, along with the scrap paper shapes, will be part of the composition. Add details such as windows on the paper cut-outs.

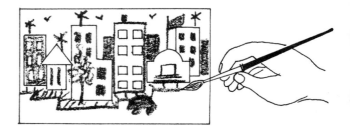

Technique:

Color, glue, printing

Tempera-Glue Relief

Materials:

- heavy paper such as tagboard, illustration, or chipboard
- white glue in a squeeze bottle
- tempera paint, assorted colors
- paint palette, muffin tin, or plastic egg carton
- container for water
- paint cloth, paper towels
- ink brayer
- black tempera, very thick, or water-soluble printer's ink
- pencil
- newspaper for the working surface

Steps:

1. Cover the working surface with newspaper. Prepare the paint palette.

2. Using a pencil, lightly sketch in a design or picture on the heavy paper. Remember to keep it simple—no tiny, detailed things.

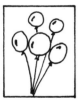   

3. Apply white glue to all pencil lines—squeeze a line of glue straight from the bottle onto the paper. Use the glue to add textured areas; fill in and build up some areas of the design or picture. For thicker areas, add more than one layer of glue. Let dry thoroughly.

4. Paint in the picture or design with tempera paint. Keep the colors bright and thick. Cover all areas of the paper, including the background. Stay within the original pencil lines and don't worry about the glue lines. If necessary, paint over them.

5. When the paint is dry, roll a brayer covered with ink or black tempera paint over the surface of the entire picture. Make sure the brayer does not have too much paint or ink on it. Roll on a piece of newspaper first. The raised glue lines will pick up the ink, accenting the lines and mass areas as well as textured areas.

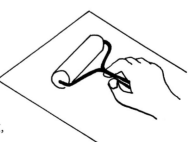

With Wallpaper

Materials:

- book of wallpaper samples
- tempera paint, assorted colors
- paint palette, muffin tin, or plastic egg carton
- #2 and #7 soft-bristle brushes
- container of water
- paper towel, paint cloth
- scraps of construction paper
- scissors
- white glue or paste
- newspaper for the working surface

Steps:

1. Select a piece of wallpaper from the wallpaper book. Trim with the paper cutter to selected size.

2. Cut solid shapes out of the construction paper scraps. Often the wallpaper itself will suggest a vase, a teakettle or a solid abstract bottle, or fruit.

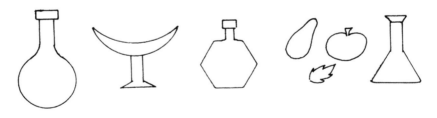

3. Arrange the cut-out shapes in a pleasing composition on the piece of wallpaper. Glue or paste into position. Be sure to glue all the edges securely in place.

4. Use the tempera paint to add areas of color, to outline construction paper shapes, and to add texture. The finished pictures are unusual and create a great deal of interest.

Technique: Color, etching

Materials:

- paper foil (red, green, blue, silver) or aluminum foil, any size
- 12″ x 9″ piece of cardboard
- rubber cement
- black tempera paint, mixed to a thick consistency
- #7 or #10 soft-bristle brush
- Bon Ami or talcum powder
- cotton
- scratching tools (pointed stick, bobby pin, or similar tool)
- Krylon clear spray paint—matte, satin, or gloss finish

Steps:

1. Cement the foil to the piece of cardboard. First, cover the back of the cardboard and the back of the foil with rubber cement. Allow both surfaces to become tacky before mounting. Fold edges over and cement to the back of the cardboard.

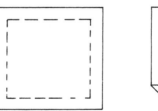 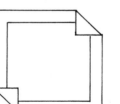 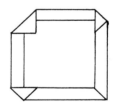

2. Clean the surface of the foil with Bon Ami or talcum powder on a piece of cotton to remove all the greasy areas.

3. Paint the surface of the foil with a contrasting color or tempera paint. Apply the paint evenly with the brush strokes all going in the same direction. Let dry.

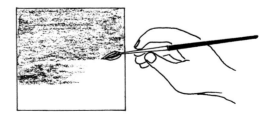

4. When the paint is dry, scratch a design on the painted surface with the scratching tool. Should the paint chip away where it was not intended to do so, it may be touched up with fresh paint.

5. Spray the surface with Krylon clear spray paint to protect the surface.

Technique: Color, etching

Materials:

- (1) 9" x 12" white construction paper, lightweight cardboard, or tagboard
- wax crayons
- black tempera paint
- liquid soap
- liquid starch
- #12 soft-bristle brush
- scratching tools
- newspaper for working surface

Steps:

1. Cover the working surface with newspaper. Mix the black tempera paint with liquid starch to a thick, creamy consistency and add a few drops of liquid soap to the paint mixture so it will adhere to the wax crayon.

2. Using the point of the crayon, apply a heavy coat of color to the 9" x 12" paper. Use many colors. These can be applied at random, in patterns, stripes, or geometric shapes. Light colors will show best. Make sure there is a good build-up of wax.

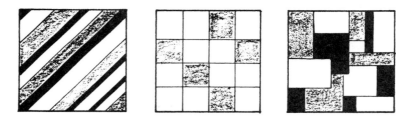

3. When the coloring is completed, paint an even coat of the black tempera paint over the entire surface of the paper. Let dry thoroughly.

4. Make lines with scratching tools (anything with a sharp point): thick and thin, wavy, straight, curved, cross-hatched; create textured effects. The under-color will show through. Lines of varying widths and areas of varying sizes will add interest to the design.

About Watercolor

Transparent watercolors are fascinating to individuals of all ages. When drops of color touch paper, they spread out magically, mingling and creating misty, hazy effects. When they are applied to dry paper, the lines are sharp and clean, with a fresh spontaneous look. But the quality of transparency also imposes special limitations—watercolors cannot be covered over, and mistakes are easier to detect and harder to correct than in other media.

Understanding and control of both brush and paint are essential to working with watercolors. The medium must be handled rapidly and directly. To become familiar with it and gain control over it, it is wise to explore watercolors in easy, enjoyable experiences, planned in sequence. Experiences should develop skills in using the brush, controlling the paint, making different color values with water, creating pictures, and combining watercolors with other media. A combination of crayon and watercolors produces wonderful resists and kinds of batiks.

This section will provide a useful sequence of experiences, beginning with activities focusing on proper use of the paintbrush to create lines, textures, and symbols. The experiences progress to experimenting with various techniques for applying paint to paper, creating individual compositions, experimenting with wet-into-wet techniques, and using watercolors with other media. Some of them involve several variations of the same technique, each requiring a little more skill and coordination than the preceding one. Others involve a single basic technique and offer suggestions for further exploration. Spend some time to learn about watercolors. It isn't always important to have a finished, framed project—there can be creative joy in just learning and experimenting.

Techniques With Watercolor

There are three basic techniques used when working with watercolors: (1) brush, (2) wet-into-wet, and (3) the wash. These techniques will be explained and illustrated in detail for easy reference.

Brush

- The brush is used as a drawing tool to create lines, textures, and symbols of a variety of subjects.
- Different ways to use the brush include:

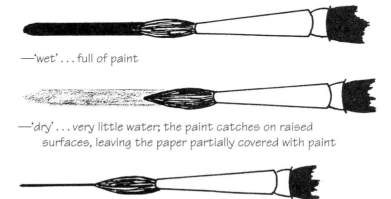

—'wet' . . . full of paint

—'dry' . . . very little water; the paint catches on raised surfaces, leaving the paper partially covered with paint

—'point' . . . for details, lines, textures, and symbols

Wet-Into-Wet

- This technique involves making the paper wet before beginning to paint. When the paint is applied to the wet paper, the colors will spread out magically, mingle together, and look hazy and misty.
- To prepare the paper for the wet-into-wet technique, follow these steps:
  — Fill a small sponge with water by dipping it in the water container.
  — Beginning at the top of the paper, make quick strokes across the surface of the paper with the wet sponge, making the entire paper wet. Don't rub the paper; keep sponge full of water so the paper doesn't roughen up.

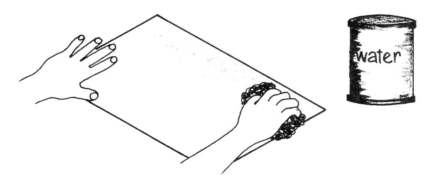

— When one side of the paper is wet, turn the paper over and smooth onto the table top or paint board. Make sure that the paper is flat, with no wrinkles. The paper will adhere to the surface. (It can be taped, but this is not necessary for the simple activities in this book.)

— Using the sponge, make the top side of the paper wet. Do make sure the sponge is full of water and use even, horizontal strokes.

- Now the paint can be applied, creating a misty, fuzzy effect, often used for backgrounds. Experience will teach 'how much' or 'how little' water is needed for the surface of the paper to create the effects desired.

The Wash

- A watercolor *wash* is applied with a brush full of paint, but not dripping, working quickly from the top of the paper with horizontal strokes. For a good wash, do not rework, mix enough paint and carry the drop from the end of a stroke across the next stroke, always working on a wet line. The colors will then mingle and blend.

- A *graduated wash* is applied by beginning with one or two strokes of full color brushed across the top of the paper. Then in succeeding strokes, dip the brush in water only and brush it across the paper. In this way more water is added gradually and the wash becomes lighter with each stroke. The result is a blending of color, graduating from the brightest to the palest; often used for skies.

- Washes can be used in various ways to obtain specific effect. For example: Paint a very wet wash of the appropriate colors across the sky portion of the paper. While still wet, use crumpled facial tissue and pick up as much paint as possible from the paper where cloud formations are desired.

Combined Brush and Wash

- The wash is used to apply the background and those objects in the background in the picture that will appear far away and misty. When the paper is dry, those objects that are in the foreground and need sharp, crisp lines are painted in with the brush: details, textures, and so forth.

- When deciding which technique, 'wet-into-wet' or brush, remember:
  — Objects appear darker and brighter when close; lighter and grayer when far away.
  — Objects overlap what happens to be behind them.
  — Close objects sometimes are drawn lower on the page; distant objects are drawn higher on the page.

With Other Media

- As a resist: Watercolors painted over crayon wax drawings with one or more colors; the wax repels the watercolors and remains exposed.
- Over-paint with watercolor on laminated paper backgrounds.
- Draw with India ink on wet or dry washes.

- Overlay: Paint with watercolor on top of tempera paint and crayon drawings.
- Combine with ink, fingerpaint, chalk, opaque paint, and pencil or ink sketches.
- Mix with white tempera paint for opaque effects.
- Rubber cement: Areas are blocked out with rubber cement; dry. Apply wash over top; when dry rub off rubber cement, exposing background paper.

Materials

The following materials will be needed to do the activities in this section:

watercolor paints	paper towels
#2, #7, and #12 soft-bristle brushes	small sponges
1" stiff-bristle brushes	scrap fabric for paint cloths
white paper: any rough-grained paper	containers for water
crayons	old newspaper
chalk	construction paper
India ink	tissue paper
pencils	facial tissue
charcoal pencil	brown paper bags
rubber cement	lightweight cardboard
liquid starch	wax paper
white glue or paste	straws
turpentine	rulers
scissors	masking tape

Additional Materials

- Watercolors may be applied to any rough-grained, light paper that is not too absorbent. Manila paper, white drawing paper, bogus paper, or watercolor paper are suitable.
- When experimenting with washes on white paper, it will soon become evident that the background color becomes an important part of the whole.
- Provide a variety of round and flat brushes in soft and hard bristles.
- Small sponges, rags, and fingers may also be used to apply paint.
- Experiment with different kinds of brushes, like a stiff-bristle brush pounced up and down makes great bushes, leaves on trees. Sponges and wads of paper make unusual textured effects.
- A little planning with a charcoal pencil may be done before you paint. Heavy lines made with a lead pencil are unpleasant because they are not absorbed by the paint and show through it. A little light blue color on the tip of the brush generally serves as well as anything for outlines.
- Make up a collection of men's old shirts for painting smocks; mothers will love having clothes protected.

The Paints

Watercolors

Watercolor paints are transparent, fluid, and fast-drying. The paints come in semi-moist pans or in tubes. Most common, inexpensive, and convenient to carry about is the box, containing eight or sixteen semi-moist pans of color. The eight-color box contains the following colors:

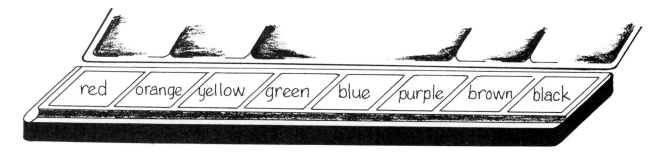

red / orange / yellow / green / blue / purple / brown / black

Water

Water is as important as the color. Water is used to dilute the paints. The lightness or darkness of the colors is altered by the amount of water used with the pigment.

It is important to remember that water runs, pours, spills, and splashes even after color has been added. Use a large container to hold water, such as a one-pound coffee can or wax milk carton. This will eliminate the need for changing water often and will stand securely on the working surface.

Preparing the Paints

Before beginning to paint, put a drop of water on each cake of color to soften the paint, making it easier to pick up with the brush.

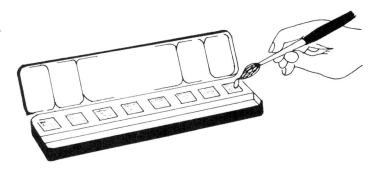

Filling the Brush

Begin by dipping the brush in water and then placing the tip of the brush around and around, at least ten times, until the brush is full of color. It is a mistake to simply dip the brush in color and, as a result, have very little paint on the brush.

Applying the Paint

When painting with watercolor paints, it is important to remember:

- The amount of water used will decide the strength of the color. The more water used, the lighter the color will be.
- Light colors are usually painted first and then dark colors. Dark colors can be painted over light colors.
- The paper serves as white so it is important to plan ahead and know when and where white will be wanted.
- Clean-looking watercolors show their freshness by tiny bits of white paper that often are left when the brush passes over the paper. Never go back over bits of white. They add sparkle and interest to the painting. Always dry paintings on a flat surface.
- When applying watercolors to paper, lay the paint on and let it alone. The more a spot is painted to improve the color or value, the worse it will look. Rubbing the brush over and over in the same place roughens the paper and muddies the color.

Mixing Colors

When additional colors are desired, they can be mixed either in the lid of the paint box or on a non-absorbent surface such as a glass or plastic plate. Styrofoam meat trays are also handy. When finished, wipe clean with a small sponge.

Cleaning the Color Cakes

It's bound to happen. Even if the brush is thoroughly rinsed, there will be occasions when the color cakes get muddy. DO NOT place the paint box under the water tap and rinse. Use a paintbrush or small sponge. When using the paintbrush, proceed as if filling the brush with paint, but then rinse and repeat the process until the color cake is clean. An alternative is to wipe each cake with a small sponge.

Before Putting the Paint Box Away

Always leave the lid of the paint box open until the color cakes are dry. Often they are very wet and will seep throughout the box if closed immediately and the box gets turned over, or if stored on its side or any which way.

The Brush

Brushes are the tools of the artist. Practice and experimentation are necessary to find out what the tools can do. It is also essential to learn the correct methods for the care and cleaning of the brushes.

Kinds of Brushes

The following round, soft-haired brushes are generally used with watercolor paints:

Holding the Brush

The brush is held as one would hold a pencil.

For some techniques the brush handle is held in the palm of the hand, rolling the color on the paper by turning the brush in one direction with thumb and forefinger.

Rinsing the Brush

When changing colors, clean the brush by gently swishing the bristles in water.

To see if all the color is out, paint several strokes on a paper towel.

When the brush has too much water, do not squeeze the bristles between the fingers. Wipe the bristles with a paint cloth or roll the bristles on a paper towel.

cleaning and storing

— Clean brushes immediately after use. Make sure no paint is left in the bristles.

— Store brushes in a drawer or on a shelf in a horizontal position, being careful not to allow the bristles to be pushed against anything. Brushes can also be stored by standing them on the handles, bristles up, in a can or similar container.

— For thorough cleaning of brushes, if there appears to be a build-up of paint in the bristles of the brush:

• Wash with warm water and soap to clean out the accumulation of color.

• Be sure to get the paint removed that collects near the ferrule.

• Rinse in clean, preferably warm water, until no soap or color remains.

• Using a paper towel or soft cloth, squeeze out the water and shape the bristles into place.

— Never leave brushes standing in paint or water containers. The bristles will be pushed out of shape.

Discovering the Brush

Discover the unlimited possibilities of the brush as a tool, become familiar with it, and develop control in manipulating the brush to create different effects.

Materials:

- (1) 12" x 18" white paper
- watercolor paints
- #7 soft-bristle brush
- container of water
- paper towels
- paint cloth

Steps:

1. Put a few drops of water on each cake of color in the paint box to soften the paint for easy use.

2. Experiment and discover with the brush, trying the following:

- "wet" brush

- "dry" brush

- "point" of bush

3. Try long continuous strokes, short up-lifted strokes, overlapping strokes, continuous strokes, wavy strokes.

4. Paint with the tip of the brush, making lines, dots, stippling.

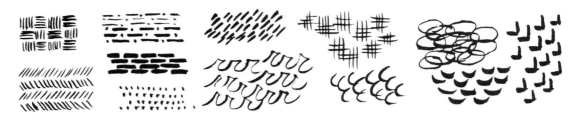

5. Try the effect of rolling the brush.

6. Create textures.

7. Create symbols of a variety of subjects with different strokes of the brush.

Technique: Brush

Materials:

- (1) 6" x 12" or 12" x 18" white paper
- black watercolor paint
- #2 or #7 soft-bristle brush
- paper towel
- paint cloth
- container of water
- newspaper

Sumi e Painting

Background:

Sumi e painting began in Japan in the 13th century. Sumi e is characterized by simplicity. It extracts the beauty of all nature and communicates it in a few strokes of the brush. Objects in nature are symbolic: The mountains symbolize peace; sun symbolizes life; etc. Humans are not subjects of sumi e painting; they become a part of the picture as they view it.

Sumi e uses brush strokes based on lines and dots. Techniques have been used for centuries and have been handed down from one master to another. There are strict rules about composition and contrast. Usually there is much of the sheet left unpainted.

Steps:

1. *Sitting position:* Sit on the floor so that you look straight down on your work. Place all equipment to the right. Rest the left hand near painting surface to balance body. Both legs are to the right. (Reverse the position and arrangement for "lefties.") Put paper directly in front. Do not move it. Only move the brush and body.

2. *How to hold the brush:* Hold the brush between the tips of thumb and forefinger. Hold handle of brush one-third of the way down from the top. Sometimes the hand may be moved down and supported on the paper by the little finger, for detailed strokes. Usually the brush is held perpendicular to the paper. It may be slanted for making wide lines.

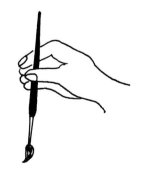

3. *Paint:* Put a drop of water in the black watercolor. A wide variety of grays can be made depending on the amount of water used. This makes sumi e painting "colorful."

4. *Paint lines:* Paint fine lines with tip of brush, thicker lines using more of the side of the brush, thick lines using the entire side of brush.

Paint dots: Print small dots with tip of brush and print groups of dots (inside of flower). Print larger shapes by pressing down a bit more on the brush. Make circles of prints. Make large brush prints by pressing down entire side of brush. Group large prints to make feathers.

Paint simple objects: pine tree, bamboo, and fish.

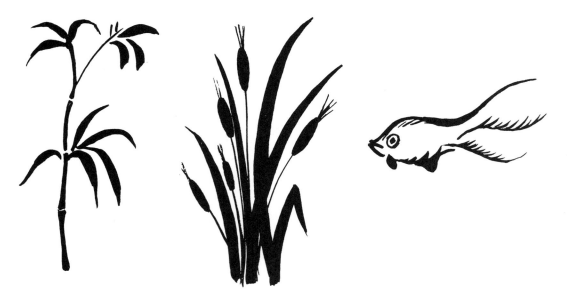

Sumi e painters paint what is important to them.

Variation:

Use sumi e painting to illustrate a haiku.

Sketching with the Brush

Technique: Line

Materials:

- (1) 9" x 12" or 12" x 18" white paper
- watercolor paints
- #2 or #7 soft-bristle brush
- container of water
- paper towel
- paint cloth

Steps:

1. Provide a subject to sketch from direct observation: flowers, still-life objects (vases, bottles, stuffed toys, and plants). To begin with, create a simple arrangement with just a few simple objects. Here are a few suggestions of objects and arrangements:

2. Using the brush as a sketching tool, draw the contour lines of the objects in the still life. Use brush lines as a means of texturing. Sketch in a simple background if desired.

Variations:

— Other subject matter may be used: illustrations and painting from memory and imagination.

— Using the wet-into-wet technique, put rows of color on the paper. When dry, use the brush to sketch in objects seen or imagined.

An "Eastern" Technique

Technique: Loading, rolling the brush

Materials:

- (1) 9" x 12" white paper
- watercolor paints
- #12 soft-bristle brush
- container of water
- paper towel
- paint cloth

Steps:

1. Hold the brush so that the handle is in the palm of the hand as illustrated.

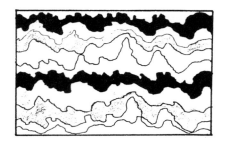

2. Place three or four drops of water on each color cake in the paint box.

3. Begin simply; try two colors such as red and yellow, which will create a third color, orange, when they mingle. When filling the brush, begin with the lightest color and work to the darkest.
   — Fill the brush with yellow paint.
   — Then dip the tip in red and swirl the brush to add red paint.

4. Holding the handle in the palm of the hand, ROLL the color onto the paper by turning the brush in one direction with the thumb and forefinger. Try horizontal lines, diagonals, curves.

5. Try using three or four colors.
   — Fill the brush with yellow.
   — Then dip the tip in green.
   — Dip in blue.
   — Finally dip the tip in violet or black.

Technique: Wet-into-wet

Materials:

- (1) 9″ x 12″ or 12″ x 18″ white paper
- (1) black crayon
- watercolor paints
- #7 or #12 soft-bristle brush
- container of water
- small sponge

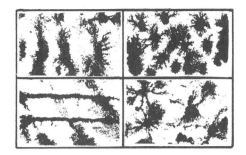

Steps:

1. Fold the white paper in half, widthwise and lengthwise, to make four equal sections. Draw black crayon lines on top of the fold lines.

2. Dip the sponge in water and make one rectangle of the paper wet by gently wiping over the surface with the wet sponge. Place drops of red paint on the wet surface. Add drops of yellow paint. The colors will mingle, creating a third color, orange.

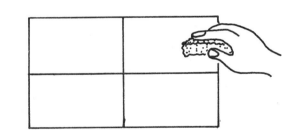

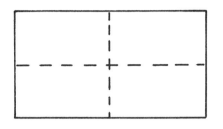

yellow/blue	red/yellow
red/blue	red/blue/yellow

3. Continue with the other rectangles in the same manner, but changing the color combinations—second: yellow and blue; third: red and blue; fourth: red, yellow, blue. This will create all the secondary colors, orange, purple, and green, as well as a neutral color, brown.

4. When dry, lines, designs, and textures can be drawn in the rectangles using crayons.

Crackled Paper

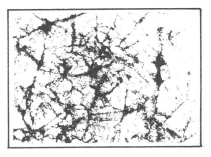

Materials:

- (1) 9″ x 12″ white paper
- watercolor paints
- #12 soft-bristle brush
- container of water
- paper towel
- paint cloth

Steps:

1. Crumple the 9″ x 12″ white paper. If a large crackle is desired, do not apply much pressure; fine crackles appear with strong pressure.

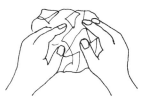

2. Gently and carefully smooth out the paper; then repeat the process, several times if desired.

3. Again smooth out the paper and place on the working surface. Paint this side of the paper with a primary color—red, yellow, or blue. Make sure the brush is full of paint.

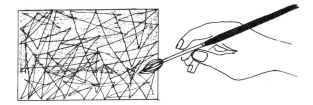

4. When the paper is damp-dry, turn it over. Paint the other side with another primary color.

5. The color will seep through the cracks that were made by crumpling and will give an interesting effect as well as a secondary color.

Variations/Suggestions:

— Try related colors, complementary colors, etc.

— Line designs can be added using crayon wax or chalk.

— The finished projects can be made into booklet covers, cards, or gift wrap.

— The crackled design provides a marvelous background to print on, using gadgets or string.

Technique: Wet-into-wet

Materials:

- (1) 9" x 12" or 12" x 18" white paper
- watercolor paints
- #7 soft-bristle brush
- container of water
- small sponge
- paper towel
- paint cloth
- straw

Spider Painting

Steps:

1. Using the small sponge, make one side of the paper wet.

2. Fill the brush with one color of paint and drop a small amount of paint on the paper. Blow the drop of paint around on the paper by blowing through the straw. Turn the paper often, blowing in many directions.

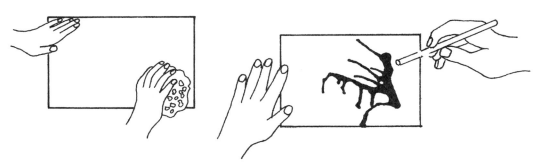

3. Repeat this procedure many times, using related colors, colors that will blend and make other colors.

4. When dry, "found" objects can be outlined with black line brush or black crayon.

Variation:

Cover paper with a wash of one or more colors. When dry, blow drops of black paint over wash.

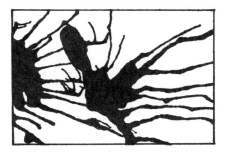

Adding the Water

Technique:
Graduated wash

Materials:

- a page of the classified section of the newspaper
- watercolor paints
- #7 or #12 soft-bristle brush
- container of water
- paper towel
- paint cloth

Steps:

1. Spread out a section of the classified ads on the working surface, making sure the columns are horizontal. Pressing heavily with a black crayon, draw over all the horizontal lines and some of the vertical lines, creating squares and rectangles. The wax crayon lines will help to keep the paint in each section.

2. Keeping in mind that the *lightness or darkness of color is altered by the amount of water used with the pigment,* paint in the various squares and rectangles with as many values of individual colors as possible.

3. When dry, use the black crayon to create lines, designs, and textures in the various squares and rectangles on top of the paint. Keep in mind the seven elements of design:

Combine two or more of the seven elements of design to create patterns, designs, and textures as illustrated.

Technique: Brush, color values

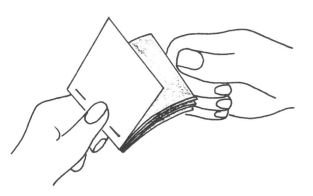

Gradated Color

Materials:

- (1) 9″ x 12″ or 12″ x 18″ white paper
- watercolor paints
- #7 or #12 soft-bristle brush
- container of water
- paper towel
- paint cloth
- small sponge
- scissors
- stapler

Steps:

1. Fold the paper in half, the width of the paper, and then in half again. Open. Fold in half the length of the paper, and then in half again. This will create 16 rectangles of equal size.

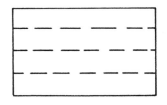 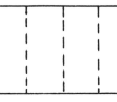

2. Select one color of paint. Fill the brush with that color and paint in one rectangle with full strength color. Continue, painting each rectangle, adding small amounts of water, each becoming lighter in value.

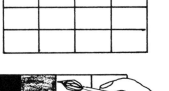

   REMEMBER: The amount of water added will affect the value of the color.

3. When dry, cut the paper into individual rectangles. Stack one under the other beginning with the full value rectangle. Staple one edge. Flip the pages to see the color changes.

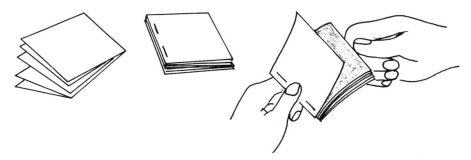

Try: Light to dark, one color to another, warm or cool colors.

Transparent Plaids

Technique: Wet-into-wet, brush

Materials:

- (1) 9″ x 12″ white paper
- watercolor paints
- #7 or #12 soft-bristle brush
- container of water
- small sponge
- paper towel
- paint cloth

Steps:

1. Prepare the white paper for the wet-into-wet technique, using the small sponge. Plaids can also be painted on dry paper.

2. Using either warm colors (red, orange, yellow) or cool colors (blue, green, purple), paint lines of varying thickness horizontally across the width of the paper. Be sure to fill the brush full of paint, and paint with sweeping strokes across the paper. Examples show strips painted on wet and dry paper.

3. Now paint the vertical stripes of varying thickness. If you wish the colors to mingle and blend, be sure to paint the vertical stripes before the horizontal stripes are dry.

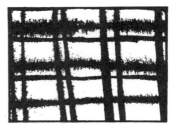

Try:

Complementary colors; dark colors on top of light colors.

Technique: Brush, crayon line resist

Materials:

- (1) 12" x 12" white paper
- watercolor paints
- #7 soft-bristle brush
- container of water
- paper towel
- paint cloth
- black crayon
- ruler
- scissors

Steps:

1. Fold the white paper in half, widthwise, lengthwise, and diagonally, as illustrated, to make eight equal sections.

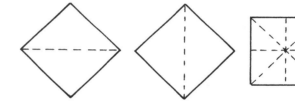

2. Using the black crayon and a ruler, draw in the fold lines so that the eight sections will be clearly marked. Make the diagonal lines 6" long from center point. Trim off corners to make an octagon shape.

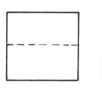 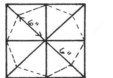

3. Draw a simple pattern or design in one section with the black crayon. Repeat it in each of the other sections so that each section is identical to the others. Make sure the crayon is applied heavily so it will resist paint.

4. Begin by painting in one section completely, using a variety of colors. Then paint in the other sections exactly the same as the first one.

People Crowds

Technique: Brush, crayon line resist

Materials:

- (1) 9" x 12" or 12" x 18" white paper
- watercolor paints
- #7 soft-bristle brush
- container of water
- paper towel
- paint cloth
- (2) black crayons

Steps:

1. Put one crayon in each hand. Place the two crayons together at a point on the paper where the top of the head is to be. Drawing with both hands at the same time, not looking at the paper, except when beginning a new figure, do the following:

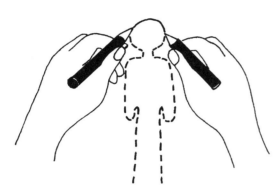

- around the head and back together
- down for the neck
- out for the shoulders
- down for the arms
- around for the hands
- straight down to the edge of the paper

2. Do this over and over, each time beginning at a different level on the paper so the people are all different heights. Let them overlap. When the paper is full, go back over each figure with the crayon so the lines are very heavy.

3. Paint the figures with watercolor paints. Paint the figures that appear to be in front one of the three primary colors. Paint the figures in the background with colors that are made with the primary color chosen. Paint the background with one of the other two primary colors.
Try: Figures in front painted with warm colors; figures behind with cool colors.

Technique: Wet-into-wet

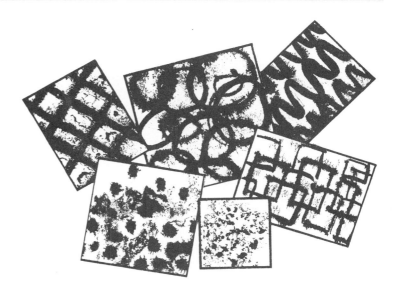

Fantasy Shapes

Materials:

- (2) 6" x 9", (2) 3" x 12", and (2) 4 ½" x 6" pieces of white paper
- watercolor paints
- #7 or #12 soft-bristle brush
- container of water
- paper towel, paint cloth
- small sponge

Steps:

1. Two pieces of each size of white paper will allow for experimentation with different ways to mingle colors, creating fantasy shapes.

2. Put drops of water on the color cakes in the paint box.

3. Prepare each piece of white paper for the wet-into-wet technique as it is used. The paper must be very wet so the colors will blend.

4. Try the following methods:
   - Fill brush with one color of paint, dab drops of color on the white paper. Repeat using a second color, letting the colors meet and mingle and blend together. Try two colors that will create a third color when they blend, such as blue and yellow, red and yellow, or red and blue.
   - Paint strips of alternating colors, letting each strip barely overlap the other.
   - Paint wavy lines, using two or more colors, each overlapping.
   - Experiment with rings, solid shapes, and designs.
   - Put dabs of color on very wet paper, pick up and tip the paper in various directions to spread color.

Suggestion:

Do not rework or go over designs.

Finders-Keepers

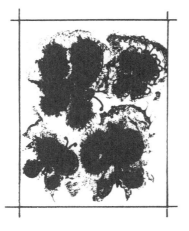

Technique: Wet-into-wet

Materials:

- (1) 9" x 12" or 12" x 18" white paper
- watercolor paints
- #12 soft-bristle brush
- container of water
- paper towel
- paint cloth
- small sponge

Steps:

1. Prepare the white paper for the wet-into-wet technique. Make sure the paper is quite wet.

2. Put drops of water on the color cakes in the paint box.

3. Fill the brush with water, then with paint. Let drops of wet paint fall here and there on the wet paper. Turn the paper from side to side so the paint will run and make lines and shapes that have fuzzy or smooth-textured edges and centers.

 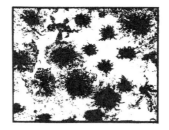

4. Add a second color by the same method while the paper is wet. Turn the paper as before and watch new colors appear as the two blend together.

5. Let the paper dry and then look for shapes of objects or animals. Outline these with a black crayon. Add details.

Variation:

On wet paper, drop colors that blend to make a dark mysterious background. This time three colors may be blended to provide a dark spooky background. When dry, look for spooks or mysterious shapes that may be outlined and enhanced as ghosts or monsters. Use crayon lines and patterns.

Technique: Wet-into-wet

Materials:

- (1) 9" x 12" white paper
- watercolor paints
- #12 soft-bristle brush
- container of water
- paper towel
- paint cloth
- small sponge
- facial tissue

Steps:

1. Prepare the paper for the wet-into-wet technique.

2. Fill the brush with blue paint.

3. Make several horizontal strokes across the width of the paper at various intervals.

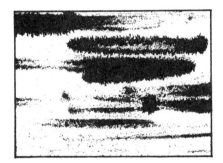

4. Fill the brush with water and paint horizontal strokes the width of the paper, overlapping edges of the blue strokes. This will spread the color and create various kinds of blue.

5. Immediately, while the wash is swimming wet, use crumpled pieces of facial tissue to pick up as much paint as possible from the paper where cloud formations are to appear.

Variation:

Try using shades of black to create a stormy sky.

Misty Flowers

Technique: Wet-into-wet

Materials:

- (1) 9" x 12" or 12" x 18" white paper
- watercolor paints
- #7 or #12 soft-bristle brush
- container of water
- paper towel, paint cloth
- black crayon, paint, or felt-tip pen
- small sponge

Steps:

1. Put drops of water on the color cakes in the paint box.

2. Prepare the paper for the wet-into-wet technique.

3. Select a color for the vase. Fill the brush with paint and paint a vase shape on the lower portion of the white paper. The paper may be placed either horizontally or vertically.

4. Select three or four colors for flowers. Using one color at a time, put drops of colors for flowers in any arrangement desired. Since these will be simple *color areas*, it is not important that the shapes resemble flower shapes. Use green paint to add leaves and stems where desired.

5. When the painting is dry, use black crayon, black paint, or a felt-tip pen and outline flower shapes, leaves, and vase.

Variations: Using the same technique, try city-scapes, landscapes, seascapes, animals, both real and imaginary.

Technique: Brush line, wet-into-wet

Materials:

- (1) 12" x 18" white paper
- watercolor paints
- #7 or #12 soft-bristle brush
- container of water
- paper towel
- paint cloth
- small sponge

Steps:

1. Fold the white paper in half, widthwise. Open and lay flat on the working surface.

2. On one half of the white paper, use paints and brush to make a line drawing or design on dry paper.

3. On the other half of the white paper, repeat the first drawing or design using the wet-into-wet technique.

4. When the two paintings are completed, compare the two halves; notice the difference in effects created by the hard and soft edges. Generally things in the background are soft, with fuzzy lines. Those objects in the foreground are sharp and clear with hard lines.

   Try: Try another picture, this time painting the background using the wet-into-wet technique. Let the background dry and then paint objects in the foreground with brush lines. Compare the results.

A Sunset Wash

Technique: Wash, cutting

Materials:

- (1) 9" x 12" white drawing paper
- watercolor paints
- #12 soft-bristle brush
- container of water
- paper towel
- paint cloth
- small sponge

Steps:

1. Prepare the white drawing paper for the wet-into-wet technique.

2. Put drops of water on the purple, red, orange, and yellow color cakes in the paint box.

3. The sky is always darker higher up so begin with purple. Fill the brush with purple paint. Begin on the side, at the top of the paper, and pull the brush horizontally across the paper. Make one or two strokes. Do not go over these strokes.

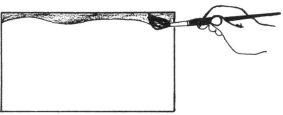

4. Rinse the brush and fill with red paint. In the same manner paint a red strip horizontally across the width of the paper, just barely overlapping the purple. This will help the colors to mingle and blend.

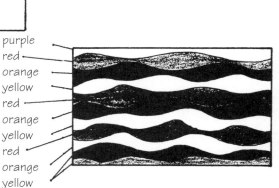

purple
red
orange
yellow
red
orange
yellow
red
orange
yellow

5. Next paint an orange strip and then a yellow strip below it.

6. Continue in the same manner, alternating strips of red, orange, and yellow to the bottom of the paper. Do not re-work. Try to end with yellow paint for a light horizon.

7. When the sunset is dry, cut silhouettes out of black construction paper and paste or glue over the top of the wash or paint on with black paint.

Technique: Wash

Materials:

A Landscape Wash

- (1) 9" x 12" white paper
- watercolor paints
- #12 soft-bristle brush
- container of water
- paper towel
- paint cloth
- small sponge

Steps:

1. Prepare the paper for the wet-into-wet technique.

2. Put drops of water on the color cakes in the paint box.

3. Add parts of the landscape: sky, mountains, land. Remember the sky is darker at the top and gets lighter toward the horizon; objects overlap what is behind them.

4. Fill the brush with blue paint. Start at the side, at the top of the paper, and pull the brush horizontally across the paper. Make several strips with full color. Then add water to the brush and spread the color to the middle of the paper, the color lighter as you near the middle.

5. Rinse the brush and fill with color for mountains: green, brown, or purple. Starting at one side of the paper, make a wavy line horizontally across the paper. Paint straight lines to fill in.

6. Rinse and fill the brush with green or brown paint for land. Start at one side of the paper and make sweeping strokes across the paper. Continue to the bottom of the paper.

7. Small strokes of various colors can be added in the foreground to give the effect of fields of flowers.

8. When the wash is dry, details in the foreground such as trees, houses, fences, and so forth can be painted over the top of the wash with brush line.

under the Sea

Technique: Wash

Materials:

- (1) 9" x 12" or 12" x 18" white paper
- watercolor paints
- #12 soft-bristle brush
- container of water
- paper towel
- paint cloth
- small sponge

Steps:

1. Prepare the white paper for the wet-into-wet technique.

2. Place drops of water on the blue, green, and purple color cakes in the paint box.

3. Fill the brush with blue paint. Start on the side, at the top of the paper, and pull the brush horizontally across the width of the paper. Do not go over it.

4. Rinse and fill the brush with purple or green paint. Make the second horizontal stroke across the width of the paper, barely overlapping the blue. Let the colors meet and mingle.

5. Rinse the brush and repeat the horizontal strokes across the width of the paper, alternating blue, green, and purple. Be sure each stroke overlaps the previous stroke. If the paper begins to dry, dampen it with the sponge. Sometimes a stroke can be made with just water to lighten colors.

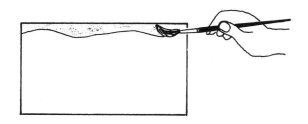

6. When the wash is dry, the underwater scene of sea life can be drawn on top with ink, black crayon, or black paint. It can also be made with cutouts of construction paper and glued or pasted on top of the wash.

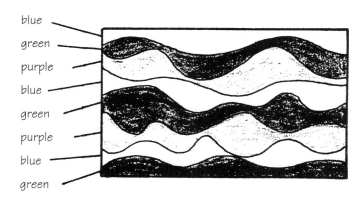

blue
green
purple
blue
green
purple
blue
green

A Simple Painting— Step by Step

Technique:

Combining wet-into-wet and brush line

Materials:

- (1) 9" x 12" or 12" x 18" white paper
- watercolor paints
- container of water
- #2, #6, and #12 soft-bristle brushes
- paper towel
- paint cloth
- small sponge
- pencil or piece of charcoal

Steps:

1. Using a pencil or a piece of charcoal, lightly sketch the whole plan of the picture to be painted on white paper. Several suggestions are shown. One will be illustrated from beginning to completion.

2. When painting, work from background to foreground or paint the foreground first and then the background.

3. Begin by painting the background, those distant objects that appear fuzzy and distant. Prepare the paper for the wet-into-wet technique.

   - Paint in water using blue and green paint; quick, free strokes with plenty of water.
   - Using just blue paint, do the sky, remembering it is lighter at the horizon. Clouds can be made with facial tissue.
   - Low scrubby hills in the background are painted with brown.
   - Paint other main parts in the foreground.

253

4. When the first part is dry, the smaller details can be painted in using a smaller brush and other colors. Light colors are always painted first and then the dark colors. Remember: Objects overlap what is behind them; close objects are lower on the paper, distant objects are higher on the paper; objects close are large, distant objects are smaller in size.

Technique: Brush, crayon line resist

With crayon Shapes

Materials:

- (1) 9" x 12" or 12" x 18" white paper
- watercolor paints
- #7 or #12 soft-bristle brush
- container of water
- paper towel
- paint cloth
- crayons, scissors
- background paper, desired color
- paste or glue

Steps:

The combination of crayon and watercolor as used in this technique offers endless possibilities. For this reason several different examples will be shown from beginning to completion.

1. Using crayons, draw selected shape(s) on the 9" x 12" or 12" x 18" white paper. Color some parts in and leave some parts white. Make a variety of sizes. Press heavily with the crayon to achieve a good wax build-up.

2. Paint a watercolor wash over each individual shape or paint each shape a variety of colors. As the shapes will be cut out, there will be no need to worry about going over the outside edges.

3. Cut out the shapes when dry.

4. Now paste or glue the shapes in an arrangement on a background of construction paper of desired color. The following illustrations will provide ideas for arrangements, additional crayon line designs, and color combinations.

Technique:
Brush, crayon line

Under a Magnifying Glass

Materials:

- (1) 9" x 12" white drawing paper
- (1) 12" x 12" black construction paper
- 9" circle template
- crayons
- watercolor paints
- container of water
- #7 soft-bristle brush
- paper towel
- paint cloth
- scissors
- paste or white glue

Steps:

1. Draw a circle on the white paper around the template. Use a black crayon, pressing hard to make the outline.

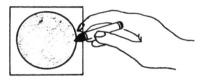

2. Inside the circle draw an insect—real or imaginary—one might see under a magnifying glass. Color parts of the insect and leave some parts white.

   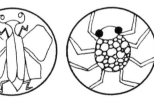

3. Use the watercolor paints to fill in parts of the insect not colored. Paint the background, the part of the circle not part of the insect, all one color.

4. When dry, cut the circle out. Place the circle on black paper and trim around it, leaving enough of the black paper to make a hand and frame to look like a magnifying glass.

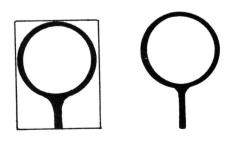

257

Tapa

Technique: Crayon line, wash

Materials:

- white and black or brown crayons
- piece of brown wrapping paper or section cut from brown paper bag, desired size
- watercolor paints
- #12 soft-bristle brush
- container of water
- paper towel, paint cloth
- warm iron, newspapers
- running water or a large container of water in which to dip paper

Steps:

1. Plan a design or pattern using either black and white or brown and white crayons. Draw on the piece of brown wrapping paper or paper bag. Press heavily with the crayon to achieve a good build-up of wax. Keep design or pattern simple. Fold in squares to aid in creating a repeat design.

2. When the coloring is complete, place the paper under running water or in a container of water to make completely wet. Then crumple the damp paper into a tight ball to crackle the surface of the paper. If a large crackle is desired, do not apply much pressure; fine crackles appear under strong pressure.

3. Open the brown paper and gently smooth out on a layer of newspaper. Paint the surface of the paper with brown paint. Let dry. Now rinse carefully under running water or dip into a pan of water and remove at once.

4. When dry, paper may be ironed flat with a warm iron. Be sure to place face-down on a pad of newspaper, so the iron does not come in contact with the crayon wax.

Technique: Crayon line, wash

Materials:

- (1) 9″ x 12″ white or manila paper
- crayons
- watercolor paints
- #12 soft-bristle brush
- running water or a large container of water in which to dip paper
- newspaper for working surface

Steps:

1. Lightly draw lines from one corner to the other, making an X to find the center of the paper. Draw a single shape in the center. Using contour lines, draw to the edge of the paper, covering the entire page with a design or pattern. Color the whole design with bright colors.

2. When the coloring is completed, put the paper under running water or in a container of water to make completely wet and then crumple it into a tight ball so the crayon cracks. Open it up.

3. Lay the wet paper on newspaper and paint over the entire picture with the brown or another dark-color watercolor paint.

4. Immediately put back in the water to wash off the paint. Spread out flat on newspaper to dry. When dry it can be ironed on the back side to make it perfectly flat.

Many Patterns from One Square

Technique:
Crayon line, brush

Materials:

- (1) 12" x 12" white paper
- crayons
- watercolor paints
- #7 soft-bristle brush
- container of water
- paper towel
- paint cloth
- small sponge

Steps:

1. Fold the paper in half twice, horizontally and vertically, so that 16 equal squares will be made.

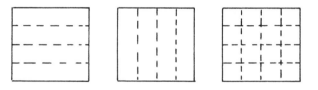

2. Decide how the squares will be filled. Here are some suggestions:

3. When the type of repeat has been chosen, build up the pattern step-by-step over the paper. Those parts to be made by crayon should be done first. Then use the watercolor paints to fill in the rest of the patterns.

260

Technique: Crayon line, wash

Materials:

- (1) 18″ x 24″ white drawing paper
- crayons (unwrapped)
- scissors
- pencil
- watercolor paints
- #12 soft-bristle brush
- container of water
- small sponge
- 4 ½″ x 6″ pieces of gray bogus or lightweight cardboard

Steps:

1. Draw two or more simple shapes on the pieces of 4 ½″ x 6″ gray bogus or lightweight cardboard and cut out. Make shapes that will relate and coordinate with each other.

2. If desired, before beginning, the 18″ x 24″ white paper can be folded into squares, rectangles, or columns to aid in developing the repeat patterns.

3. Place the first shape under the top left-hand corner of the white paper. Hold the paper down firmly with one hand. Rub the side of the crayon back and forth or with a circular motion over the paper directly above the shape until it shows through bright and clear. Move shape and repeat process, in rows across the paper.

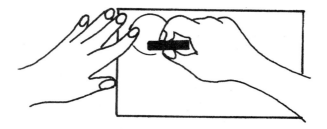

4. Now place the second shape partially overlapping the first and, using a contrasting color of crayon, repeat the same process.

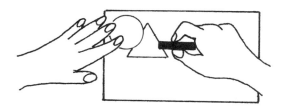

5. The process can be repeated with a third and even a fourth shape if desired. Cover the entire paper.

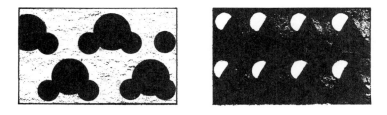

6. When the crayon rubbing has been completed, apply a wash or repeated splashes of color over the paper. Put on wet or dry paper.

7. Additional accents may be added with crayon when the watercolor paint is dry.

The results of such wallpaper projects are often as imaginative as they are colorful and gay.

Variations:

— Use the same technique to create greeting cards for specific occasions such as Christmas or Hanukkah.

— Try using leaves with prominent veins, pieces of textured fabric, sandpaper, or any other objects with a surface texture suitable for rubbing, and then apply watercolor paint.

— A variety of effects may be achieved by using any of the following techniques:
  • Blend several shades of one color or several different colors.
  • Use greater pressure on some parts of the imprint for a shaded effect.
  • Let the type of objects in the design suggest the colors to be used, such as fall colors for leaf designs, gay colors (red, yellow, blue, green) for a circus motif, etc.
  • Use manila paper strips with simple patterns cut in them for an all-over striped or plaid pattern.
  • Textured materials may be cut into abstract shapes and their imprints can be arranged to make an attractive design. Try overlapping them.

Technique:

Wet-into-wet, chalk line

Materials:

- (1) 12" x 18" white drawing paper
- watercolor paints
- #12 soft-bristle brush
- container of water
- paper towel
- paint cloth
- small sponge
- brightly colored chalk

Wallpaper Patterns with chalk

Steps:

1. Prepare the 12" x 18" white paper for the wet-into-wet technique.

2. Apply the watercolor paint to the white paper using one of several techniques: paint stripes, place drops of color at random over the paper, or one color wash.

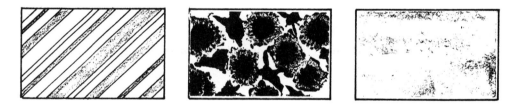

3. While the watercolor paint and paper are still wet, draw designs, patterns, or a picture over the surface of the paper with the colored chalk. The wet paper will help the chalk to adhere and to move smoothly over the surface of the paper.

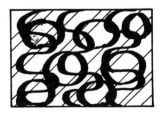

Variations:

— Try light blue construction paper, dark blue paint, and white chalk.

— Let the watercolor paint dry. Then draw with chalk, dipping the ends of the chalk in liquid starch before drawing on the dry paper.

A Resist With Rubber Cement

Technique: Wash, resist

Materials:

- (1) 9" x 12" white drawing paper
- watercolor paints
- #12 soft-bristle brush
- container of water
- paper towel
- paint cloth
- rubber cement and pencil
- newspaper for working surface

Steps:

1. Cover the working surface with newspaper.

2. The rubber cement can be applied in one of two ways, It can be dribbled in a free and accidental pattern over the surface of the paper, or a design or picture can be planned. Lightly sketch a design or picture on the white paper and paint out some parts of the paper with rubber cement. Let dry thoroughly.

3. Cover the paper with a watercolor wash and allow to dry thoroughly. The color may be brushed or sprayed on or splashed on, depending on the effect desired.

4. After the paint is thoroughly dry, erase the rubber cement and watch the white areas magically appear.

Variations:

Method #1: — Paint out some areas with rubber cement and let dry.
— Cover the entire paper with a light color and let dry.
— Paint out additional areas with rubber cement and allow to dry.
— Cover the paper with a darker color or colors and allow to dry.
— Erase the rubber cement and watch the colors and paper appear as if by magic.

Method #2: — Plan a picture and mask some areas with rubber cement, taking care to let the paint or rubber cement dry before going on to the next step.
— When finished and thoroughly dry, "erase" the cement to reveal the areas that have been masked out.

Technique: Wash, wax resist

Materials:

- (1) 9" x 12" white paper
- (1) 9" x 12" piece of very waxy wax paper
- watercolor paints
- #12 soft-bristle brush
- container of water
- paper towel
- paint cloth
- pencil, paper clips

Steps:

1. Place the wax paper on top of the white drawing paper. Secure in place with several paper clips.

2. Draw a design or picture on the wax paper with the pencil. Press down hard. Remember to fill the whole paper; the more lines, the more interesting the effect will be.

3. Take off the wax paper.

4. Paint over the entire paper with a light or dark color paint. Watch the wax line resist the paint. Dark colors of paint do give the greatest contrast. Apply paint with single strokes across the width of the paper . . . do not scrub the paper with the brush.

Variation:

Use ends of candles to draw on the paper before painting it.

A Kind of Mosaic

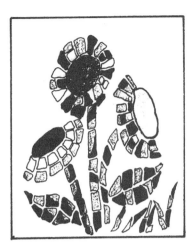

Technique: Wet-into-wet

Materials:

- (1) 9" x 12" white paper
- (1) 9" x 12" construction paper, any color
- watercolor paints
- #12 soft-bristle brush
- container of water
- paper towel, paint cloth
- paste or glue

Steps:

1. Prepare paper for wet-into-wet technique.

2. Beginning at the top of the paper, paint stripes of color horizontally the width of the paper or use a variety of related colors, making sure each stripe of color touches the other. Paint all the way to the bottom of the paper, completely covering the paper. Let dry.

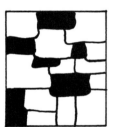 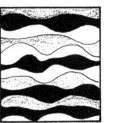 

3. When the paper is dry, tear it into small pieces of various shapes and sizes.

4. With these pieces create a design or picture on the construction paper, gluing each into place.

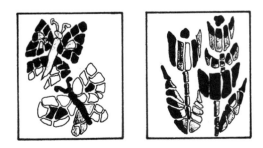

Variation:

Specific objects such as butterflies or flowers can be made and when completed the construction paper can be trimmed, leaving just a small border of color around the edge of the mosaic object.

Technique: Brush

Materials:

- (1) 9" x 18" white paper
- watercolor paints
- #7 or #12 soft-bristle brush
- container of water
- paper towel
- paint cloth
- oil or turpentine in small container
- rag or brush to apply oil or turpentine
- black crayon or black paint

Stained-Glass and Parchment Effect

Steps:

1. Lightly sketch a design, pattern, or picture on the white paper with a pencil.

2. Paint in the pencil lines with black paint. Let dry.

3. Fill in the outlined portions of the picture with different colors of watercolor paint.

4. When the watercolor paint is dry, brush the back of the paper with oil or turpentine to increase the transparency of the paper and the colors.

A Picture in Layers

Technique:
Tempera, crayon line, wash

Materials:

- (1) 9" x 12" or 12" x 18" white paper
- white tempera paint
- stiff-bristle brush
- watercolor paints
- #7 soft-bristle brush
- container of water
- paper towel
- paint cloth
- crayons
- newspaper

Steps:

1. Paint the 9" x 12" or 12" x 18" white paper with white tempera paint, covering the entire surface with two coats, the first with the brush strokes going horizontally and the second with the brush strokes going vertically. Use a stiff brush to get fine-textured lines. Dry thoroughly.

2. Draw a picture, using both the end and side of the crayon. The side of the crayon will let the textured tempera coat of paint show through. Do not cover the entire surface with crayon.

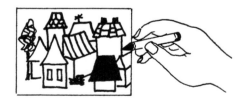

3. Add a watercolor wash to those areas of the drawing that are not heavily crayoned. The watercolor adds extra dimension to the drawing because of its transparency.

Note: Be prepared to have this activity take several art sessions, as the white tempera paint must be thoroughly dry before applying the crayon drawing.

Technique: Wet-into-wet, printing

Materials:

- (1) 9″ x 12″ or 12″ x 18″ white paper
- (1) 9″ x 12″ or 12″ x 18″ hard cardboard
- watercolor paints
- #12 soft-bristle brush
- container of water
- paper towel
- paint cloth
- small sponge
- pencil
- white glue
- printer's ink and brayer
- thick string

In Focus/out of Focus

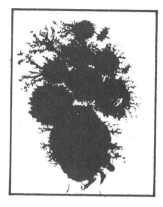

Steps:

1. Lightly sketch a simple design or picture on the white paper.

2. Using the wet-into-wet technique, flow rich colors onto the sketch areas. The dampness of the paper will prevent hard edges. Let dry.

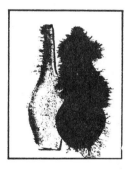 

3. Redraw the design or picture *in reverse* on the hard cardboard. Using white glue, attach heavy string on the outline of the design or picture to form a printing plate.

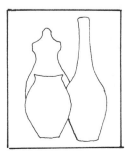 

4. Using a brayer, apply ink to the surface of the cardboard and string. Place the dry painting face down over the cardboard and string. Rub the paper with a soft cloth or roll over the surface of the paper with a clean brayer.

Results:

Crisp, clean outlines printed on misty, hazy painted backgrounds. This technique produces beautiful results.

About Printing

Printmaking or "printing" is one of the oldest and most popular of all art forms. When very young we learn to make prints the way that people long ago learned about printmaking: footprints or handprints made over and over again in wet sand or earth. Art prints are created in a similar way. One material is pressed against another to create a picture or design that can be repeated many times.

The repetitive nature of any of the printing techniques makes printing one of the best methods of developing the concept of pattern and design. Printmaking encourages creativity and yet imposes disciplines. As one becomes absorbed in the texture, line, and light and dark patterns, it will be discovered that the only limits are the techniques themselves. Print projects provide hours of pleasure—the moment the first print is pulled is one of great expectation and suspense. Suddenly there is an awareness of all the things around, their shapes, textures; a desire to experiment, try making prints.

The activities in this section utilize simple, inexpensive equipment, basic printing materials, and found or discarded items and household supplies. They range from the simple process of inking and printing fingerprints to the more complex preparation of stencils and incised surfaces. The techniques are designed to enable anyone to achieve fascinating and intriguing effects.

Techniques for Printing

The following techniques will be used in the printing activities in this section. The section is divided into several parts, each dealing with one of the printing techniques. At the beginning of each part are detailed explanations and illustrations of the skills, materials, and procedures for using each technique.

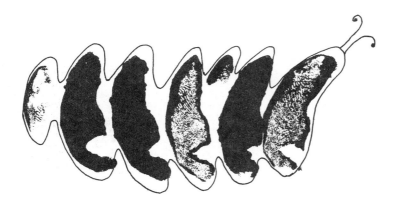

With Fingers

When a fingertip, finger, or the side of a finger is pressed on a paint pad and then pressed on paper, a print is made; then come flowers, patterns, designs, and many more wonderful things.

Stamping

Surfaces of various objects are moistened on a pad coated with paint or ink and stamped on paper.

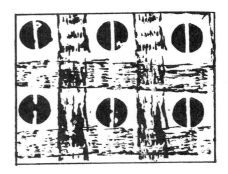

Stencils

In stenciling, printing is done through a surface called a stencil. Stencils are made by cutting away an area and using what is cut away or what remains to control the application of color.

Monoprints

A single print can be made by applying thick tempera paint or water-soluble printer's ink on a nonabsorbent surface with etched designs, then blotting with an absorbent paper.

Relief Prints

Paper, string, cardboard, and felt are just a few of the things that can be used to create a raised surface.

Incised

Incised printing is printing from a flat surface with ink imbedded into etched or engraved lines as in etching.

Materials

A limited budget need not limit printmaking activities; materials generally found in the average classroom can be combined with found or scrap materials to produce an exciting collection of handsome prints. The following materials and tools will be used in the activities on printmaking in this section:

Printing Medium

- **tempera paint:** equal parts of powdered tempera paint, powdered Ivory or Tide soap and liquid starch mixed with a small amount of water to a "puddly" consistency.
- **water-soluble printer's ink:** comes in tubes, available in many colors.
- **India ink:** water-soluble only for easier clean-up; comes in colors as well as black.
- **poster paint:** ready-mixed water-soluble paints; in jars, many colors.
- **acrylic paints:** water-soluble, in tubes, thinned with water or in bottles in a more liquid form.

Paper to Print on

construction paper	drawing paper	brown paper bags
gray bogus	newspaper	onionskin
tissue	shelf paper	paper toweling
copy paper	parchment	butcher's paper
wallpaper	magazine pages	typing paper
gift wrap	newsprint	

Also experiment with textured papers, glossy and matte finish paper, and foil.

Applying the Medium

- **paint/ink pad**
  - *pad:* made from a sponge, a piece of foam rubber, piece of old carpeting, several pieces of paper towel folded together.
  - *container:* disposable aluminum tins, a flat dish, or pan for each pad and color to be used.
  - *To assemble:* Dip the material that is to be the pad in water and then gently squeeze out some of the water. Place the wet pad in/on the flat container. Pour on the ink or paint and spread over the pad surface evenly with a piece of cardboard.
  - *A hint:* When many colors of paint or ink are needed in small amounts for small objects, use a muffin tin, egg cartons, a plastic meat tray; put a small piece of sponge in the bottom of each section.
- **brayer:** a rubber roller specifically designed for printing, used to apply paint or ink to flat surfaces such as a printer's block.
- **inking block:** a smooth, nonporous surface for rolling out the paint or ink to coat the brayer. For an inking block try:
  - scrap of smooth floor covering such as a vinyl tile
  - cookie sheet, glass baking dish
  - piece of heavy wax paper, foil, or oil cloth taped to a piece of sturdy cardboard or chipboard
  - piece of Masonite™, smooth side
- **stencil brush:** short-handled, stubby brush with short, stiff bristles. Stencil brushes are best, but a substitute can be made from old easel brushes or others by cutting the bristles about $3/4''$ below the metal band which holds the bristles together.
- **soft-bristle brushes:** watercolor brushes, #7 and #12

Also Needed

- **printing pad:** It is easier to get good clear prints when a padded surface is under the paper on which the print is made.
  - many layers of newspaper
  - an old sheet or other smooth fabric, folded over several times to be thick, smooth, and flat: size of the container used to hold it
  - a piece of thick, smooth carpeting
- **cutting board:** used when cutting stencils with sharp tools to protect the working surface
  - a piece of thick cardboard or chipboard
  - a piece of plywood or Masonite™

- **objects to stamp:** Make a collection of objects that can be used for stamping, creating relief prints.

vegetables	wood	wire
fruit	twigs	toothpicks
dried cereals	sponges	paper clips
macaroni	erasers	nuts and bolts
corks	straws	kitchen tools
nails	hair clips	pencils
combs	pipe cleaners	clothespins
keys		

- **carving, incising tools:** used to etch designs in flat surfaces; can be anything with a sharp point. These activities should be for older children.

- **cutting tools:** used to cut complex stencils, needing details. These tools should be used by the teacher or older children, under supervision.

X-acto blades	single-edged razor blade	sharp pointed knife

- **blocks:** can be made of any of the following materials:

cardboard	chipboard	blocks of wood	sticks
cylinders	tin cans	thread spools	doweling
Styrofoam			

Additional Materials

wax crayons	sponges	clothespins	chalk
pencils	foil	strings, yarns	rickrack
white glue	wax paper	sandpaper	wire screen
scissors	stapler	cotton	cheesecloth
toothbrush	burlap	paper towels	
masking tape	straight pins	facial tissue	

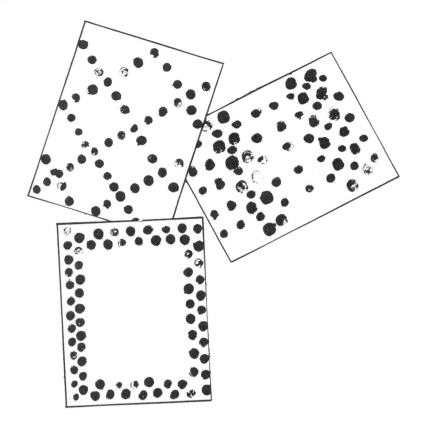

Fingerprints

When a fingertip or finger is dipped into paint and pressed on paper, a print is made. Intriguing and interesting prints can be made from hands, fingers, and fingertips.

Materials:

- paint or ink for printing
- paint/ink pad: one for each color
- wet cloth or paper towel to wipe fingers
- paper to print on
- newspaper for working surface
- printing pad

Steps:

1. Cover the working surface with newspaper.

2. Place printing paper on printing pad.

3. Touch the tip of one finger to the paint/ink pad and then press against the printing paper to make a print. Try making rows of fingertip prints, dipping into the paint pad to pick up more paint as needed.

 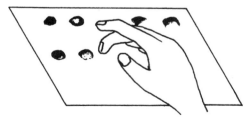

4. Press the underside of one finger on the paint pad and make a print. Print rows of fingers at diagonals, horizontally and vertically. Do not slide finger on paper or the image will be blurred.

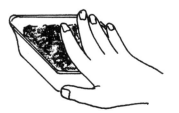 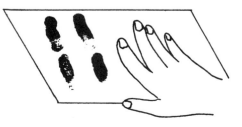

Technique: Fingerprinting

Materials:

- paint or ink for printing
- paint/ink pad: one for each color
- wet cloth or paper towel to wipe fingers
- paper to print on
- newspaper for working surface
- printing pad

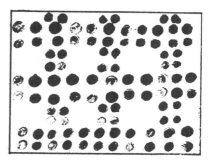

Steps:

1. The use of many colors will make this experience more exciting so several paint/ink pads will be needed, but very little paint or ink. Use a muffin tin, the lid of an egg carton, or a large flat dish. Place a wet pad in each section or far apart in a flat dish. Put a different color paint on each pad.

2. Place printing paper on printing pad.

3. Touch the tips of two or more fingers to paint/ink pad of one color. Press one finger on the printing paper and make a print. Continue by "walking" fingers in paint and then across the paper.

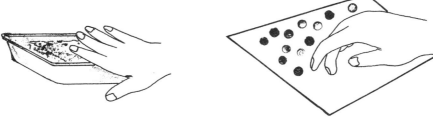

4. Wipe color off fingertips with a wet cloth or paper towel. Continue with a second and then a third color.

5. Cover the paper with prints or plan a definite pattern. Try combining fingerprints with other printing media.

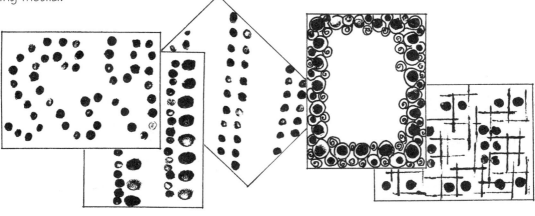

Finger Creatures

Technique:
Fingerprinting

Materials:

- paint or ink for printing
- paint/ink pad: one for each color
- wet cloth or paper towels to wipe fingers
- paper to print on
- newspaper
- newsprint for experimental prints
- crayons

Steps:

1. Cover working surface with newspaper and make a padded newspaper printing surface. Place paper for printing on top.

2. Prepare paint pad or pads if several colors are to be used.

3. Try:

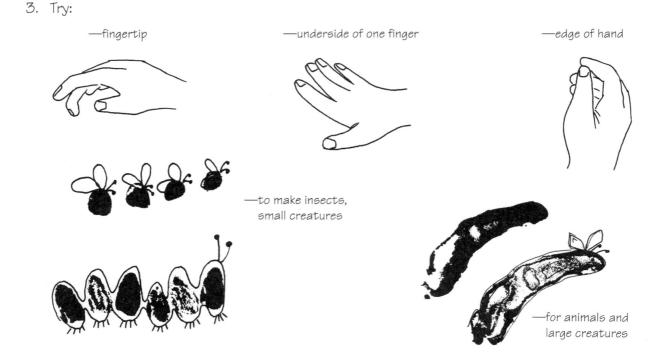

—fingertip

—underside of one finger

—edge of hand

—to make insects, small creatures

—for animals and large creatures

4. When the print or prints are dry, use black crayon to add accent lines and facial features.

Technique: Fingertip printing

Materials:

- brown crayon
- (1) 6" x 18" white drawing paper
- thick gray tempera paint
- wax paper or small container
- paint pad: one for each color
- small pieces of cotton, glue or paste
- printing pad
- newspaper for working surface

Steps:

1. Draw stems for the pussy willows with the brown crayon on the 6" x 18" white drawing paper. If the pussy willows are to be in a vase, cut the vase from a 4 ½" x 6" piece of construction paper and glue or paste to the paper. Draw the stems coming out of the vase.

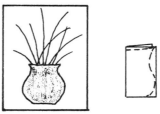

2. Put a small amount of the gray tempera paint on a piece of wax paper or in a small container. Dip a fingertip in the paint and print a pussy willow on the stem. Do all the stems and let dry.

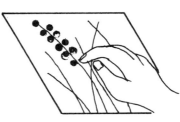

3. When the paint is dry, put a small piece of cotton on the tip of each pussy willow, using glue or paste.

Variations: Create other flower shapes by combining different fingertip prints.

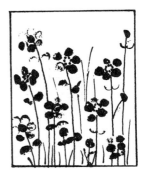

Iris in Bloom

Technique: Hand and finger printing

Materials:

- tempera paint mixture
- paint/ink pad: one for each color
- paper for printing
- printing pad
- newspapers for working surface
- crayons

Steps:

1. Prepare a paint pad for each color of paint to be used. Suggested colors: shades of purple, yellow, green.

2. To print the shape of the iris flower:

Press the side of the hand, little finger on the paint pad and then on paper; first right and then left hand so the petals cup around the center.

To make the small petals that curve down, print with just the side of the small finger.

3. To make the stems, use a brush or the side of a piece of cardboard. The full-length print of the small finger can be used to make leaves. Add stamens and accent the flower shapes with crayon.

Try:

Create other flower shapes by combining different fingertip, finger, and hand prints.

Stamping

Materials:

For the stamp pad

- a sponge, piece of foam rubber, piece of old carpeting, or several pieces of paper towel folded together for each color of paint to be used

- a disposable aluminum tin, flat dish, or pan for each color of paint to be used

Paint for printing

- tempera paint mixture: equal parts of powdered tempera paint, powdered Ivory or Tide soap and liquid starch, mixed with a small amount of water to a "puddly" consistency

- water-soluble printer's ink

- poster paint

- India ink, water-soluble

Preparation:

The stamp pad

1. Make the material to be used as a paint pad wet with water.

 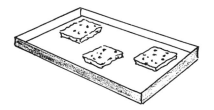

   Place the wet pad in the bottom of the flat container.

2. When stamping with small objects and many colors of paint or ink are desired, use a plastic egg carton or muffin tin. Put a small pad of sponge or folded paper towel in each section for each color to be used.

3. Pour paint or ink of desired color on the wet pad. Spread the paint evenly over the surface of the pad with a brush or piece of cardboard. Re-soak the pads if they become dry.

Objects to stamp

Stamping prints can be made with anything. The possibilities are endless. The following list suggests just a few ideas:

vegetables	wood	wire
fruit	twigs	paper clips
dried cereals	sponges	screws
macaroni	spools	nails
corks	erasers	nuts and bolts
clothespins	straws	kitchen tools
combs	hair clips	pencils

Some objects will be small and difficult to hold. It is best to mount them on something larger for easier handling and clean fingers.

—Clip sponges with clothespins.

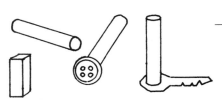

—Glue individual small objects to the ends of pieces of doweling or wood.

Strips of lightweight cardboard can be folded and glued to small squares of cardboard to make printing stamps. Glue the small object to the underside of the cardboard square.

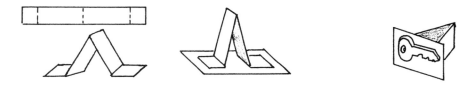

Printing:

1. Place the printing paper on printing pad (see page 274).

2. Press the printing object firmly and evenly on the paint/ink pad. Before printing, check the surface to make sure it is evenly saturated without dry areas or puddles of paint.

3. Now press the object firmly and evenly on the printing paper. Try the first print on newspaper or scrap paper. If the print is badly smudged, too much paint has been used. If the print fuzzes around the edges, the paint is too thin.

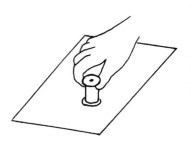

Technique: Stamping
Materials:

With Vegetables

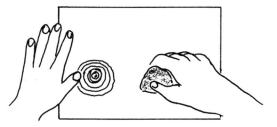

- vegetables: potato, onion, carrot, celery stalk, okra, turnip, and/or any other firm vegetable
- paint or ink for printing
- paint/ink pad
- soft-bristle brush
- knife to cut vegetables
- paper towels
- sponge
- paper to print on, any size
- 9" x 12" newsprint for sample prints
- newspaper for working surface
- printing pad

Steps:

1. About one hour before beginning, cut the vegetables in half and put face down on paper towels to dry.

2. Cover the working surface with newspaper. Position the printing pad and prepare ink pad.

3. To print: Press the flat, cut surface of the vegetable firmly and evenly on the ink pad. Before printing, check the surface to make sure it is evenly saturated, without dry areas or puddles of paint. Do the first print on the 9" x 12" newsprint to make sample prints before printing on other paper.

It will be easier to coat the surfaces of some vegetables with a paintbrush.

4. Make sample prints of several vegetables to get ideas for combining two or more into repeat designs and patterns. When another color is desired, wash or wipe the printing surface of the vegetable with a paper towel or sponge.

Technique: Stamping

Materials:

- fruit: oranges, grapefruit, apples, lemons, limes, any other fruit
- paint or ink for printing
- paint/ink pad
- soft-bristle paintbrush
- knife to cut fruit
- paper towels
- sponge
- 9" x 12" newsprint for sample prints
- paper to print on, any size
- newspapers for working surface
- printing pad

With Fruit

Steps:

1. About one hour before beginning, cut the pieces of fruit in half and put face down on paper towels to dry.

2. Cover the working surface with newspaper. Make a padded printing surface.

3. To print: Press the cut surface of the fruit firmly and evenly on the paint pad. Before printing, check the surface to make sure it is evenly saturated without dry areas or puddles of paint. Do the first print on the 9" x 12" newsprint to check the quality of the print.

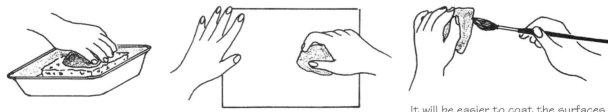

It will be easier to coat the surfaces of some fruits with a paintbrush.

4. Make sample prints of several fruits to get ideas for combining two or more into repeat designs and patterns. When another color is desired, wash or wipe the printing surface of the fruit with a paper towel or sponge.

285

The Versatile Potato

Materials:

- a potato
- kitchen or paring knife
- paint or ink for printing
- paint/ink pad
- soft-bristle paintbrush
- 9" x 12" newsprint for sample prints
- paper towels
- sponge
- paper to print on
- newspapers for working surface
- printing pad

Steps:

1. Cut the potato in half. Trim away the outside edges to make a flat, distinct printing surface. Cut away parts to make a design at least ½" deep. The design can be drawn on first before beginning to carve.

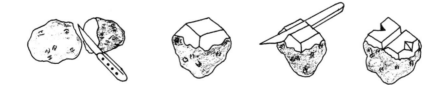

2. Prepare the paint pad and cover the working surface with newspaper.

3. To print, press the potato stamp on the paint pad or paint the carved surface with a brush. Then press firmly and evenly on the 9" x 12" newsprint for sample prints. Lift the stamp carefully so the print will not be smudged. Before final printing, always check the printing surface to make sure it is evenly saturated, without dry areas or puddles of paint.

4. Instead of printing "helter-skelter" over the paper, attempt to work out repetitive designs and patterns. To help in printing, put chalk lines on the paper before beginning to print to act as guidelines.

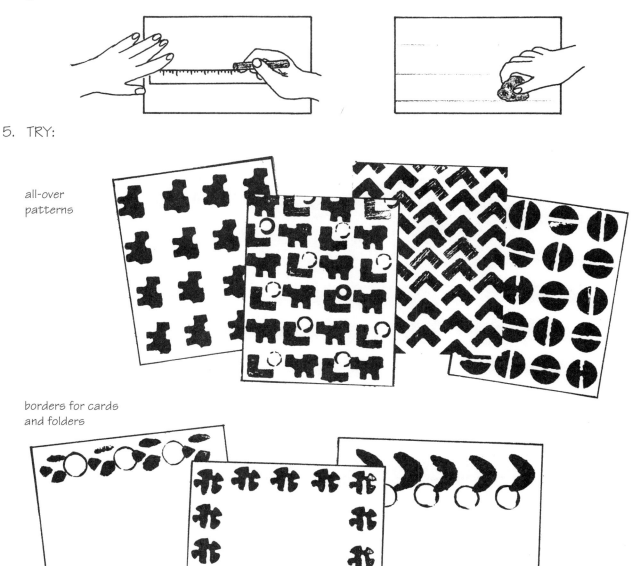

5. TRY:

all-over
patterns

borders for cards
and folders

pictures

book plates

With Sponges

Technique: Stamping

Materials:

- a variety of small sponges in different sizes and shapes
- a clothespin for each piece of sponge used
- tempera paint mixture: a variety of colors
- a small flat container for each color of printing paint—egg cartons or muffin tin
- newsprint for sample prints
- 9" x 12" or 12" x 18" paper to print on
- newspaper for working surface

Steps:

1. Cover working surface with newspaper. Clip wet sponges in clothespins, one for each color of paint to be used.

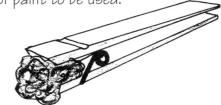

2. Prepare the printing paint by pouring a small amount in a flat container. To avoid many separate containers, use a muffin tin or an egg carton, a different color in each section.

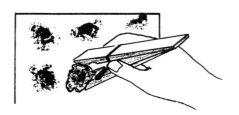

3. To print: Dip the sponge in paint, wiping excess paint off on the edge of the paint container. Dab sponge on the printing paper.

4. Try dabbing, pulling, pushing, and twisting the sponge. Experiment on newsprint before printing on other paper.

5. When the paint is dry, outline or add accents to the sponge shapes with crayon. The crayon lines do not need to conform to the painted shapes.

Variations: Use sponge prints to make trees, flowers, animals, repeat patterns, and border designs. Combine with gadgets, cardboard printing.

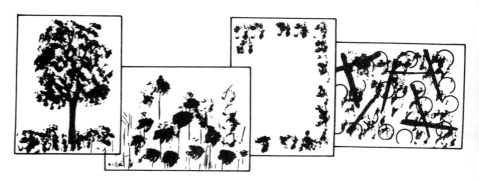

Technique: Stamping

Materials:

- gadgets: corks, combs, kitchen utensils, bottle caps, keys, nails, buttons, screws, tacks, tin cans, cookie cutters, spools, etc.
- paint or ink for printing
- paint/ink pad
- printing pad
- soft-bristle paintbrush
- newsprint for sample prints
- paper to print on, any size
- newspaper for working surface

With Gadgets

Steps:

1. Cover the working surface with newspaper. Position printing pad. Prepare paint/ink pad.

2. To print: Press the surface of the object to be printed firmly and evenly on the paint/ink pad. Before printing, check the surface to make sure it is evenly saturated, without dry areas or puddles of paint.

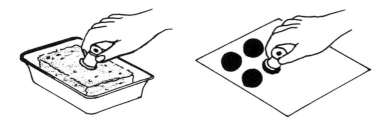

It will be easier to coat the printing surface of some gadgets with a paintbrush.

3. Instead of printing "helter-skelter" over the paper, attempt to work out repetitive designs and patterns. To help in printing, put chalk lines on the paper before beginning to print to act as guidelines.

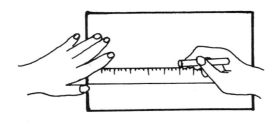
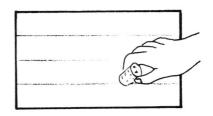

4. Make sample prints of many objects. Here are just a few of the many possibilities.

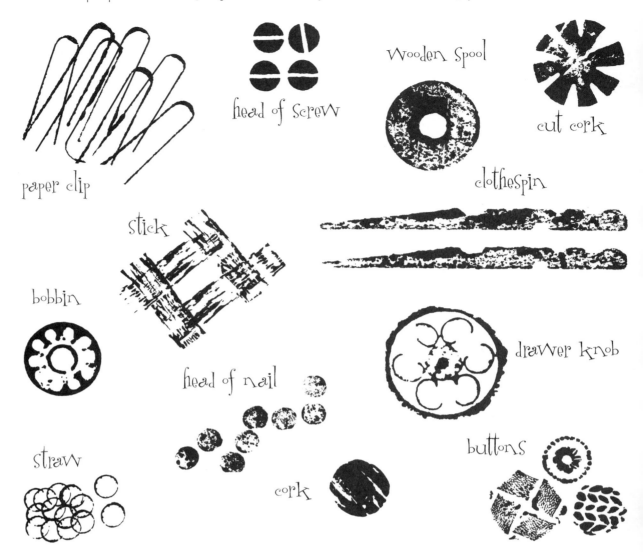

paper clip

head of screw

Wooden Spool

cut cork

clothespin

stick

bobbin

drawer knob

head of nail

straw

buttons

cork

5. Experiment with combinations of two or more gadgets to create patterns and overall designs.

6. Combine gadget printing with other media such as crayon or watercolor washes.

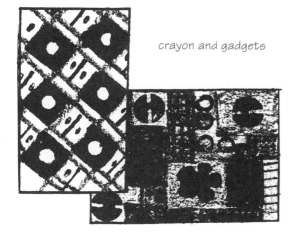

crayon and gadgets

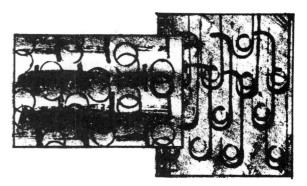

gadget printing on watercolor washes

7. Experiment with gadget printing on top of tissue collages, the classified section of the newspaper, on top of fingerpaint designs, or anything else that comes to mind.

Print borders, stationery, book plates, wrapping paper, cards, and folders.

With Wood Scraps

Technique: Stamping

Materials:

- scraps of wood salvaged from home and/or lumber yards
- paint or ink for printing
- paint/ink pad
- soft-bristle paintbrush
- newsprint for sample prints
- paper to print on, any size
- newspapers for working surface
- printing pad

Steps:

1. Analyze shapes of wood available. See how many shapes there are to work with. Notice the similarities and differences in shapes; the ways of achieving variety in shape and color. Shapes can be created by printing one shape next to or overlapping another.

2. Prepare the paint pad, and working and printing surfaces.

3. To print: Press the wood pieces on the paint and/or paint the surface of the wood with a paintbrush. Place on printing paper and press down firmly and evenly. The printing pad should be thick so the grain of the wood will print.

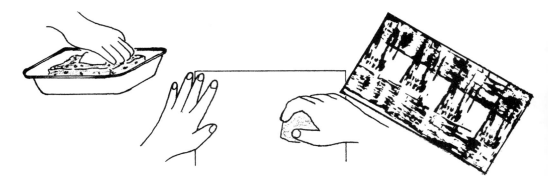

4. Using a variety of shapes and colors, continue to build new shapes by placing them next to one another and overlapping. All sides of wood block can be utilized. Remember to wipe off first color of paint before using the wood with another color.

Variations:

Try combining with other printing media such as gadgets, fruits, or vegetables.

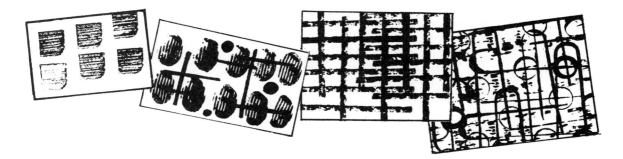

With sticks

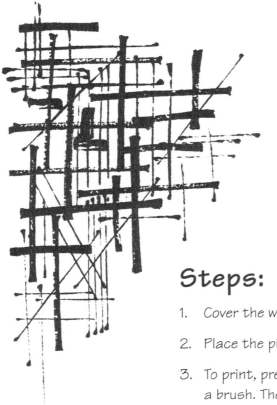

Technique: Stamping

Materials:

- small sticks of various sizes, shapes, and thickness
- paint or ink for printing
- paint/ink pad: one for each color
- paper to print on, any size
- newsprint for sample prints
- printing pad
- newspapers for working surface

Steps:

1. Cover the working surface with newspaper.

2. Place the piece of newsprint on the printing pad for sample prints.

3. To print, press the side or end of the stick on the paint pad or paint with a brush. Then press firmly and evenly on the paper. The printing pad should be thick so the grain of the wood will print.

4. Experiment with the amount of paint and pressure applied to the stick when printing; try groupings of various stick-printed shapes to create animals, flowers, birds, fish, and so forth.

Variations: Combine stick prints with other printing media such as gadgets.

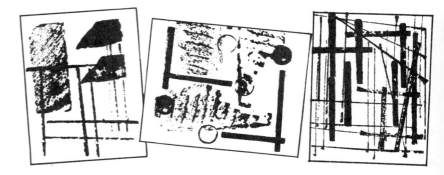

Monoprints

Materials:

- hard surface such as sink counter, tray, plate of thick glass, heavy cardboard, oilcloth, desk top, or smooth wood
- thick tempera paint, mixed with liquid starch, water-soluble printer's ink, or fingerpaint
- brayer
- tools: fingers, hands, sticks, notched cardboard, pencils, combs, erasers, paper clips, clothespins, plastic forks, etc.
- sponge
- soft cloth

Steps:

1. Roll or brush the paint or ink onto a hard surface. As the paint and ink are water-soluble, it can be put on a desk top or counter top and later wiped away with sponges.

2. Using fingers, hands, or tools, make a design in the paint or ink. Several different designs can be tried before making the print.

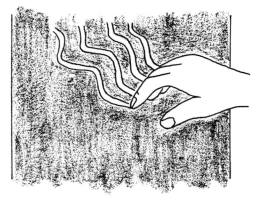

295

3. The print: Lay a piece of paper over the surface of the wet paint or ink. Gently smooth the top surface of the paper carefully with fingers and palms or a soft cloth. Peel the top paper off immediately, gently and carefully.

Variations:

— Make a print, using one color; let dry thoroughly. Use another color, make a different design, and print on top of the first.

— Using black paint or ink, make monoprints on interesting papers such as wallpaper, the classified section of the newspaper, gift wrapping paper, or on top of a tissue collage, fingerpaint, crayon, or chalk design.

— Using blue or green paint or ink and paper, create underwater seascapes.

— Using black or orange paint or ink, black or white paper, create spooky Halloween pictures.

several colors

still lifes

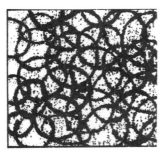

overall designs

plaids, patterns

impressionistic

Technique: Monoprint

With Fingerpaint

Materials:

- fingerpaint paper
- white drawing paper, construction paper, or butcher's paper
- fingerpaint or tempera paint mixed very thick with liquid starch
- newspaper for working surface
- soft cloth

Steps:

1. Cover the working surface with newspaper.

2. Place one sheet of the paper in the middle of the working surface. Put two or three tablespoons of paint in the middle of the paper. With fingers and the palm of the hand, spread the paint over the entire surface of the white paper.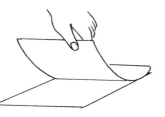

3. Using fingers, palm of hand, notched cardboard, or anything else, create a design or pattern in the fingerpaint.

4. When the design is complete, place the second sheet of white paper on top of the fingerpaint. Gently smooth the paper with a soft cloth or the palm of the hand. Then carefully peel off the top sheet.

Variations:

— Make a crayon design on the white paper before doing a fingerpaint design and monoprint.

— Cover the paper with tissue paper collage, adhering with liquid starch. When dry, do a fingerpaint design on top and make a monoprint.

With string

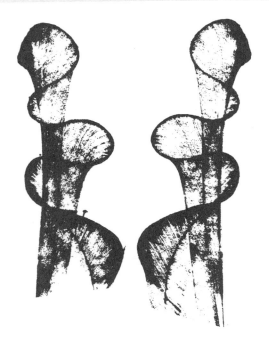

Technique: Monoprint

Materials:

- a variety of 15–18" length string
- tempera paint in flat pans mixed very thin in consistency
- white drawing paper, any size (several pieces of 6" x 12" good for experimentation)
- newspapers for working surface
- a book or other flat heavy object

Steps:

1. Fold the 6" x 12" pieces of white paper in half, vertically or horizontally.

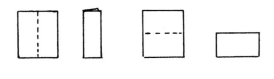

2. Put string, except for a few inches of one end, into the paint. Take it out, pulling the string through the thumb and forefinger to remove the excess paint.

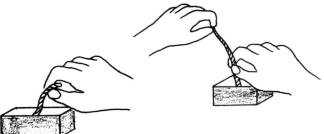

3. Lay the string in a wavy pattern on one half of the white paper. Let the unpainted tail stick out of one end. Fold the other half of the paper on top of the string. Hold secure with a book or other heavy object. Carefully pull out the string with a swift continuous pull.

Variations:

— Use more than one color. Let the first color dry before adding another.

— Make more than one print on the paper. Lay the string in another position on half of the paper and repeat the process.

— Combine with other media: on top of tissue collages, fingerpaintings, watercolor washes.

With Ferns and Leaves

Technique: Monoprint

Materials:

- leaves and ferns
- tempera paint mixture or printer's ink
- paint/ink pad
- soft-bristle brush
- printing pad
- 9" x 12" pieces of newspaper
- newsprint for sample prints
- paper to print on, any size
- newspaper for the working surface

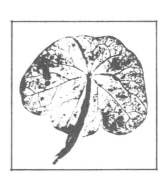

Steps:

1. Place a leaf or fern frond, vein side up, on a 9" x 12" piece of newspaper. Apply paint or ink with a paintbrush, keeping the brush fairly dry to prevent blobbing.

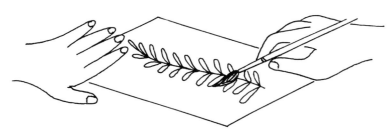

2. Move the painted leaf or frond to a clean piece of 9" x 12" newspaper placed on the printing pad. Position the printing paper on top, checking to make sure the leaf shape will be in the center of the paper. Rub gently with fingers and palms of the hand.

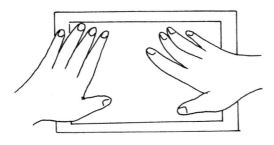

3. Pull the print paper away carefully and gently so the print does not smear.

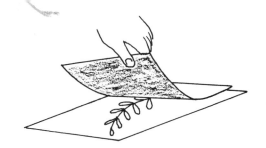

4. Some samples of various leaves and fern fronds:

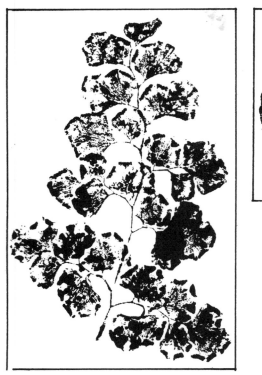

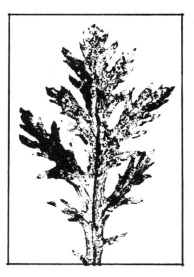

300

Hints:

— Some plants are easier to handle if they are pressed in a book between layers of paper towel to flatten before printing.

— A plastic bag is useful to preserve fresh specimens so they may be stored in the refrigerator until ready to use.

— Blossoms and ferns should be printed right away since the petals sodden, fern fronds curl up, and soft delicate leaves stick right to the paper.

Variations:

— Try leaf and fern prints on thin, porous paper such as rice paper, onionskin, or tissue paper. Use as cards, note paper, or folders.

— Make a collection of prints in black and white. Mount them on black construction paper folded like a fan; this will stand freely to display the prints.

— Use prints to make note paper, book plates, or bookmarks.

Making Stencils

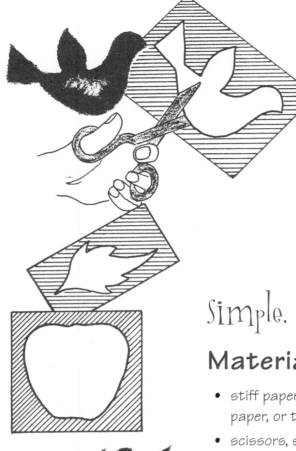

The only limiting factors in stenciling activities are one's own resourcefulness and creativity. Nature will suggest many ideas for stencils such as leaves, flowers, and trees, as well as numbers, initials, abstract shapes, and other symbols.

There are three basic steps to stenciling:

1. Design the stencil.
2. Choose the surface on which to transfer it.
3. Select the method of transfer.

Simple, Symmetrical Stencils

Materials:

- stiff paper: tagboard, gray bogus, heavy drawing or construction paper, or thin cardboard
- scissors, small with sharp points
- pencil
- ruler

Steps:

1. Fold the piece of stencil paper in half. Mark a 1″ border on the three open edges.

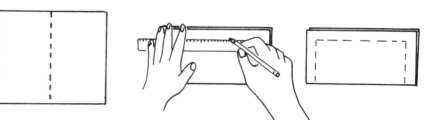

2. Draw half of any simple symmetrical shape or symbol, the center on the fold. Keep within the 1″ border. This will add strength to the stencil.

3. Cut out the shape, beginning and ending on the fold. The cut-out shape is the *positive stencil* and the paper with the cut-out shape is the *negative stencil*.

negative stencil

positive stencil

Asymmetrical Stencils

Materials:

- stiff paper: tagboard, gray bogus, heavy drawing or construction paper, thin cardboard
- scissors, small with sharp points
- pencil
- ruler

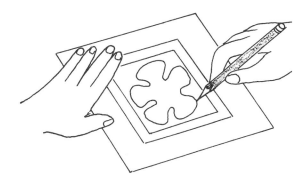

Steps:

1. Draw a 1″ border on all four edges of the stencil paper.

2. Draw one or more simple shapes in the middle of the paper, keeping within the 1″ border.

3. Poke the point of the scissors through the center of the shape. Cut to the edge of the shape and then proceed to cut out the shape. Illustrated below are just a few of the many possibilities.

Complex, Detailed Stencils

As the fascination with stenciling develops, so will the desire to create more intricate stencils. Scissors will not always produce the fine details desired. A cutting tool such as a single-edged razor or a matte knife will cut small tiny details.

Materials:

- stencil paper
- ruler and pencil
- cutting tool: single-edged razor, matte, or X-acto knife
- cutting board: a piece of heavy cardboard, chipboard, or wood such as plywood or Masonite™

Steps:

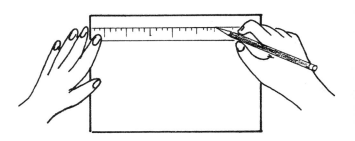

1. Mark a 1″ border on all four edges of the stencil paper.

2. Draw shapes, symbols, or a single motif inside the 1″ border.

3. Place the stencil paper on the cutting board and cut out the shapes with the cutting tool.

Variations: To print two or more colors, sometimes several stencils will be needed. Draw design on newsprint. Decide on colors and cut a separate stencil for each color to be used, cutting out only the parts of the design to be that color.

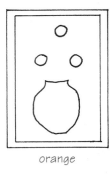

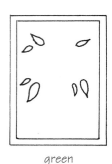

orange   yellow   green

When printing, do one color at a time, dry, and then do the next color.

Technique: Stencil

Materials:

- stencils
- colored chalk
- piece of cotton, facial tissue, or cheesecloth
- paper to print on
- newsprint for sample prints
- newspaper for working surface

With chalk

Steps:

1. Prepare the stencil: See pages 302–303.

2. Place the negative or positive stencil on the paper. Fasten or hold it firmly with one hand. Make short brisk strokes with the chalk, starting on the stencil, to the surface of the paper.

3. To achieve a softer, feathered look: Make a chalk line around the edge of the stencil. Using cotton or facial tissue, rub the chalk from the stencil onto the paper. Always rub from the stencil onto the surface of the paper to prevent the chalk from going under the surface of the stencil.

4. Try combining the positive and negative stencils, using two or more stencils together:

With crayon

Materials:

- stencils
- wax crayons
- newsprint for sample prints
- paper to print on
- eraser
- facial tissue or piece of soft fabric
- newspaper for working surface

Steps:

1. Prepare the stencil: See pages 302–303.

2. There are two basic techniques for crayon stenciling.

end of the crayon

Negative stencil: Use the crayon to make short brisk strokes over the edge of the stencil toward the center of the cut-out shape onto the paper.

Positive stencil: Use the crayon to make short brisk strokes over the edge of the stencil shape onto the paper.

With an eraser

To create a softer, feathered look, draw heavily with the crayon onto the stencil paper around the edge of the shape. With the eraser, piece of facial tissue, or soft cloth, rub the crayon from the stencil paper onto the surface of the printing paper.

Variations:

Overlap shapes, or make rows, patterns, or borders. Blend two or more colors, combine with other printing techniques and other media such as tissue paper.

Stencil Brush

Technique: Stencil

Materials:

- paint or ink for printing
- stencils
- paper to print on
- newsprint for sample prints
- stencil brush (short, stiff bristles)
- paper towels
- newspaper for working surface

Steps:

1. Prepare the stencil: See pages 302–303.

2. Very little paint or ink is used on the stencil brush, so small amounts of different colors can be put in egg carton cups, a muffin tin, or on many small pads placed on one large tray.

3. Place the stencil in position on the paper and hold firmly in place with one hand.

4. Dip the stencil brush lightly in the paint or ink and wipe the excess paint off the brush onto some scrap paper or paper towels. Apply the paint with strokes that start on the stencil and run off onto the paper.

5. Try using positive and negative stencils separately or together in various combinations; overlap stencils, using different colors.

Technique: Stencil

Materials:

- stencils
- tempera, showcard, or poster paint
- small sponges
- clothespins
- small flat containers, one for each color of paint, or an egg carton or muffin tin
- newsprint for sample prints
- paper to print on
- newspaper for working surface

With a Sponge

Steps:

1. Prepare the stencil: See pages 302–304.

2. Cover the working surface with newspaper.

3. Make the small pieces of sponge wet and clip each one with a clothespin. Use one for each color of paint to be used.

4. Prepare the printing paint. Pour a small amount of paint in each flat container. Using a muffin tin or an egg carton with a different color in each section will avoid having to cope with many individual containers.

5. Place the stencil on the paper and fasten or hold firmly in place with one hand.

6. To print: Put a small amount of paint on the sponge. When dipping, wipe the sponge on the edge of the paint container to remove any excess paint. Dab the paint on with the sponge. DO NOT SCRUB but DAB the paint so that it will not work underneath the stencil.

7. Try: Repeat patterns, borders, combining the positive and negative stencils.

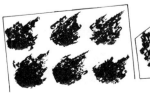

Spatter

Materials:

- stencils
- liquid tempera, showcard, or poster paints
- newsprint for sample prints
- paper to print on
- piece of wire screen
- stiff-bristle brush or old toothbrush
- newspaper for working surface
- straight pins or masking tape
- cardboard box (optional)

Steps:

1. Prepare the stencil: See pages 302–304.

2. Cover a large working surface with newspaper. Make a pad of several thicknesses of newspaper.

3. Since very little paint is used on the brush, place small amounts of paint of different colors on felt or fabric pads on a large tray or put in an egg carton or muffin tin.

4. Position the stencil on the printing paper and place on the pad of newspaper. Secure in place with straight pins or masking tape.

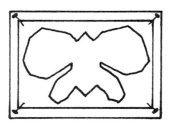

5. Apply paint to the brush or toothbrush. Hold the wire screen over the stencil and rub the brush briskly over the wire to spatter. Spattering may also be accomplished by flicking the brush with the finger or a small stick.

Suggestion:

To eliminate the possibility of paint spattering where it is undesired, cut down the sides of a cardboard box. Place the printing paper and stencil on the bottom of the box. Then spatter paint, holding the wire and brush over the top of the box.

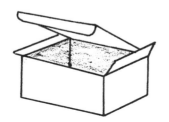 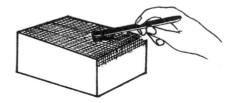

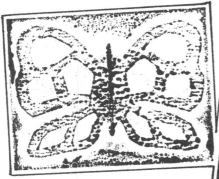

Relief Prints

Since relief prints are made by printing from a raised surface, the shapes, symbols, or motifs to be printed must be placed on a "block."

Kinds of Blocks

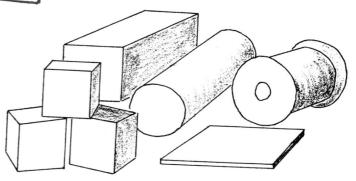

— Almost anything can be used as a block for printing. Spools, small pieces of wood or doweling, small boxes, tin cans, cardboard cylinders, all lend themselves to becoming blocks.

— Larger motifs can be put on pieces of cardboard cut from cardboard boxes, chipboard, pieces of plywood, or Masonite™.

— Easily disposable blocks can be made from lightweight cardboard or chipboard. Needed are strips, 2" x 6" or 8", and small squares or rectangles of chipboard or cardboard. Fold and glue or staple as illustrated. The object to be printed is glued to the surface of the small rectangle or square.

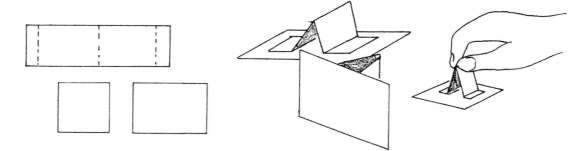

Preparing the Block

— Small objects can be glued directly to the flat surface of the block. Allow glue to dry thoroughly.

— If a large design or motif is sketched first and is to be transferred to a large "block," use a graphite carbon; that is, rub pencil lead over the back of the drawing and trace onto the cardboard or wood that is to be the "block." The sketch can also be used as a pattern to cut pieces of cardboard, fabric, or other material to be used.

Felt/Fabric

Technique: Relief prints

Materials:

- scraps of felt
- blocks
- scissors
- white glue
- paint/ink pad
- paint or water-soluble ink for printing
- printing pad
- newsprint for sample prints
- paper to print on
- newspaper for working surface

Steps:

1. Part of the fun of making felt blocks is that almost anything can be used for the "block" itself. Spools, small pieces of wood or doweling, small boxes, or disposable "blocks" made from cardboard are just a few. They will, in fact, often suggest ideas for the actual felt stamps. See page 312.

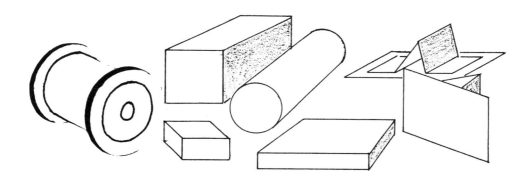

2. Cut shapes, symbols, or a single motif from the scraps of felt. Glue to the surface of the block and let dry thoroughly.

3. Prepare the paint/ink pad and cover the working surface with newspaper.

313

4. To print: Press the block on the paint/ink pad. Check to make sure all of the felt shape has been saturated with paint or ink. Then press firmly and carefully on the printing paper. Lift the block carefully so as not to smudge the print.

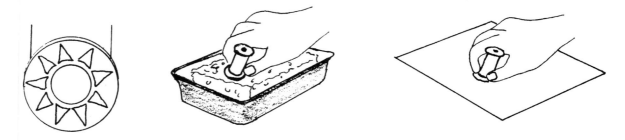

5. Experiment with horizontal and vertical rows, borders, patterns, combining two or more shapes or symbols. To aid in printing rows, make lines on the printing paper with a ruler and chalk before beginning to print.

Technique: Relief prints

Materials:

- cylinder containers: tin cans, salt or oatmeal containers, etc.
- strings and yarns, varying in thickness
- scissors
- white glue
- paint for printing
- paint pads: one for each color to be used, or a paintbrush
- paper to print on: butcher's or shelf paper, long strips
- newsprint for sample prints
- newspaper for the working surface

Steps:

1. If using tin cans, cut out the top and bottom of the can with a can opener, leaving a cylinder. For safety, bind the edges of the can with masking tape so there will be no sharp edges. If using a cardboard cylinder such as an oatmeal container, you can punch a hole in the middle of the top and bottom; insert a piece of wooden dowel to facilitate the rolling of prints.

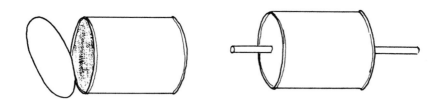

2. Glue string or yarn in any desired pattern around the outside of the cylinder. Let dry thoroughly.

3. To print: Either press the cylinder on the paint/ink pad or paint the string with a brush, thoroughly saturating the string with paint. Place hands inside the can at either end and roll across the paper.

4. Experiment with over-prints in different directions. If the painting is done carefully, several colors may be put on the roller at one time.

5. Combine with other printing techniques such as potato prints, roller prints over watercolor washes, fingerpaintings, or chalk or crayon designs.

6. Combine felt or fabric cut-outs, rickrack, fabric trims with string and yarn to create interesting rolled prints.

Technique: Relief prints

Materials:

- scraps of materials whose surface will yield textures and patterns when printed: burlap, wire mesh, sandpaper, vinyl tiles, corrugated paper, wood, fabric, etc.
- white glue
- scissors
- large piece of cardboard for plate, at least 9" x 12"
- brayer
- paint or ink for printing
- inking block
- paper for printing
- newsprint for sample prints and layout of design
- newspaper for working surface

Steps:

1. Arrange materials on a piece of newsprint that is the same size as the cardboard plate in order to experiment with composition. Some can be cut or torn to create interesting shapes. Remember that pieces should all be about the same thickness or height above the surface plate.

2. Transfer and glue all the pieces into position on the cardboard plate and let dry. Do make sure all pieces are securely attached.

3. Prepare the inking block and brayer with paint or ink.

4. To print: Roll the inked brayer over the surface of the collage print, using only one color. Be sure to cover the entire plate, including the corners. Do not use too much paint as it will blur the edges of the textured areas.

5. Move the printing plate to a clean piece of newspaper. Place the printing paper on top of the inked plate. Use a clean brayer to roll over the paper or press firmly and carefully with the palm of the hand.

6. Lift the printing paper carefully so the print will not be smudged.

Cardboard: Repeat Patterns

Technique: Relief prints

Materials:

- scraps of lightweight cardboard, chipboard, tagboard, gray bogus, or any other fairly thick paper
- blocks
- white glue
- scissors
- paint or ink for printing
- brayer or paintbrush
- inking block or paint/ink pad
- newsprint for sample prints
- paper to print on
- newspaper for working surface

Steps:

1. Fold strips of cardboard 6" to 8" long as illustrated, and glue to small squares or rectangles of cardboard to make printing blocks. Small blocks of wood or spools can also be used for blocks. See page 312.

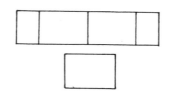 

2. Cut simple shapes or symbols from the cardboard scraps. Glue to the small squares or rectangles of thick cardboard to be used as printing blocks.

3. The paint or ink can be applied with a brush or the block can be pressed on a paint/ink pad.

4. To print: Place printing paper on printing pad. Press inked block on the printing paper. Lift carefully so the print will not be smudged.

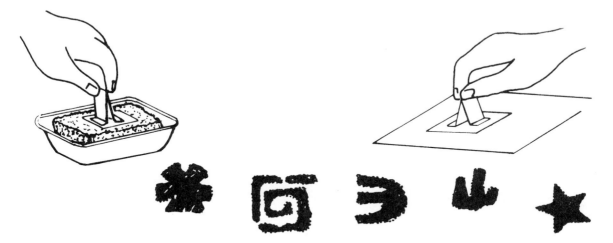

Cardboard: Picture Plate

Technique: Relief prints

Materials:

- scraps of lightweight cardboard, chipboard, tagboard, or any other fairly thick paper
- scissors
- white glue
- paint or ink for printing
- brayer
- inking block
- newsprint for sample prints and sketches
- paper to print on
- newspaper for working surface

Steps:

1. Decide on the subject matter: figures of birds, animals, people, designs, landscapes, underwater-scapes, or city-scapes. Sketches can be made on a piece of newsprint the same size as the plate and then used as patterns when cutting the cardboard.

2. Cut the larger shapes first. Glue down well on a piece of cardboard or chipboard the size desired.

3. Add details cut from thinner paper such as tagboard or gray bogus. Several layers can be built up. The effects of texture can be created by overlapping, varying thickness, and cutting. The added details will make the print more interesting.

4. All parts of the cardboard "block" should be carefully glued and set aside to dry completely.

5. Prepare the inking block. Squeeze about 1" of the water-soluble ink or about two tablespoons of paint mixture on the inking block. Run the brayer back and forth until it is evenly coated and the paint or ink "crackles."

320

6. Roll the inked brayer over the cardboard block. Ink all parts of it. Roll the brayer in different directions to make sure that the entire block is inked. A halo will be left around all parts of the design where the ink cannot reach the cardboard.

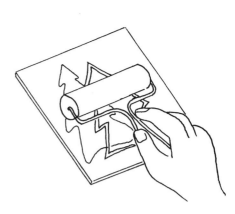

7. Place the cardboard block on a clean piece of newspaper. Put the printing paper, larger than the plate, on top of the inked plate. Roll a clean brayer over the paper or rub firmly and carefully with the palm of the hand. Check the results by lifting the corners of the printing paper to see if all areas have printed. If not, continue to rub.

Variations:

— Glue string or textured materials on the block in combination with cardboard shapes.

— Try printing with more than one color.

— Make a crayon rubbing from a cardboard block.

— Use this technique to make cards, folders, invitations, stationery, and wrapping paper for special occasions.

— Make the actual plate long and thin, a circle, hexagon, or any shape other than a square or rectangle.

string

Technique: Relief prints

Materials:

- string, varying in thickness
- blocks
- white glue
- scissors
- brayer
- paint or ink for printing
- inking plate
- printing pad
- newsprint for sample prints and sketches
- paper to print on
- newspaper for working surface

Steps:

1. Draw sketches of simple shapes, symbols, or a motif on newsprint. Select one and transfer to the printing plate. Use a *graphite carbon*, that is, rub pencil lead over the back of the drawing and trace on the *block*. See page 312 on blocks. Remember, the design will reverse when printing.

2. Squeeze glue on the lines of the shape and apply the string, pressing into position. Let dry thoroughly.

  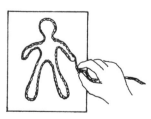

3. Put one or two tablespoons of paint or about 1″ of water-soluble ink on the inking plate, rolling out with the brayer until it "crackles." Roll the inked brayer over the printing plate, saturating the string, and be sure to cover the entire plate including the string. In some cases it may be easier to apply the paint or ink to the printing plate with a soft-bristle brush.

4. Move the inked plate onto a clean piece of newspaper. To print, the paper can be placed on top of the printing plate and rubbed with the palm of the hand or rolled over the paper with a clean brayer. If the printing block is small, the inked surface can be pressed on the paper using a thick printing pad. Lift the paper or printing block carefully so the print will not smudge.

5. Experiment with various printed and textured backgrounds. Bits of torn tissue paper and previously printed papers such as wallpaper or newspaper can add to the excitement of the final print.

6. Try combining prints of two or more blocks, borders, words, repeat patterns; use with crayon, watercolor, or tissue techniques.

Art Gum Eraser Incised Prints

Materials:

- 1 ½" x 1 ½" art gum erasers
- carving tools
- paint or ink for printing
- paint/ink pad
- printing pad
- newspaper for working surface
- newsprint for sample prints
- paper to print on

Steps:

1. The art gum eraser usually measures about 1 ½" x 1 ½". It can be used to make one "block" or be cut in halves and/or quarters to make several. The smaller pieces are useful for printing borders on stationery or book plates, and also provide more opportunities for different designs.

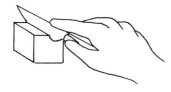

2. Using the carving tools, incise simple shapes or symbols on the flat surface of the eraser. This should be demonstrated by the teacher first; safety must be stressed for this procedure. The following illustrations provide a few examples; shaded areas represent those carved away.

3. To print: Press the incised surface of the eraser on the paint/ink pad and then on the newsprint placed on the printing pad. Make several sample prints, experimenting with possible designs for borders, patterns.

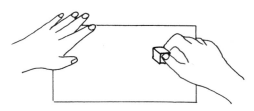

4. If desired, chalk lines can be made on the printing paper before beginning to print to aid in keeping lines straight and to create definite patterns.

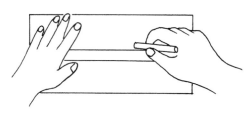

Technique: Incised prints

Materials:

- Plasticine™ clay
- paint/ink for printing
- paint/ink pad
- printing pad
- carving tools
- newsprint for sample prints
- paper to print on
- newspaper for working surface

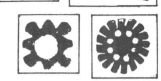

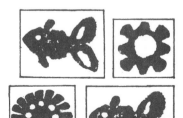

Steps:

1. Make the Plasticine™ into a shape: square, rounded, or any other. Do not handle the clay any more than necessary since the Plasticine™ will then become too soft. Press the "block" down firmly on newspaper-covered working surface to make a flat surface.

2. Using the carving tools, incise simple shapes or symbols on the flat surface of the Plasticine™. This should be demonstrated by the teacher first; safety must be stressed for this procedure. The following illustrations provide a few examples; shaded areas represent those carved away.

3. Prepare the paint/ink pads. Place paper on the printing pad.

Plasticine™ Prints

4. To print: Press the incised surface of the Plasticine™ on the paint/ink pad and then on the paper. Using the newsprint, make trial prints to discover how much paint or ink should be used and the right amount of pressure needed.

5. Be sure to use a good thick printing pad. Clogged or disappearing lines may be incised again at any time.

6. The Plasticine™ may be washed clean with water and used again.

Soap Prints

Technique: Incised prints

Materials:

- bar of Ivory soap
- paring or kitchen knife
- carving tools
- paint or ink for printing
- inking block
- brayer
- printing pad
- newsprint for sample prints
- paper to print on
- newspaper

Steps:

1. The bar of soap can be cut in halves or quarters to make smaller blocks or used whole as one large block. Use a kitchen or paring knife to cut and also to make a flat surface on which to carve.

2. The design or motif can be drawn directly on the flat surface or sketched on paper and transferred by means of a graphite "carbon."

3. Using the carving tools, use one of two methods:

   — Carve away the background of the design to a depth of about $^3/_{16}$" so that the subject matter remains.

   — Carve away the subject matter so that only the background remains.

The portions that are carved away will not print. The parts that remain raised will print. Take care when carving, as the soap is very soft and will chip easily. Demonstrate carving first, stressing safety all the while.

4. Prepare the inking block by rolling the brayer back and forth in the ink or paint until it "crackles." Then roll the inked brayer over the surface of the soap. Check to make sure the surface is evenly coated with paint or ink.

5. Place paper to be printed on the printing pad. Press inked surface of soap on the printing paper. Lift carefully so the print is not smudged. Continue in the same manner.

Variation: Use paraffin in blocks instead of soap.

Technique: Incised prints

Materials:

- pieces of soft wood scrap, approximately 2″ x 2″ or any available size
- hammer and nails and saws or wood files
- paint or ink for printing
- inking block
- printing pad
- newspaper for sample prints
- paper to print on
- newspaper for working surface

Steps:

1. Explore use of dots, lines, and shapes that can be made with:
   - Hammer and nails: Pound nail part way into wood. Remove nail. Make a pattern with nail holes.
   - Wood files: File lines in different directions to make a design.
   - Saw: Remove wood from edge of shape.
   - A combination of two or more of the above.
2. Make desired design on the wood block.
3. Prepare the brayer by rolling it on the inking block, using either paint or ink. Then roll the inked brayer over the incised surface of the wood block. Make sure there is an even coat and that the entire surface is inked.

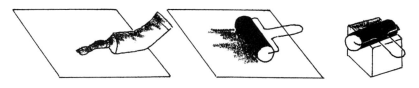

4. Print by putting block down on paper (placed on a thick printing pad) and pressing down with hand, or print by putting block down face-up and then rubbing with the palm of the hand on the printing paper.

5. Try an arrangement of four prints in a square, printed edge to edge; borders, patterns involving two or more blocks; printing on paper bags; printing on fabric with textile paint.

About Mobiles

Delight in movement in our daily lives is as great as our pleasure in color or sound. The soaring, swooping flight of a bird, a leaf falling, a flag fluttering, kites flying, sails in the wind—all are movements that provide visual excitement or peace, depending on our moods. A mobile is created for the sake of movement and it is the manner in which it moves that captures our attention and intrigues us.

As an art form, mobiles are related to sculpture, painting, drawing, and design. Because they are three-dimensional, art critics often refer to them as mobile sculptures. First created in the 1930s, mobiles are fascinating to children and adults alike.

A mobile has width, height, and depth, and its parts move. Gentle air currents keep the separate parts moving in graceful motion, changing its appearance as it moves. None of the parts rest on or touch others as it moves. It has been said that a mobile should not merely hang in the air and move like a weathervane—its parts passive, static objects which are made to move in a limited way by the force of the wind—but should give the feeling of floating or dancing gently through space. This statement might be applied to the single-string or bar mobile, and yet these mobiles do have their own form of moving and turning in the breeze. They delight the youngest child and their construction makes excellent experiences with mobiles.

In this section we will explore the endless possibilities of mobiles, beginning with simple string mobiles and progressing to bar, string, and ring mobiles as well as the more complex, multiple-arm mobiles that involve balance as well as motion. Included are a variety of media combined with various techniques in creating mobiles. Each in its own way will enchant and be visually pleasing to watch as it moves in a breeze.

Techniques With Mobiles

A mobile has width, height, depth, and its parts move. Gentle air currents keep the separate parts moving in graceful motion, changing its appearance as it moves. None of the parts rest on or touch others as it moves. Begin with a simple single-string mobile and progress to bar, ring, and spring mobiles as well as the more complex, multiple-arm mobiles that involve balance as well as motion. The following techniques will be used in constructing mobiles in the activities in this section.

single-string mobile

two-string bar mobile

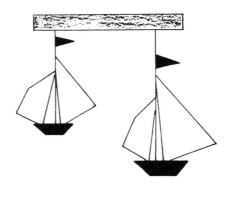

ring mobile

multiple-string bar mobile

shaped bar mobile

spring mobile

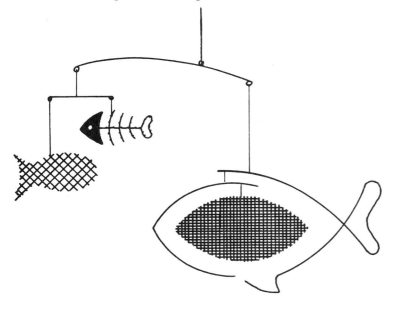

complex, multiple-arm mobile

As balance is the essential element to be considered, each portion must be balanced. One works with a combination of arms and pendants or objects to develop the rhythm of balance and motion.

Arms

The linear elements of a mobile to which the pendants or objects can be hung.

These can be made from coat hangers, reeds, plastic rods or tubes, wooden dowels, twigs, wire, branches, plastic straws, or any lightweight, rigid material.

To Balance

The two smallest elements are balanced one against the other and each is hung by a nylon thread. When it balances, it is attached to an arm that has a counterweight so that a perfect balance is attained. The following are a few examples:

— Two objects balanced at either end of a wire. The string toward the center, which holds the mobile, is adjusted to the right or left until the two units are in straight balance.

— Two Christmas tree balls and a star are balanced horizontally as in the first. The two small shapes are balanced asymmetrically by the large star.

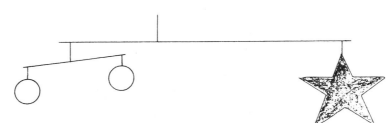

— Two shapes balanced asymmetrically. The angle of the wire is established by moving the string, which suspends it, to the left or right.

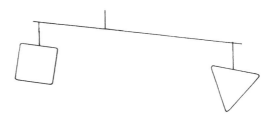

It is possible to make many combinations of "arms." The following are a few examples:

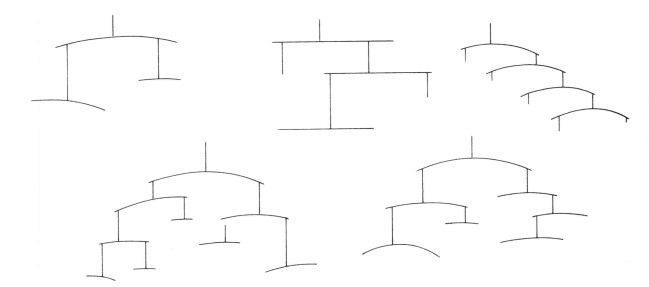

Stabiles

These are a combination of moving and stationary parts, with planned movements, dependent on balance. Generally it has a fixed base with the mobile attached.

Base

This can be made from blocks of wood, driftwood, Styrofoam, coiled wire, lumps of clay, or coat hangers anchored in a tin can with plaster of Paris. The following are a few examples:

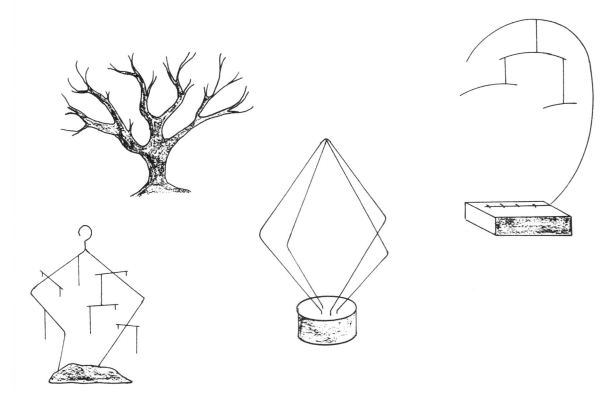

Materials

The most essential ingredients of a mobile are an individual's own ingenuity, imagination, and skill, but also needed are the following materials and tools for the activities in this section:

For Construction of Mobiles

- **arms:** the linear elements of a mobile to which the pendants or objects are hung. These can be made from:

coat hangers	1/8–1/4" wooden dowels
reeds	twigs, branches
plastic rods or tubes	plastic or paper straws
cocktail picks	kabob bamboo sticks

- **wire:** #16, #18, and #19 gauge galvanized wire is about the cheapest, most easily obtainable wire, and it is easy to handle. Brass, copper, and aluminum wires are more expensive and difficult to use.

- **thread:** Nylon thread or thin nylon fishing line are lightweight, thin, transparent, and attractive as they do not distract from the mobile itself. Fishing line is cheapest when purchased on a large spool. For single-string and bar mobiles, thin yarn or string or heavy-duty sewing thread work well and are easily handled by younger students.

- **pliers:** long-nosed, 3–4 inches, with a wire cutter at the side.

Paper

construction paper	butcher's paper	wallpaper	glossy and matte finish paper
drawing paper	illustration board	paper toweling	railroad board
tissue paper	gift wrap	tagboard	chipboard
newspaper	metallic paper	facial tissue	old greeting cards
pages from magazines	wax paper	textured papers	
	aluminum foil		

Collectibles

buttons	wire coat hangers	old keys	paper plates
clothespins	dried weeds and flowers	toothpicks	seashells
egg cartons	beads	small paper boxes	spools
scraps of felt	driftwood	ice cream sticks	pipe cleaners
corks	feathers	plastic lists	tin cans
braids, tapes	scraps of fabric	blown eggs	sponges
drinking straws		gourds	glitter, sequins

Additional Materials

#7 and #12 soft-bristle
   brushes
crayons
pencils
tempera paint
small containers for water
   (milk cartons are best)

liquid starch
white glue
paper towels
brads
yarn, roving, string
needles (embroidery)

paste
scissors
small sponges
paper clips
stapler
paper punch

Suggestions

- Keep boxes of construction paper scraps, one for large pieces and one for small pieces, as well as a box for "collected" or found papers such as wallpaper, gift wrap, etc.
- Keep another box for "collectibles" so they will always be handy when you need them for special projects.
- Remember that the small milk cartons are ideal as containers for water or paint as they are free, easily disposed of, and do not tip easily while work is in progress. Many of the new kinds do not need to have tops cut off; the tops simply pull off.

Displaying Mobiles

A mobile should be hung wherever there is enough room to permit it to move freely and not look closed in. A mobile is best hung at eye level or a little higher to be seen and fully appreciated.

- **an overhead wire:** It is possible to suspend a wire the length of a room, attaching it to either wall in a "discreet" manner which will not damage anything. Small eye hooks screwed in the side of molding around windows, edge of cabinets or doors, or edge of hinges will cause no visible damage and are strong enough to hold a wire stretched the length of a room. Try taking one screw out of a hinge on a high cabinet and replacing it with an eye screw.

an eye screw

- **in a corner:** Place wires across a corner, anchored with t-pins or tacks (hidden behind the molding, not through the wood), or use small hooks or eye screws.

- **long hooks:** Make from wire or coat hangers to hang mobiles throughout a room from objects or beams overhead.

- **several:** To hang several mobiles, such as single string or bar mobiles, try one of the ideas illustrated below:

Suspend the mobile from a fishing swivel and it will turn more freely.

Any of these methods can be used while working on mobiles. The more complex mobiles are much easier to construct and balance if they can be hung while working on them. Some people prefer to work from the bottom up and others prefer to start at the top. This is an individual preference . . . experimentation will tell which works best for you.

Geometric Shapes

Materials:

- (2) 3" squares of 4 colors of construction paper
- scissors
- glue or paste
- 3' piece of string of yarn

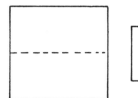

Steps:

Two of each shape cut will be needed, so remember to fold and cut two squares of construction paper at the same time.

1. CIRCLE: Fold two squares of paper in half, together. Hold in the middle of the fold, open edges up. Trim off the top, open corners.

Begin at the middle of the side, cut to the middle of the top.

2. CIRCLE RINGS: While still holding the folded circle, cut half a circle within the first. Begin at the folded edge, leaving ½" to ¾" margin, and cut to the folded edge. For more rings, repeat the process.

3. TRIANGLE: Fold two squares of paper in half, together. Hold the folded edge. Cut from one corner to the opposite corner.

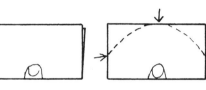
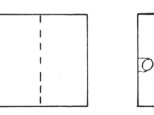

4. TRIANGLE RINGS: Turn the triangle shape so the open edges are up. Leaving a ½" to ¾" margin, cut from the fold up to the corner, turn, and cut to the folded edge. For more rings, repeat the process.

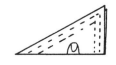

338

5. DIAMOND: Fold two squares of paper in half, together. Hold the folded edge, with the open edges up. Begin at one folded corner. Cut to the middle of the top, turn, and cut down to the other folded corner.

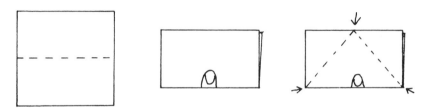

6. DIAMOND RINGS: While still holding the diamond shape, cut a half diamond within the first. Leave a ½″ to ¾″ margin. Begin at the folded edge, cut to the top, turn, and cut down to the folded edge. For more rings, repeat the process.

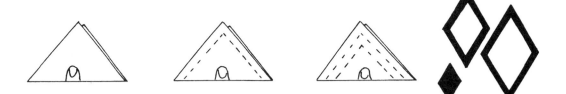

7. SQUARE RINGS: Fold two squares of paper in half, together. Hold the folded edge, with the open edges up. Begin at the folded edge, leaving a ½″ to ¾″ margin. Cut half a square within the first. Repeat the process for more rings.

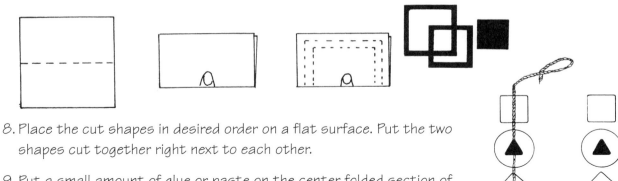

8. Place the cut shapes in desired order on a flat surface. Put the two shapes cut together right next to each other.

9. Put a small amount of glue or paste on the center folded section of each piece. Beginning at the bottom, lay the string on top of the glue, leaving the excess string at the top for hanging.

10. Glue the entire surface of the second group of shapes and place on top of the first, covering the string at the same time. Make sure all the edges are glued down.

Variations:

— Try using printed papers such as wallpaper or gift wrap, as well as metallic papers combined with construction paper.

— Try using larger pieces of paper, such as 9″ x 12″; cut just one geometric shape with many rings. Suspend as many of the rings as possible with the largest shape cut.

string of Hearts

Technique: Single-string

Materials:

- squares and rectangles of construction paper, an equal number of each color: red, white, pink
  - 3" x 3"
  - 4" x 4"
  - 3" x 4"
  - 4" x 6"
- scissors and pencil
- 3–4' length of string or yarn
- glue or paste

Steps:

1. Fold *two pieces of construction paper of equal size in half together.* Pencil half a heart on the paper, center on the fold. Make it as large as possible. Trim away the excess paper.

2. Leaving a ½" to ¾" margin, cut a second "half a heart" within the first to make a heart ring. For more rings, repeat the process.

3. Repeat the process with other squares and rectangles of construction paper. Remember to fold and cut two pieces of paper at a time.

4. Place the hearts in a straight line, on a flat surface, putting the two shapes cut together next to each other. Put some smaller shapes within the larger hearts.

4.

5. Put some glue or paste in the center of each heart. Place the string on top of the glue, beginning with the heart at the bottom, leaving the excess string at the top for hanging.

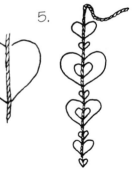
5.

6. Put paste or glue over the entire surface of the second set of hearts and place on top of the first set, covering the string at the same time.

7. Tie a loop at the top with the excess string.

Technique: Single-string

Materials:

- (2) 9″ x 9″ pieces of lightweight paper: fadeless paper, or a combination of a printed paper and construction paper, one of each
- white glue
- scissors and pencil
- 5 or 6 paper clips
- object(s) to hang
- nylon thread and a piece of string

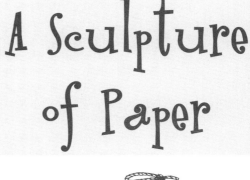

Steps:

1. Spread the glue over the entire surface of one piece of paper. Place the second sheet of paper on top and rub gently, making sure all the edges are secure. The two sheets become one heavy sheet of paper.

2. Make many cuts in the paper: curved lines, straight lines, angular cuts, being careful not to make any cut completely through the paper (thus cutting it into pieces). The paper will have many long cuts but still *be in one piece*. (These lines may be planned and drawn in with a pencil before cutting.)

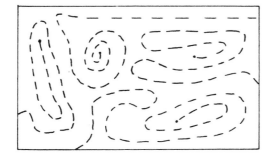

3. After cutting, bend and twist the strips gently into loops. Attach the end of each loop to another section or strip of paper. Hold with a paper clip until the glue is dry.

4. Look for new shapes and color contrasts. Keep looping, twisting, and attaching the strips until all the loose ends are attached to other sections.

5. Suspend one or more objects such as small plastic ornaments or bells within the sculpture, using nylon thread. Attach a piece of string to the top of the sculpture so it can be suspended.

A Spinning Sun

Technique:
Single-string

Materials:

- (1) 9" x 9" yellow construction paper
- scissors
- circle template or compass
- needle and nylon thread
- pencil

Steps:

1. Draw a circle on the yellow construction paper right to the edge of the paper. Then draw a smaller circle in the middle of the large circle. Draw a design around the edge of the circle. This can be any kind of design desired. The circles can be drawn with a circle template or compass.

 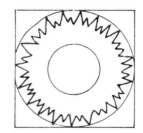 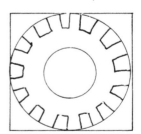

2. Cut out both circles and then trim the small inside circle a bit smaller so it will swing in the middle of the large circle.

3. Write or draw something on the center circle. Try a "sun verse" such as "smiles are personal sunshine," or "smiles are meant to be shared."

4. Sew the small circle into the middle of the sun.

Tie here and sew up to the top.
Leave some string to hang the sun.

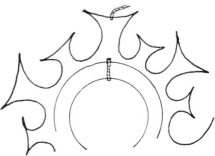

Technique: Single-string

Materials:

- scraps of construction paper: black and flesh colors
- scissors
- glue or paste
- 3–4' length of string or yarn
- black crayon

A Wiggly Witch

Steps:

1. Cut out 2 bodies, 2 heads, 4 legs, 1 circle, 2 shoes, and 2 hands. (See suggested shapes.) All can be cut from construction paper and made to any size. For one size, see measurements needed below each piece.

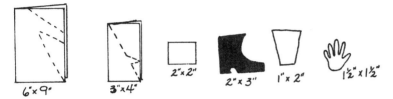

6"x9"   3"x4"   2"x2"   2"x3"   1"x2"   1½"x1½"

2. Glue or paste circle to head, shoes onto legs, and hands onto bodies.

3. Turn the parts face down on the table and lay the second set next to them in the order that you want them to hang.

4. Glue a long piece of string from the top of the hat to the body, leaving a space between the head and shoulders. Glue short pieces from the body to each leg, leaving spaces between.

5. Glue the second set of parts over the first to cover the string. Make sure all edges are glued down.

6. Use the black crayon to draw a face and hair. Add any other details desired, such as a broom, pumpkin in hand, etc.

A Jack-o'-Lantern

Technique:

Single-string

Materials:

- (1) 9" x 12" orange construction paper
- light orange and green crayons
- scissors and pencil
- scraps of black construction paper
- white glue or paste
- needle and nylon thread

Steps:

1. Fold the 9" x 12" orange construction paper in half, widthwise. Using the pencil, draw half a pumpkin on the paper, center on the fold. Cut out.

2. With the paper still folded, cut the nose and mouth on the center fold. To cut the eyes, fold the paper as illustrated or poke a hole with the tip of the scissors and cut out eyes.

3. Using black construction paper scraps, cut out eyes, nose and mouth to fit in the shapes cut out of the pumpkin.

4. Use the green and orange crayons to add accent lines and color the stem.

5. Cut short pieces of thread and glue to the black pieces and then glue to the pumpkin so they hang in the holes cut. A needle and thread can be used to hang the pieces as well.

Technique:

Single-string

Materials:

- (2) 9" x 12" green construction paper
- scraps of construction paper and metallic paper
- optional: glitter and sequins for decorations
- scissors and pencil
- glue or paste
- 3–4' length of string or yarn

Steps:

1. Fold the two 9" x 12" pieces of green construction paper in half, lengthwise. Draw half a Christmas tree on the paper, middle on the fold. Make it as large as possible. Cut out.

 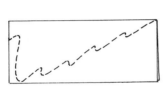

2. While the tree is still folded, draw a second and a third tree shape within the first, leaving a ½" to ¾" margin between each. Cut out.

3. Open the tree "rings" and lay on a flat surface. Discard the middle tree. Place the smallest tree in the middle of the largest tree ring.

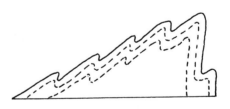

4. Put glue down the middle of the center tree and on the folds of the tree ring. Place the string on top of the glue, beginning at the bottom of the tree. Leave the excess string at the top for hanging. Put glue over the surfaces of the second pieces and place on top of the first, covering the string at the same time.

5. Using the scraps of construction paper and bits of metallic paper, cut and glue decorations on the tree. Remember—the tree will be observed on both sides. Add glitter and sequins, if desired.

Bird in a Cage

Technique: Single-string

Materials:

- (8) 1″ x 12″ strips of brown construction paper
- *bird: any paper colors desired*
  body: (1) 3″ x 4″
  wings: (2) 2″ x 3″ scraps
- (2) 1″ brads
- scissors and paste or glue
- nylon thread and needle
- piece of yarn or string

Steps:

1. Glue the ends of two 1″ x 12″ strips together, overlapping 1″. Join the others, making four long strips in all.

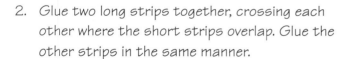

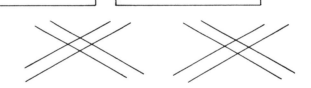

2. Glue two long strips together, crossing each other where the short strips overlap. Glue the other strips in the same manner.

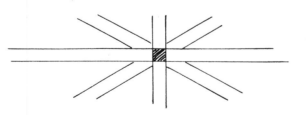

3. Join all the strips together, placing one set of four across the top of the other set of four, and secure in place with a brad.

4. Repeat the process with the other ends to complete the circular cage.

5. Cut the shape of a bird from the 3″ x 4″ piece of construction paper. Use the 2″ x 3″ rectangles for the wings. Cut the headpiece, tail, and other details from scraps of construction paper. Glue or paste.

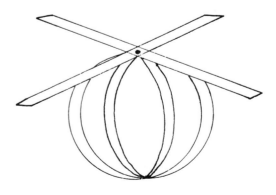

6. Using a needle and thread, hang the bird in the cage. Use a piece of yarn or string to suspend the cage.

346

Single-string Mobiles—other Ideas

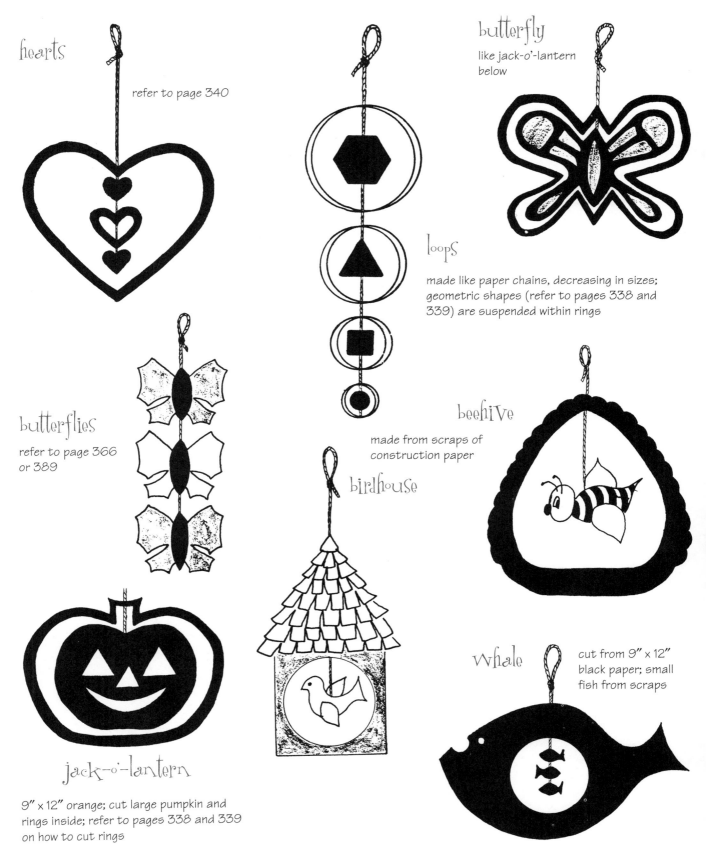

hearts

refer to page 340

butterfly

like jack-o'-lantern below

loops

made like paper chains, decreasing in sizes; geometric shapes (refer to pages 338 and 339) are suspended within rings

made from scraps of construction paper

butterflies

refer to page 366 or 389

birdhouse

beehive

Whale

cut from 9" x 12" black paper; small fish from scraps

jack-o'-lantern

9" x 12" orange; cut large pumpkin and rings inside; refer to pages 338 and 339 on how to cut rings

Dancing Snowman

Technique: Bar mobile, two-string

Materials:

- white construction paper:
  (4) 6" x 6" squares
  (4) 4" x 4" squares
  (4) 2" x 2" squares
- (4) 2" x 3" construction paper, any color, for hats
- (2) 3" x 9" construction paper, any color, for bar
- scraps of black construction paper for arms, eyes, buttons, etc.
- (2) 2' lengths of string or yarn
- scissors
- glue or paste
- black crayon

Steps:

1. BODY: Trim the corners of the squares of white construction paper, two at a time, to make circles.

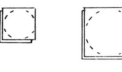

2. HATS: Use the 2" x 3" pieces of colored construction paper to make hats. Cut two at a time so they will be the same size.

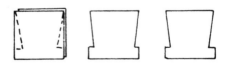

3. Place the circles and hats in order on a flat surface. Overlap pieces a little and glue or paste. Add strips of black paper for arms. Put glue down the middle for one snowman. Place the string, beginning at the bottom, on the glue, leaving the excess at the top for hanging.

4. Cover the second set of circles with glue or paste and place on the first set over the string. Be sure to secure all the edges. Use scraps of paper and black crayon to add details.

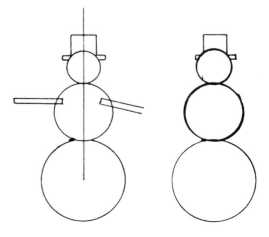

5. Make the second snowman in the same manner.

6. BAR: Glue string to the outside edges of one 3" x 9" strip of construction paper. Glue the second strip over the top of the string. Tie the ends of the string together for hanging.

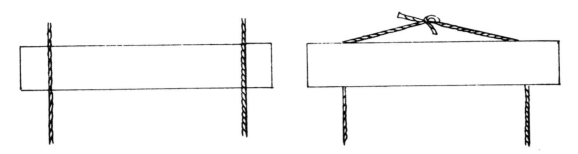

Two-String Bar Mobiles —other Ideas

butterflies
refer to page 366
or 389

hearts
refer to page 340

sailboats
made from scraps of construction
paper, a toothpick or kabob stick
for mast

fruit
scraps of construction
paper—and imagination!

trees
refer to page 345

350

Technique:

Shaped bar

Materials:

- (1) 9" x 12" white construction paper
- orange construction paper:
  (1) 6" x 9"
  (1) 4 ½" x 6"
- black construction paper:
  (1) 6" x 9"
  (1) 1" x 9"
  (1) 3" x 3"
  (2) 2" x 6"
- scraps of construction paper, all colors
- scissors
- glue or paste
- needle or paper punch
- nylon thread or fishing line
- pencil and black crayon

Steps:

1. GHOST: Draw a ghost shape on the 9" x 12" white construction paper with a pencil, almost touching the edges of the paper at its head, hands, and lower edge. Outline with a black crayon if desired. Cut out.

2. JACK-O'-LANTERN: Fold the 6" x 9" and 4 ½" x 6" pieces of orange construction paper in half, widthwise. Draw half a jack-o'-lantern shape on each piece, middle on the fold. Cut out. Add facial features with black crayon on both sides or cut out like the jack-o'-lantern on page 344.

3. SPIDER: Make a cylinder of the 1″ x 9″ black construction paper. Use thin strips of black paper to make legs; glue on the inside of the cylinder. Fold down and bend strips to give shape to legs.

4. BAT: Fold the 3″ square of black construction paper in half. Trim the corners to make a circle. Open. Cut a slit half way up the fold to the center. Overlap the edges of the cut and paste or glue. Cut wings from the 2″ x 6″ strips of paper as illustrated. Glue to the underside of the head.

5. BLACK CAT: Draw a black cat freehand on the 6″ x 9″ black construction paper with a pencil and cut out. Add facial features and whiskers with scraps of construction paper.

6. Attach a string or thread to the top of each object, either with a needle or a paper punch. Tie at various intervals onto the ghost.

7. Tie a string to the top center of the ghost's head and suspend.

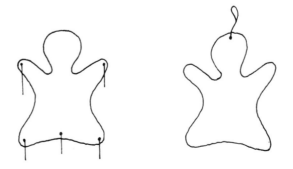

Variations:

This idea can be adapted to almost any holiday theme desired, such as Thanksgiving with Pilgrim's hat or turkey and attached symbols.

Technique: Bar
mobile, multiple-string

Translucent Trees

Materials:

- 9" x 12", 6" x 9", and 4 ½" x 6" green construction paper, two of each size
- (2) 12" x 18" pieces of wax paper
- scraps of bright-colored tissue paper, glitter, sequins, etc.
- an iron
- stack of newspapers for an ironing pad
- scissors
- glue or paste
- paper punch or embroidery needle
- nylon thread or string
- (1) 6" x 12" construction paper for bar, any color

Steps:

1. Place one piece of wax paper on a stack of newspapers which will act as an ironing pad. Scatter scraps of tissue paper over the entire surface of the wax paper. Bits of glitter, foil paper, and sequins may be added.

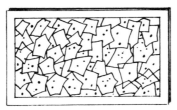

2. Place the second sheet of wax paper on top of the tissue, etc. Iron over the surface of the second sheet of wax paper with a moderately warm iron. The heat will seal the two sheets of wax paper together. If the iron is too hot, the wax will burn away and the two papers will not adhere to one another. Put aside to cool.

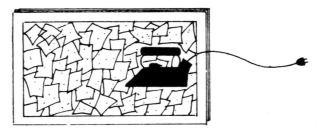

3. TREES: Fold each two pieces of equal size green construction paper in half, lengthwise, together. Draw half a tree on the paper, middle on the fold. If you begin with a basic triangle, variations in shape are easy to develop. See illustrations:

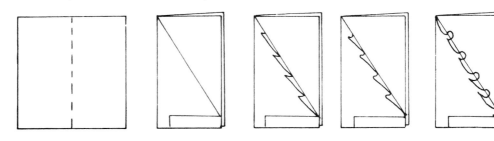

4. Hold the fold and cut out. While still holding the tree shape, cut a second tree within the first tree, leaving a ½″ to ¾″ border. Open.

5. Glue one ring each of each size onto the ironed wax paper. Cut out, trimming the excess wax paper away.

6. Turn over each shape and glue the second tree ring to the other side, covering the edges of the wax paper.

7. Using a paper punch and string or a needle and thread, tie a string to each tree.

8. BAR: Fold the 6″ x 12″ pieces of construction paper in half, lengthwise, to make the bar. Put glue on one half of the bar, lay ends of strings attached to trees on glue and fold over the other half of the bar. Press firmly to secure. Add another piece of string or thread to the top of the bar for hanging.

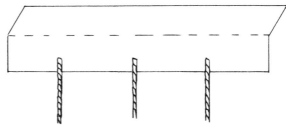

Variations:

— Additional strings may be suspended from the bar, adding the center trees made when cutting the tree rings.

— Pieces of tissue or sequins may be glued to the strings suspending the trees for additional color and sparkle.

— Use other ring shapes such as hearts, geometric shapes, etc., with translucent wax paper centers.

Technique: Bar mobile, multiple-string

Materials:

- (1) 6″ x 18″ green construction paper
- (1 each) 6″ x 9″ lengths of white, light blue, pink, and light green construction paper
- (1 each) 6″ x 9″ lengths of white, light blue, pink, yellow, and light green thick yarn
- scissors
- paste or glue
- crayons

Steps:

1. SYMBOLS: Fold the 6″ x 9″ pieces of construction paper in half, widthwise, and cut out symbols of Easter. Make sure the bottom edge of each shape is on the fold.

3. BAR: Fold the 6″ x 18″ green construction paper in half, lengthwise. Holding the folded edge, cut a wavy edge around the open edges.

4. Open the green construction paper and apply a line of paste or glue down the center of one half. Space the ends of yarn inside on the glue. Fold the other half over and press down. Hold until the glue or paste dries. Add facial features, designs, etc., on both sides of each shape with crayons.

2. Open each shape. Put paste or glue all over one side of a shape. Lay the end of the yarn on top of the shape and fold the other half of the shape over the string, pressing firmly in place.

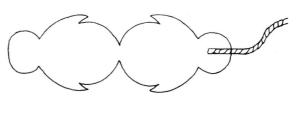

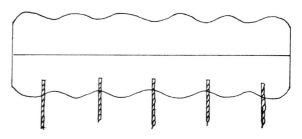

355

Under the Big Top

Materials:

- construction paper or printed paper, such as wallpaper or gift wrap, the following sizes:
  (4) 6″ x 9″
  (2) 2 ½″ x 3″
- (4) 2″ x 2″ flesh construction paper
- (4) 1″ x 2″ white construction paper
- (1) 6″ x 18″ or 12″ x 18″ construction paper, any color for big top
- scraps of construction paper, all colors
- scissors
- paste or glue
- needle or paper punch
- nylon thread or string
- crayons

Steps:

1. CLOWNS:

body

Fold the 6″ x 9″ paper in half, lengthwise. Cut as illustrated.

hands and ears

Cut from scraps of flesh-colored paper.

shoes

Cut four from scraps of black paper.

face

Trim the corners of the four 2″ x 2″ flesh-colored squares.

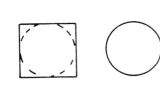

Fold the 2 ½″ x 3″ paper in half, lengthwise, and cut like a triangle.

hat

collar

Cut wavy edges on all four 1″ x 2″ pieces of white paper.

2. Place all pieces of two clowns in correct order, face down, on a flat surface. Glue or paste the pieces together. Put glue down the center of one clown and place string on top, beginning at the bottom, with the excess at the top for hanging. Glue the second set of pieces on top, covering the string. Do both clowns.

3. Add facial features, hands, ears, shoes, and collars as well as any additional details desired. Remember, there's a front and a back, and both sides will be observed.

4. BIG TOP: Fold the 6" x 18" or 12" x 18" construction paper in half, widthwise. Trim as illustrated to make the big top. This can be made most attractive with added decorations of bits of metallic paper, yarn, etc.

5. BALLOONS: Cut circles from scraps of construction paper. Refer to page 338 on how to cut circles.

6. STARS: Refer to page 367 on how to cut stars.

7. Suspend each completed object from the big top with nylon thread or fishing line and a needle. Add a string at the top for hanging.

Variations:

— Try adding circus animals or other performers to the big top.
— This same idea can be adapted to almost any theme desired. Below are a few suggestions, but do let the imagination go:

umbrella	barn	sailboat	north wind
raindrops	silo	beach umbrella	things that blow
boots	cows	shovel and pail	in the wind
ducks	horses	rubber raft	
rain coat	haystack	bathing suits	

under the Sea

Technique: Bar mobile, multiple-string

Materials:

- construction paper, any color, cut to the following sizes, one for each fish to be made: 2" x 4", 4" x 6", 3" x 4", and 6" x 9"
- scissors and pencil
- wire coat hanger
- nylon thread or fishing line
- needle or paper punch

Steps:

1. FISH: Fold the rectangles of construction paper in half, lengthwise. Pencil half a fish shape on each, center on the fold. Holding the fold, cut out the fish shape.

2. SPRING: While still holding the fish shape, cut half a circle from the center of the fish shape. Remember to begin and end on the fold. Open both shapes. Cut the circle into a spring.

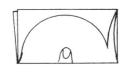

3. Repeat the preceding steps for each fish to be made. Make many fish of all sizes and shapes.

4. Attach a piece of nylon thread or fishing line to each fish and spring made. Tie onto the wire hanger at various intervals. The coat hanger may be left in its original shape or pulled and bent to make other interesting shapes.

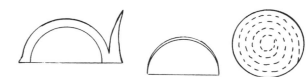

Variations:

— Cut out fish shapes, leaving whole. Use scraps of paper to make mosaic decorations on fish and springs for seaweed.

— Use crayons to decorate whole fish shapes.

With "Rice Paper"

Technique: Bar mobile, multiple-string

Materials:

- (3) 2-ply pieces of facial tissue
- (1) 12" x 18" wax paper
- colored tissue paper scraps
- flat dried weeds (flowers, ferns)
- scissors and soft-bristle brush
- small container and water
- white glue
- newspaper
- wooden dowel or stick
- nylon thread and needle

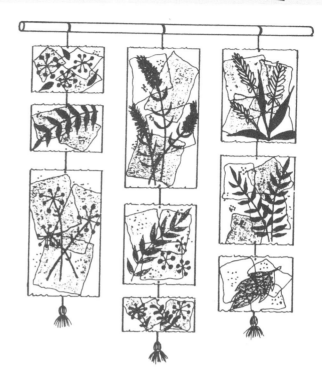

Steps:

1. Spread newspaper on the working surface. Place the piece of wax paper on the center of the newspaper.

2. Make a glue mixture of 2 parts glue to 1 part water. Stir with a small wooden stick to a thick creamy consistency.

3. Paint the surface of the wax paper with the glue mixture. Arrange cut or torn pieces of colored tissue paper on the wax paper in any manner desired, covering each piece with the glue mixture. Arrange the dried weeds on top of the tissue paper design. Cover the weeds with glue mixture.

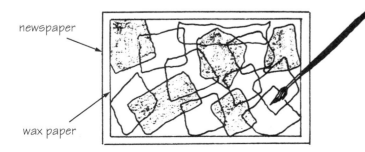

newspaper

wax paper

4. Separate each 2-ply piece of facial tissue into two single pieces. Place one piece on top of the design on wax paper, putting one edge of the facial tissue along the top of the wax paper. Pull the opposite edge until it is taut. Press down on top of the design. Use a brush or sponge to cover the surface of the facial tissue with glue mixture. Continue with the other piece of facial tissue until the entire piece of wax paper is covered, overlapping the edges. **NOTE:** Be sure to give one final coat of glue mixture over the top.

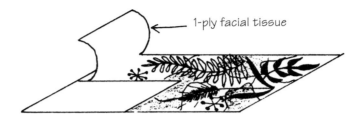

1-ply facial tissue

5. When completely dry, cut into rectangular shapes of varying sizes. Using a needle and nylon thread or fishing line, string the shapes in rows and tie each to the piece of doweling or wooden stick.

Variation:

Instead of one large sheet, make each shape individually.

Multiple-String Bar Mobiles —other Ideas

branch and birds

—branch may be real or made from 3" x 18" brown construction paper

—leaves: 3" x 4" green construction paper: refer to page 376

—birds: refer to page 391

butterflies

—large: 9" x 12" construction paper

—others: 3" x 4", 4 ½" x 6", 2" x 4", refer to pages 366 and 389

crayon batik discs

—circles of various sizes cut from white drawing paper

—refer to page 389 for batik process

Snowflakes

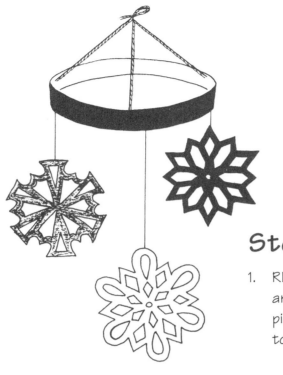

Technique: Ring mobile

Materials:

- (1) 3" x 18" lightweight cardboard for ring
- (3) 9" x 9" tissue squares for each snowflake, all the same or different colors
- (1) 12" x 12" wax paper for each snowflake
- liquid starch
- soft-bristle brush
- scissors
- glue or paste
- needle or paper punch
- nylon thread or string

Steps:

1. RING: Overlap one end of the 3" x 18" strip over the other end and glue to make the ring. To hang, attach three evenly spaced pieces of string around the ring. Bring the ends of the string together and tie in a loop for hanging.

2. SNOWFLAKES: Fold each square of tissue paper in the following manner to prepare and cut the snowflakes. (Remember, each snowflake to be hung will need three tissue snowflakes.)

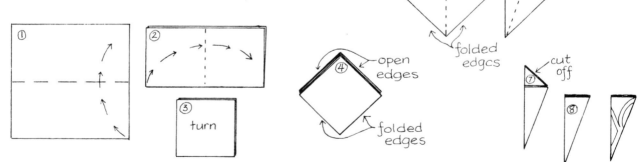

3. Place a piece of wax paper on top of a piece of newspaper.

4. Paint the wax paper with a coat of starch. Place one snowflake on this. Cover with starch. Place the second snowflake on top of this and cover it with starch. Repeat with the third snowflake. Paint carefully as the snowflakes are fragile.

5. Let the tissue dry thoroughly, overnight if possible. When the tissue is dry, the wax paper will peel away, leaving a stiff layered tissue snowflake. Attach string or thread to each and suspend from the circle ring.

Technique: Ring mobile

Materials:

- black construction paper:
  (3) 3" x 3"   (6) 2" x 6"
  (2) 4" x 4"   (4) 2 ½" x 9"
- (1) 3" x 18" lightweight cardboard, any color, for ring
- scraps of green, yellow, and red construction paper
- scissors
- paste or glue
- embroidery needle or paper punch
- nylon thread or string

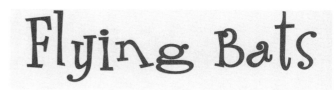

Steps:

1. BODY: Fold the 3" x 3" and 4" x 4" squares of black construction paper in half and trim off the corners to make five circles. Open.

   Cut a slit half-way up the fold line, overlap the edges of the cut, and paste or glue. This will make it curve, like a little hat. Do each circle.

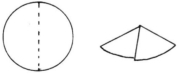

2. WINGS: Place the 2" x 6" and 2 ½" x 9" pieces of black construction paper in pairs, on top of each other. Cut off the top corners and the lower parts as illustrated to make wings.

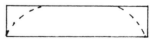

   Paste or glue each pair of wings to the back of a head (the circle).

3. BODY PARTS: Cut eyes, nose, etc., from the scraps of construction paper and paste or glue onto the heads.

4. RING: Bend one end of the 3" x 18" strip around and overlap the other. Glue or paste. If necessary, secure in place with a staple. To hang, attach three evenly spaced pieces of string around the ring. Bring ends together and tie into a loop for hanging.

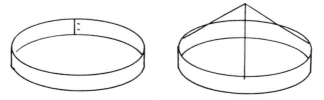

Insects in Flight

Technique: Spring mobile

Materials:

- (1) 6″ × 6″ construction paper or lightweight cardboard, any color
- for insects: (construction paper)
  ladybug (1) 3″ × 9″ orange
  (1) 2″ × 6″ black
  ant (1) 1 ½″ × 12″ black
  (1) 1″ × 6″ black
  bee (1) 1 ½″ × 12″ yellow
  (2) 1″ × 6″ white
  (1) 1 ½″ × 12″ black
  spider (1) 1 ½″ × 9″ black
- scraps of red and black construction paper for legs, eyes, mouth, antennae
- scissors
- glue or paste
- embroidery needle or paper punch
- nylon thread or string

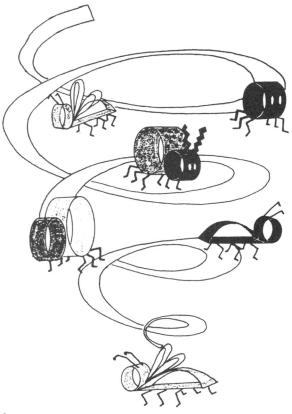

Steps:

1. SPRING: Trim away the corners of the 6″ × 6″ paper to make a circle. Beginning at the edge, cut in and around to the middle of the circle to make the spring. Cut about ½″ to ¾″ from the edge.

2. ANTENNAE AND LEGS: These are made from long thin (⅛″) strips of black construction paper. The antennae can be straight or accordion-pleated and are glued to the head. Legs are attached inside the body cylinder and bent two or three times for leg joints.

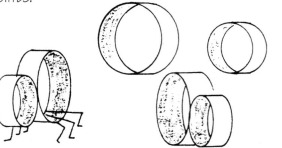

3. LADYBUG: Make rings of the orange and black construction paper. Glue the small black cylinder onto the large orange cylinder. Use scraps of construction paper cut in strips for legs. Add antennae to the head.

4. ANT: Make a cylinder of the 1″ x 6″ strip of black paper. Make a loop of the 1 ½″ x 12″ black strip by joining the ends. Glue the small black cylinder on top of the loop where the ends are joined. Add legs and antennae as in step 2.

5. BEE: Make a small circle at one end of the yellow strip of paper. Stick the other end of the strip under the circle and glue down. Make loops of the strips of white paper and glue right behind the small yellow circle. Use scraps of paper for eyes, mouth, antennae, and legs.

6. SPIDER: Make a cylinder of the 1 ½″ x 9″ strip of black construction paper. Add legs as in step 2.

7. After making one of each, it will be easy to make any insect, real or imaginary, just using scraps of paper.

8. Suspend the spring from an overhead string or wire. Using a paper punch and string or needle and thread, suspend the insects at various intervals on the spring.

Variations:

Refer to pages 379 and 380 for ring creatures.

Butterflies of Foil

Technique: Spring mobile

Materials:

- (1) 6" x 6" construction paper, tagboard, or other lightweight cardboard
- foil paper, any color, cut to 4 ½" x 6", 3" x 4", and 3" x 3" for butterflies of all sizes
- scissors and pencil
- needle
- nylon thread or fishing line

Steps:

1. SPRING: Trim away the corners of the 6" x 6" paper to make a circle. Beginning at the edge, cut in and around to the middle of the circle to make the spring. Cut about ½" to ¾" from the edge.

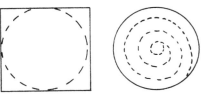

2. BUTTERFLIES: Fold the rectangular pieces of foil in half, widthwise. Lightly sketch half a butterfly shape on each piece. Be sure to include the body, not just the wings. See illustrations.

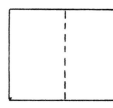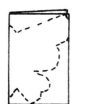

3. Fold the wings up, next to the body, about ¾" to 1" from the center fold. Attach the nylon thread through the fold between the wings to hang. Prepare all the butterflies in the same manner.

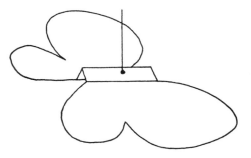

4. Suspend the spring from an overhead string or wire. Tie the butterflies to various parts of the spring.

Technique: Spring mobile

Materials:

- (1) 6″ x 6″ light blue construction paper
- 4 ½″ x 6″ and 6″ x 9″ rectangles of red, white, and dark blue light-weight paper
- scissors
- needle or paper punch
- nylon thread or string

Steps:

1. SPRING: Trim away the corners of the 6″ x 6″ paper to make a circle. Beginning at the edge, cut in and around to the middle of the circle to make the spring. Cut about ½″ to ¾″ from the edge.

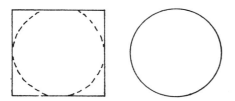

2. STARS: To make, fold and cut each rectangle of lightweight paper as follows, folding in the direction of the arrows:

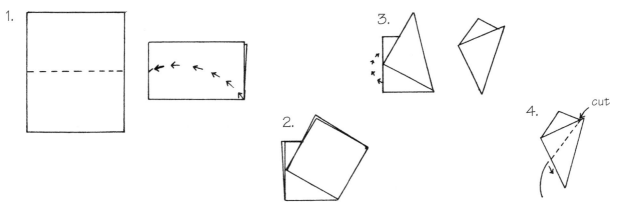

   NOTE: The deeper the cut, the sharper the points will be.

3. Tie a piece of string to one end of the spring and hang from an overhead wire or string. Using a paper punch and string or needle and thread, suspend the stars from the spring at various intervals.

Shower of stars

Technique: Multiple-arm

Materials:

- small paper boxes: gelatin, cereal, paper clip, jewelry, etc.
- scraps of all kinds of paper: wallpaper, construction paper, etc.
- collectibles: yarn, buttons, feathers, glitter, sequins, fabric
- scissors and glue
- needle and nylon fishing line
- arms for mobile

"Birds of a Feather"

Steps:

As the dimensions of the boxes will vary, it is impossible to give exact measurements.

1. Cut two rectangles of paper, one for the top of the box and one to cover the bottom. Make them as wide as the box and a bit longer to wrap over the sides. Glue the bottom. Using a needle and fishing line, run through middle of the top piece before gluing over the top. The line will hang loose until ready to attach to the arm of the mobile.

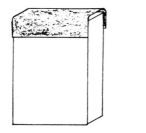

2. Cut one or more strips of paper long enough to wrap all the way around the box and have the ends overlap about ½" in back or on the side. Glue into place.

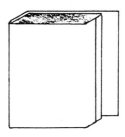

369

3. Now begin creating the bird. Use pieces of paper curled, twisted, and folded. Remember to include a flap (piece of paper folded back and used to attach to box). See illustrations. For more exciting and eye-catching creations, add yarn, feathers, glitter, buttons, or anything else.

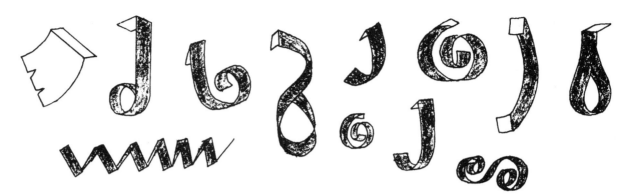

4. When three or more birds are complete, assemble the arms of the mobile. Attach birds to arms of mobile, varying lengths of line.

Technique: Multiple-arm

Materials:

- for each fish: 1" x 12" strips of construction paper, 3 of one color and 3 of another
- glue or paste
- scissors
- arms for mobile
- nylon thread or fishing line
- needle or paper punch

Woven-Paper Fish

Steps:

1. Fold all six strips in half.

2. Slip one strip over another to interlock as shown, and glue into place.

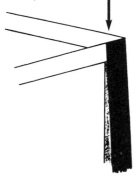

3. Slip two strips on cross strip, the two outside ones on one part of the folded strip and one on the other as illustrated.

4. Weave in the other three strips in the other direction, doing a sort of double weaving; one half of the strip on one side and the other half of the strip on the other side. You will in fact be able to slip your hand in the middle of the fish. It can also be stuffed with tissue paper to give an added three-dimensional effect.

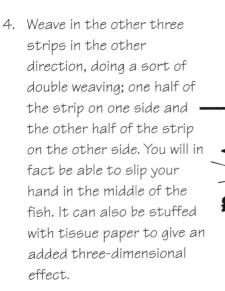

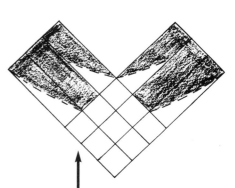

5. Secure all strips in place with glue or paste. Trim the unwoven portions of the strips as illustrated (cut away the shaded areas.) Attach a nylon thread or fishing line to each fish and tie to the arms of the mobile.

Creative Creatures

Technique:
Multiple-arm

Materials:

- white drawing paper: 4 ½" x 6", 6" x 9", or 3" x 4" for each creature to be made (depending on size desired)
- tissue paper, all colors
- crayons and scissors
- soft-bristle brush
- collectibles: sequins, glitter, yarn, string
- liquid starch
- piece of wax paper
- newspaper for the working surface
- arms for the mobile

Steps:

1. Draw a simple shape on the size white drawing paper chosen. Any design or object can be drawn, but preferably something with an inner pattern . . . birds, flowers, butterflies, animals, or seasonal objects. Draw the outline very dark with black crayon.

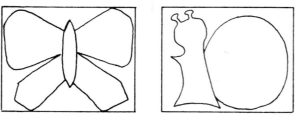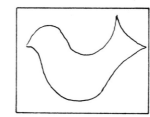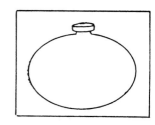

2. Lay a piece of wax paper over the top of the drawing. Place a piece of tissue paper on top of the wax paper. It will still be possible to see the crayon outline if it is dark enough.

3. Place long lengths of string or yarn in liquid starch in small container, and squeeze the excess starch away with fingers as you pull it out. Place the string on the tissue following the outlines of the drawing underneath.

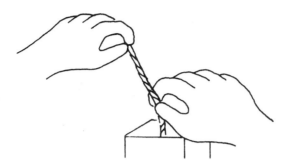

4. Add individual touches and decorations with glitter, yarn, sequins, tempera paints (somewhat difficult), and pieces of tissue paper, attaching all with liquid starch.

5. Paint liquid starch over the entire figure and place the second sheet of tissue paper on top. Paint another layer of liquid starch to seal the layers of tissue and yarn or string together. Allow to dry thoroughly.

6. When dry, the wax paper will peel away. Trim the excess tissue beyond the outline of the yarn or string. Attach a nylon thread or string to each object and suspend from various parts of the arms of the mobile.

Falling Leaves

Materials:

- scraps of tissue paper, all colors
- liquid starch
- scissors and soft-bristle brush
- large piece of wax paper
- needle or paper punch
- nylon thread or fishing line
- arms for mobile
- newspaper for working surface

Steps:

1. Cover the working surface with newspaper. Place the piece of wax paper in the center. Cut or tear the scraps of tissue into pieces of all sizes and shapes.

2. Using the soft-bristle brush, cover the wax paper with a coat of starch. It will not cover evenly but this will be remedied when the tissue is applied.

3. Place one piece of tissue paper at a time on the wax paper and cover with starch. The pieces may be picked up with the tip of the brush. Overlap the pieces of tissue paper, and continue until the entire piece of wax paper has two or three layers of tissue paper.

4. Let dry thoroughly, overnight at least. When the tissue paper is dry, the wax paper will peel away, leaving a sheet of tissue collage.

5. Cut the tissue collage into shapes: butterflies, fish, flowers, etc. A template or pattern may be made from a piece of construction or bogus paper, and traced around on the tissue before cutting for better planning and less waste. Add a string to each shape and tie to arms of mobile.

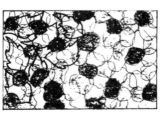

Variations: Here are a few ideas for other shapes:

Technique:

Multiple-arm

A Harvest of Fruit

Materials:

- 1" x 12" strips of construction paper, assorted sizes
- white glue or paste
- scissors
- 2" x 3" and 3" x 4" pieces of green construction paper for leaves
- arms for mobile
- nylon thread or fishing line
- needle

Steps:

1. Using one or more of the 1" x 12" strips of construction paper, glue or paste ends together to make the shape of a fruit. Apples, lemons, and oranges usually need only one strip. A banana takes two strips and grapes do not need a beginning shape. The rings will not stay in exact shape until they are filled with paper rolls.

2. Each shape will be filled with a number of rolled paper strips. To begin each roll, fold about ⅛" of one end down and roll the strip so it looks like a spring. Glue or paste the end of the strip to the roll.

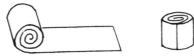

3. Make enough paper rolls to fill the shape of the fruit. Place them in the shape to test how many are needed. Then take out the rolls, put paste or glue around the edge of each one, and put them back in the shape, sticking all the rolls together.

4. LEAVES: Fold scraps or rectangles of green construction paper in half. Cut one half a leaf. To create a three-dimensional effect, cut out parts in the center as illustrated. Glue on fruit.

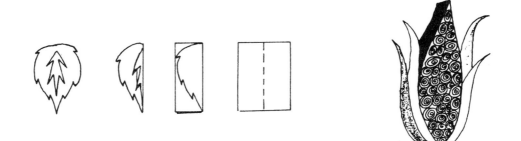

5. Using needle and nylon thread or fishing line, attach fruit to arms of mobile.

    Variations: Try other fruits and also vegetables such as corn. Fill a cornucopia at Thanksgiving.

Technique: Multiple-arm

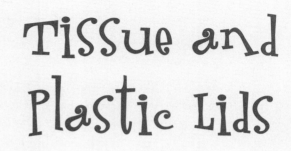

Materials:

- clear plastic lids (from coffee, candy, and nut cans, etc.)
- white glue
- soft-bristle brush
- small container and water
- scraps of tissue, yarn, string, glitter, sequins, construction, and other kinds of paper
- arms for mobile
- nylon thread or fishing line
- needle or paper punch
- scissors
- newspaper for working surface

Steps:

1. Cover the working surface with newspaper. Using the needle or paper punch, put a small hole in each plastic lid, near the outside edge. This will be used to hang it and will also be a reminder of where the top is while working.

2. Make a mixture of 2 parts glue and 1 part water in the small container. Use a small wooden stick to stir the mixture to a creamy consistency. The glue is applied to the plastic lids with a paintbrush and will dry clear.

3. Using the scraps of construction paper, tissue paper, yarn, string, glitter, and sequins, create designs, patterns, or pictures for each plastic lid to be hung. Try various designs on the lids before gluing into place. The following are a few ideas:

4. When all the final designs are made, remove "pieces" from one lid. Paint the surface of the lid with the white glue mixture. Place one piece of the design on the lid at a time, painting a second coat of the glue mixture over the top of each piece. Let dry thoroughly. Do all in the same manner.

Variations:

Jack-o'-lanterns

orange tissue

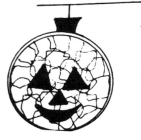

christmas tree balls

tissue, glitter, sequins

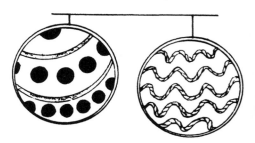

Spring flowers

yarn and tissue

Technique: Multiple-arm

Ring Creatures

Materials:

- 1" wide strips of construction paper, assorted colors, cut into the following lengths: 4", 6", 9", and 12"
- scissors
- glue or paste
- needle or paper punch
- nylon thread or fishing line
- arms for mobile

Steps:

The possibilities are endless . . . once begun there is no end to the number of creatures that can be made from paper curls and rings. These are a lot like the Scandinavian wood-shaving creatures made into mobiles. As sizes and dimensions will vary, only the outlines of a few creatures are illustrated; from there let the imagination take over.

1. Begin by making the outside outline of the shape of the creature. It will generally take several strips combined to create one creature. It will help to have some paper clips handy to hold ends glued until dry. Remember—the shape will not stay until rings or rolls are inside.

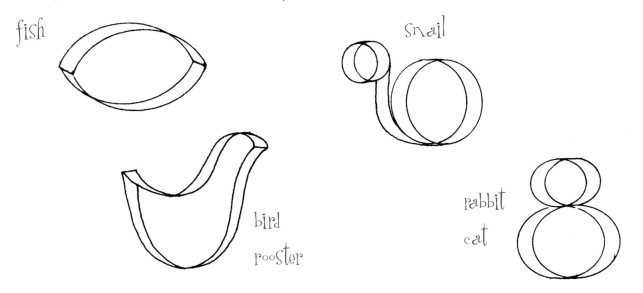

fish

snail

bird
rooster

rabbit
cat

2. Using paper rolls (see page 375), rings, curls, and accordion-pleated strips, fill in the shape desired. Notice the owl has many paper rolls to create the effect of feathers on his chest. The tail of the rooster has loose paper curls for his tail and rings for his headpiece. The rabbit has two paper rings for a tail within the large ring used to create his body.

3. Assemble arms of the mobile. Attach nylon thread or fishing line to the creatures and tie to arms.

Technique:

Multiple-arm

Like "Stained Glass"

Materials:

- black construction paper:
  (2) 4 ½" x 6" for each object
- 4 ½" x 6" colored tissue
  paper for each object
- needle or paper punch
- nylon thread or fishing line
- scissors and paste or glue
- arms for mobile

Steps:

1. Fold two pieces of the black construction paper in half, lengthwise. Cut out half the shape of a butterfly; you may wish to pencil in the shape first.

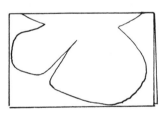 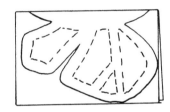

2. While the paper is still folded, draw in wing designs. Cut into wing shapes and cut out the design sections. The arrows show the best place to cut into the wings so as to leave a shape that can easily be glued to the tissue paper.

3. Unfold the shapes, paste or glue one side of one shape, and lay it on the tissue paper. Put paste or glue on the other shape and glue to the other side of the tissue paper right behind the first shape so they match exactly, back to back.

4. Trim the extra tissue paper away when the paste or glue is dry.

5. Using the needle and thread or paper punch and string, attach a string or thread to the shape so it can be hung from an arm of the mobile.

6. Almost any shape desired can be made in the same manner:

— Fold in half, together, two pieces of construction paper the same size, and cut out a shape.

— Cut into the shape and cut the center out while it is still folded (see dotted lines).

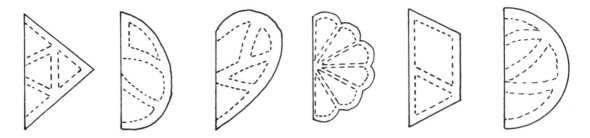

— Open shapes, put paste or glue on one shape, and lay it on the tissue paper. Put paste or glue on the other shape and place on the other side of the tissue paper right behind the first shape so they match exactly.

— Trim away the excess tissue paper when the glue or paste is dry. Add thread or string and attach to arms of mobile.

Technique: Multiple-arm
Materials:

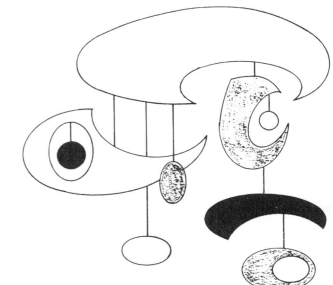
- pieces of any kind of *stiff* paper such as construction paper, tagboard, railroad board, chipboard, etc.
- pieces of any kind of *printed* paper such as wallpaper, gift wrap, magazines, etc.
- glue or paste
- scissors
- needle or paper punch
- nylon thread or fishing line
- arms for mobile, if needed

Steps:

1. Before beginning to cut out shapes at random, try sketching a few ideas on a piece of newsprint. A little planning saves time and materials. Illustrated are a few ideas for free-form shapes that can be made using a geometric shape as a base. It is sometimes easier to begin with a familiar shape such as a square and proceed from there.

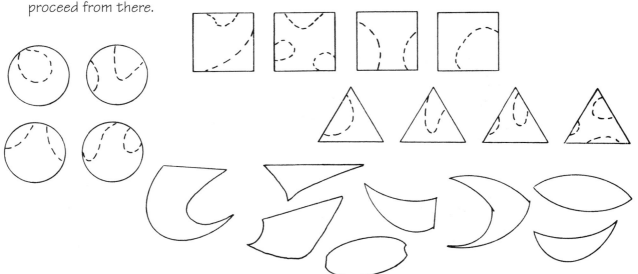

2. Cut out shapes desired from the scraps or pieces of paper, tagboard, illustration board, etc. When using some paper, only one side will have color or pattern so it will be necessary to cut two shapes and glue them back to back. Always remember that the parts of a mobile are visible from all sides.

3. When all the shapes are cut out, attach a nylon thread or fishing line to each. Attach pieces either to one large shape or arms to make the mobile.

Birds in Flight

Technique: Stabile

Materials:

- construction paper scraps, bits, and pieces
- glue or paste
- scissors
- crayons
- needle or paper punch
- nylon thread or fishing line
- dried branch or piece of tumbleweed

Steps:

1. Fold pieces of construction paper in half and cut out the body of a bird. No particular size is given as there should be birds of all different sizes.

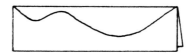

2. Fold scraps of construction paper in half and cut wings and tails, center on the fold. See illustrations for suggestions:

tails

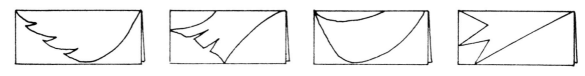

wings

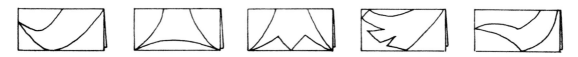

3. Glue or paste wings and tail onto the body of the bird. Use crayons, pencils, ink, or felt-tip pens to add eyes and beaks.

4. The birds can be made as elaborate as desired with additional pieces of construction paper, glitter, or sequins.

5. Using the needle and thread or fishing line, sew through the back of the bird and tie to the branch. A paper punch can also be used.

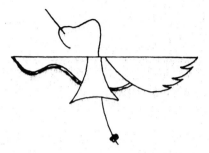

Variations:

— Make the birds of all shades of one color or in a variety of colors.

— Try a combination of construction paper and printed papers such as wallpaper, gift wrap, or pages from magazines.

An Egg Tree

Technique: Stabile

The egg tree is an Easter custom of the Pennsylvania Dutch who are descendants of the early German settlers in Pennsylvania.

The eggs to be hung on the tree can be real blown eggs or eggs made of paper, such as construction or tissue. A list of materials and steps for several techniques are given below.

Blown Eggs

Materials:

- raw eggs
- egg dye
- toothpicks
- nylon thread or fishing line

Steps:

1. To prepare the egg:
   — Put something soft, like a towel or rumpled tissue paper, on a table.
   — Place the egg, small end up, on the towel. It is easier to balance the egg on a soft surface.
   — Drive a needle through the shell at the top of the egg and wiggle the needle around to make a hole about the size of a pea.
   — Make a hole at the other end.
   — Blow the contents of the egg into a dish.

   Suggestion: Blow the eggs at home and bring the shells to school.

2. Before decorating the eggs, make fasteners with nylon thread and toothpicks. Break a toothpick in half and tie a thread about 12″ long to one of the halves. Lower it through the hole in the egg. Pull the thread and the stick will fall into a horizontal position and will not pull out.

3. Decorate the eggs, using egg dye or any other technique desired. When the eggs are decorated, tie them to the various branches of the tree.

   Hint: Short of time, purchase plastic eggs at your local craft store; they don't break.

Construction Paper Eggs

Materials:

- 3" x 4", 4" x 6", and 2" x 3" white construction paper
- scraps of all colors of construction paper
- scissors
- paste or glue
- needle
- nylon thread or fishing line

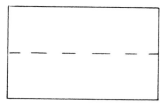

Steps:

1. Fold the white construction paper rectangles in half, lengthwise. Hold the fold and cut away the open corners to make an egg shape. Open.

2. Using scraps of construction paper, cut all kinds of shapes such as circles, rings, triangles, flowers, butterflies, etc., to decorate both sides of each egg.

3. Glue or paste the cut shapes onto the egg shape. Using a needle and nylon thread or fishing line, hang the eggs on the various branches of the tree.

Other Ideas for the "Tree" or Branch Mobiles

The "egg tree" makes an attractive addition to any room at any time of the year. The following illustrations suggest other ways to use the tree throughout the year.

refer to page 366

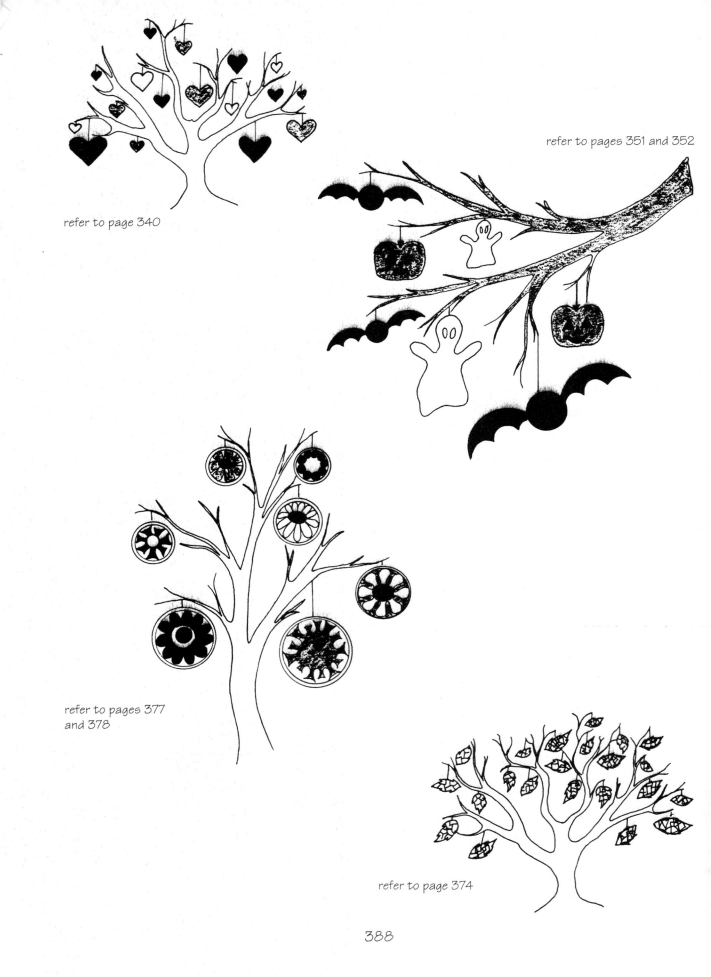

refer to page 340

refer to pages 351 and 352

refer to pages 377
and 378

refer to page 374

Batik Butterflies

Technique: Stabile

Materials:

- (1) 9" x 12" or 12" x 18" white drawing paper
- crayons and scissors
- thin brown tempera paint
- soft-bristle brush
- newspaper
- running water or a large container of water
- coat hanger and piece of wood
- nylon thread or fishing line
- needle or paper punch

Steps:

1. Using a black or brown crayon, draw many butterflies on the white drawing paper. Make them all different sizes. Color in the butterflies with bright colors, pressing heavily to get a good build-up of wax.

2. When the coloring is completed, put the paper under running water or in a container of water to make it completely wet. Then crumple it into a tight ball so the crayon cracks. Open it up again.

3. Lay the wet paper on newspaper and paint over the entire picture with the brown tempera paint. Immediately put it back in the water to wash off the paint. Spread out flat on newspaper to dry. (It can be ironed later with a warm iron to make it completely flat before cutting.)

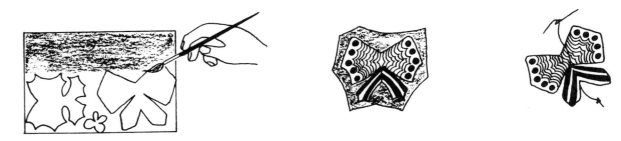

4. When the paper is dry (overnight), cut out the butterflies. Glue or paste each butterfly to a piece of construction paper. Trim away the excess construction paper with scissors. This will give the butterfly a colorful back. Using a needle and nylon thread or fishing line, hang each butterfly from the wire arms attached to the main wire of the stabile.

5. To make the stabile, refer to page 334.

Technique:

Stabile

Tirol Swallow Tree

Materials:

- (2) 3" x 4" paper for each bird: construction paper, printed papers, any kind desired
- scissors and crayons
- glue or paste
- *tree: materials and instructions below*
- needle or paper punch
- nylon thread or fishing line

Steps:

1. One 3" x 4" piece of paper is for the body of the bird. This can be one of several shapes and can be cut freehand or penciled on the paper before cutting. The following are two ideas for basic shapes:

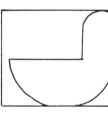 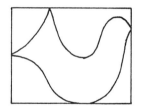

2. Fold one 3" x 4" piece of paper in half, widthwise, to make the wings. Cut freehand or draw shape on first with pencil before cutting. Remember, the fold should be the center, keeping the wings in one place.

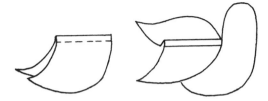

3. To attach wings to the body, use one of the following techniques:

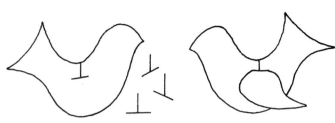

   —Glue the folded wings to the top part of the body.

   —Cut a slit in the body, the angle of the slit deciding the direction of the wings.

4. Using nylon thread or fishing line and a needle, attach a string to each bird made.

5. Decorate the birds with crayons, scraps of all kinds of paper, or anything else desired.

collectibles

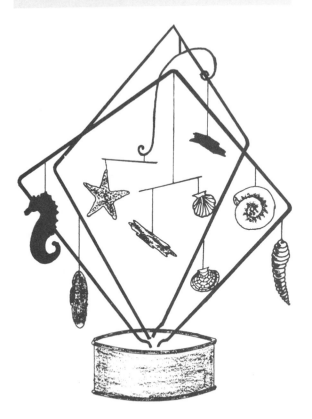

Technique: Stabile

Materials:

- small found objects, natural or man-made: driftwood, shells, small toys, nails, metal objects, etc.
- small tin can (tuna or cat food can)
- plaster of Paris
- 2 wire hangers
- nylon thread or fishing line
- scissors
- newspapers

Steps:

1. Pull the two wire hangers, one at a time, into triangular shapes. Holding the top of the hanger with one hand, pull the bottom of the hanger with the other hand to make a diamond shape.

2. Mix plaster of Paris according to directions on the package. (Do be careful with this as it can clog sinks, etc. Be sure to stay with it as it dries fast.) Pour enough plaster of Paris in the tin to almost fill it. Allow to set a few minutes until it begins to harden. Then insert the "hanging" part of the hanger into the plaster. Hold until firm enough to stand alone. Let dry thoroughly.

3. Attach nylon thread or string to the objects to be hung. Tie at various intervals to the wire hangers.

Variations:

Any ideas in this book can be substituted for the "collectibles." Check the *Paper* section for a variety of cut-out objects.